AVID

READER

PRESS

THE FOUR TESTS

*WHAT IT
WILL TAKE
TO KEEP
AMERICA
STRONG AND
GOOD*

DANIEL BAER

AVID READER PRESS

New York   London   Toronto   Sydney   New Delhi

AVID READER PRESS
An Imprint of Simon & Schuster, Inc.
1230 Avenue of the Americas
New York, NY 10020

First Avid Reader Press hardcover edition September 2023

AVID READER PRESS and colophon are trademarks of Simon & Schuster, Inc.

For information about special discounts for bulk purchases, please contact
Simon & Schuster Special Sales at 1-866-506-1949 or business@simonandschuster.com.

The Simon & Schuster Speakers Bureau can bring authors to your live event.
For more information or to book an event, contact the
Simon & Schuster Speakers Bureau at 1-866-248-3049 or
visit our website at www.simonspeakers.com.

Interior design by Ruth Lee-Mui

Manufactured in the United States of America

1   3   5   7   9   10   8   6   4   2

Library of Congress Cataloging-in-Publication Data

Names: Baer, Daniel Brooks, 1977– author.
Title: The four tests : what it will take to keep America strong and good / Daniel Baer.
Identifiers: LCCN 2023023288 (print) | LCCN 2023023289 (ebook)
| ISBN 9781668006580 (hardcover) | ISBN 9781668006597
(trade paperback) | ISBN 9781668006603 (ebook)
Subjects: LCSH: Security, International—History—21st century. | Political
leadership—United States—History—21st century. | Power (Social sciences)—United
States—History—21st century. | United States—Foreign relations—History—21st
century. | United States—Politics and government—History—21st century.
Classification: LCC JZ5588 .B32 2023 (print) | LCC JZ5588
(ebook) | DDC 320.97309/05—dc23/eng/20230613
LC record available at https://lccn.loc.gov/2023023288
LC ebook record available at https://lccn.loc.gov/2023023289

ISBN 978-1-6680-0658-0
ISBN 978-1-6680-0660-3 (ebook)

*For Stela Sears, and for immigrants who,
like her, choose to bet on America.*

*And for my nieces, Denver, Ines, and Sasha,
with hope for the future we will give them.*

Contents

1. **A WAGER ON THE FUTURE**   1

2. **FROM HEGEMON TO COOPERATOR-IN-CHIEF**   19
   The Scale Test

3. **FROM MONOPOLY TO START-UP**   69
   The Investment Test

4. **RIGHT MAKES MIGHT**   113
   The Fairness Test

5. **TAKE A CHANCE ON WE**   171
   The Identity Test

6. **WHAT CHOICE DO WE HAVE?**   219

Acknowledgments   227
Notes   231
Index   243

1

A WAGER ON THE FUTURE

1.

"It's never, ever been a good bet to bet against the United States of America," Joe Biden said at the 2023 State of the Union address. Most every U.S. president in recent memory has offered some version of the same sentiment. It's a good line, even if such rhetoric is less an expression of analysis and more an incantation, an attempt to speak into existence strength that many see as slipping away, or already gone. For, in truth, in the last 150 years there has never been a better time to bet against America.

"I volunteer, I donate, I vote, I write to my member of Congress . . . and I marvel that so much still gets worse and I wonder if what I'm doing matters at all." How many millions of Americans have uttered, or at least thought, something like that? At times, feeling hopeless becomes a kind of reprieve; caring about the future is hard work. But while many aspects of the United States have changed over nearly two and a half centuries, including some of the mechanics of our democracy, power still lies with citizens. We decide America's fate.

This is not a book intended for academics or foreign policy insiders. This book is for those who wake up and look at their phone or turn on their computer and feel like the news is coming for them from every direction, and who want a way to focus their attention on the future with neither despair nor naïve hope that "it'll all work out." This book is about the problems we face. But it is not meant to sound the alarm—between the challenges to American democracy at home, increasing competition in the world, and global threats like climate change, most Americans are already concerned. Many of us feel like the problems we face are both insurmountable and innumerable.

My interest is to organize our principal challenges, show how they connect to each other, and to suggest that they are neither impossible to confront nor innumerable. The notion of a polycrisis—a mot du jour of the early 2020s—is useful for saying "there's a lot going wrong all at once" but it can discourage us from saying "okay, where to begin?"

Consider this thought experiment: If you and I separately made lists of the top ten problems that the United States faces, our lists would probably substantially overlap. Maybe seven or eight of the problems would be more or less the same. And if the United States made progress on just two or three of those, we'd probably feel as if things were moving in the right direction, enough so that we'd contemplate capturing that momentum to tackle the other challenges.

If we're going to use polycrisis as a concept, we should allow ourselves to conceive of polyprogress too.

2.

One of the supposed features of democracy is that it allows for societal evolution without political revolution. Democracies, when they work well, hold the things constant that ought to be constant—institutions and the principles that underlie them—while also allowing the things to change that need to change for a society to adapt to new realities.

The U.S., along with its allies, built the global economic and political realities of the twentieth century. Geographic good fortune was one source of American advantage—not only the moat formed by the Atlantic and Pacific Oceans that shielded it from nineteenth-century geopolitics but also the fertile land, the climate, the timber, the minerals, the oil. Demographic bounty was another—the immigrants who came, particularly between the U.S. Civil War and World War II, and who mined and farmed and laid railroad ties and filled factory floors to build the economic engine that would—along with the outsized sacrifice of Soviet bodies—be indispensable to the Allies' victory in 1945. The combination of the two gave the United States a competitive edge that could be leveraged to take the central role in designing, building, and leading the world order of the last seventy-five years.

In the twenty-first century, as the world economy, technological capabilities, and global politics have changed dramatically, the United States has, so far, failed to achieve a necessary political-economic evolution. One need not indulge in hyperbole to acknowledge that the United States' current trajectory does not encourage confidence. It's not just that it has social and economic woes of the kind that have always been present and continue to impose a tax on the well-being of too many Americans. Our deep political divisions and dysfunctions suggest that the United States is failing at basic functions of successful states. It no longer has the confidence of the majority of its citizens when it comes to two fundamental tasks: creating the conditions that give citizens a belief that, over the medium to long term, general welfare will improve; and providing citizens with a sense of adequate security in their way of life. The pessimists have plenty of compelling and real datapoints to support a dark view of the future of the United States.

At the same time, if the idea that "it has never been a good bet to bet against America" has a kernel of truth in it, it is of course *not* that the history of the United States has been but a string of triumphs. Quite the contrary, it is in the weaker, darker, more difficult moments of its history that the strength of its democratic system has—imperfectly, crudely, but effectively—averted what appeared to be inevitable and often existential catastrophe. Intelligently understood, it is not a claim to a certain fate, but instead a hypothesis about the function of the democratic system: it won't always work well, it may allow problems to fester for too long and at enormous cost, but eventually it will be able to generate both the ideas and the political will to address the challenges it faces, including its own failures.

When commentators speak of the end of the American-led world or remark on American decline today, they most often focus on the relative decline of U.S. national performance and power compared to other world powers, particularly China. My argument here is not that that kind of decline is ephemeral or unimportant; it is not. However, focusing on those measures of relative influence in geopolitics will not effectively address their most problematic implications. Ensuring continued military superiority may be a tactic, but it is not, on its own, a sustainable strategy for the long run. As King Canute could have told us a millennium ago, there's no holding back a tide. America's unipolar moment has receded. And rather than allowing an ongoing attempt to maintain eroding unipolarity to dominate our strategic thinking about global competition, we should focus on how the United States succeeds and fails on its own terms to make good on the promise of American democracy. That should be the guiding objective that defines its strategic approach to domestic and foreign policy. The goal is not to beat China because of its weaknesses; the goal is for America to succeed because of its strengths.

That may not seem a particularly novel claim. But it is still a relevant one. And for all the politicians who aver that "a strong foreign policy depends on a strong America" or "a strong America begins at home," we've made insufficient progress on demonstrating the truth behind that cliché. Republicans have ignored necessary investments in favor of short-term profit for corporatist backers and Democrats have been too impressed with their own social justice moralism and have failed to compellingly connect domestic policy to national competitiveness. The notion of a "foreign policy for the middle class" animated the first years of the Biden administration. But even more important than making sure our foreign policy is designed with working Americans in mind is a strategy for rebuilding the middle class in service of a strong America.

America needs to succeed *as* America because, for all the despots and authoritarians that remain, the influence of popular opinion—of so-called ordinary people— is growing in the world. (Indeed, one feature of the current political moment in the advanced democracies of what we still anachronistically call the West is that popular opinion has broken free of the mediating influence historically imposed by elites, often with alarming effect.) If one believes that the liberal principles that underlie American democracy attach to basic truths about the human condition and have universal appeal, the progress of the United States toward "a more perfect union" is not only essential for the prosperity, security, and freedom of its citizens but also for the appeal and influence of the United States in the world, and for its ability to shape international politics in the decades to come.

3.

It is a perennial challenge for strategists—in politics and war, as in business—to take the right lessons from history while at the same time guarding against the shackles or blinders it might impose. History can bequeath insight, but also encourage analytical mistakes in the form of assumptions that stowaway in our minds as we look to the future. Those assumptions affect both our beliefs about what tools or approaches are likely to be effective in future iterations of strategic competition and our beliefs about what the goals of that competition are.

In the postwar years it was a realistic objective of the United States to consolidate its position, having inherited the place of the United Kingdom as the dominant global power, and, to that end, to subdue the challenge to U.S. dominance from the Soviet Union. At the time, U.S. success was not considered a given, but the goal was not far-fetched given the relative strength of global powers at the end of World War II. That goal—and its ultimate achievement—defined seventy-five years of world politics.

Too many discussions today either implicitly or explicitly assume that the goal of the United States for the next seventy-five years should be to retain its hegemony. There is no question that would be the most advantageous outcome for the United States and would provide it maximum scope of maneuver in international politics. It would be nice to maintain unambiguous dominance. But it is simply not realistic, at least not in the way that we think of it when looking backward at the last seventy-five years. If that is the goal, then the contest is already lost.

The good news is that the United States does not need to dominate world politics unilaterally for Americans to have an expectation
of good and happy lives in generations to come. There can be a good
life for Americans in a post-American-hegemony world. There was a
good life for British people after the end of British hegemony. Even
so, there is reason for concern. After all, two world wars coincided
with the empire's decline. And a principal reason for the U.K.'s post-
hegemonic success was that its closest ally and fellow democracy, the
United States of America, took its place as the dominant global power
and shouldered the burdens attached to that role.

4.

An understandable but perverse lesson that has been drawn from
some of the more salient episodes of the history of U.S. foreign policy
in the last seventy-five years—including its support for dictators and
anti-leftist coups in the Cold War and its catastrophic invasion of Iraq
in 2003—is that the accumulation and exercise of U.S. power in the
world is bad and that therefore we should welcome America's forced
withdrawal from the world stage as its relative power declines. This
view—which finds adherents both on the left and the right in American politics—is as misguided as the crude neoconservative thesis that
the exercise of U.S. power has been unambiguously to the good. A
tally of U.S. sins and good deeds will always be incomplete and, at
least for some, inconclusive. And it is beside the point. Clearly the
U.S. could have been better, measured by its own standards.

The relevant question is whether the last seventy-five years were
better than the realistic alternatives of Soviet communist triumph in
the Cold War, or of global politics defined by the absence of a dominant power and a continuation of the kind of geopolitical jockeying

that preceded World War I and World War II. One can acknowledge that the United States has taken actions that have been extraordinarily damaging to the lives of millions of people both elsewhere in the world and in the U.S., where misguided wars have imposed enormous costs on American servicemembers and their families, yet still believe Americans are better off—as, by and large, are those living around the world—than they would be if the United States had not enjoyed its dominant position, given the plausible counterfactuals. We weren't ever competing with a perfect world, even if we should always be credibly working toward one.

As we look to the future we must be clear: there can be a good life for Americans in a world without American hegemony; but there cannot be a good life for Americans—or at least it would be unreasonable to expect a good life for Americans—in a world dominated by the Chinese Communist Party or by Vladimir Putin or by another authoritarian state. The United States does not need to be a hegemon but it cannot abide authoritarian hegemony. Those who counsel calm about the implications of the relative decline of U.S. power and the apparent possibility that China—with its current system of government—will surpass the United States in comprehensive national power misjudge the seriousness of that prospect even as others misjudge the likelihood of it.

For the next seventy-five years, the goal is no longer a world that the United States controls in some significant measure, but rather a world that is hospitable to the continuation of the American experiment and in which the United States can compete and flourish economically, and can sufficiently influence the outcomes of international politics to defend the security of its people.

Putin's brutal invasion of Ukraine reminded the world that authoritarian regimes cannot be pretended away as threats. It has also become common to predict or warn against a so-called new Cold War with China. Particularly in Europe, but also in much of the Global South, many warn against such a contest because they do not want to repeat the Cold War and live through its divisions, deprivations, and costs once again. Fair enough. But that backward-looking concern misses a bigger problem with using the Cold War as a frame for our own strategic thinking: the goal of the contest with China is not the same as the goal once was with the Soviet Union. Or, rather, it's only half the same. It is important to avoid a potential future in which an authoritarian China asserts hegemony in world politics. In that sense, what we're trying to prevent is similar to the Cold War aim of preventing Soviet domination. However, what we are seeking is not the U.S. hegemony that was the oft unspoken but barely hidden goal in the Cold War. Instead we have to aim at a new way of managing world politics. What was once done by the seats of empire, and later by the exercise of power by a superpower hegemon, must now be done by a web of alliances, agreements, pooled resources, and cooperation between countries. U.S. leadership remains essential and consequential, but the task is more challenging and requires more political finesse.

The loss of hegemony means that the U.S. must adapt to a future in which it has less coercive power over other states, and this reality is colliding with another decades-in-the-making change, which is that a greater share of the security challenges that the U.S. faces are phenomena that are not primarily controlled by particular governments at all. Pandemics, climate change, human migration—these are not challenges that the U.S. can confront by twisting arms of one or a few governments; they are problems that require coordination rather than coercion. The future demands more effective global governance, that is, systems for managing global challenges collectively. At the same time, the system of global governance that the U.S. and its partners developed in the last seventy-five years (a system that includes the U.N., the international financial institutions, the World Trade Organization, and so on) is increasingly under strain both from the number of problems that are placed at its doorstep and the bad behavior of states that seek to extract concessions from others with a mix of sabotaging the international system and holding it hostage.

5.

The U.S. cannot successfully approach the contests and challenges of the twenty-first century in the frame of the geopolitical competition of the twentieth. Not only is the definition of what it means to "win" different, the means by which the U.S. will win or lose are different too. The twenty-first century will *not* be won—at least not by the United States and the free world that, by default if not by right, it still leads—in a head-to-head contest between states. Nor will it be won with the same things that generated geopolitical advantage in the twentieth century—larger nuclear arsenals or a U.S. economy that comprised 40 percent of the world's economic output in 1960.[1]

Traditional aspects of national power, particularly military power, will continue to be important in guarding against the threats posed by authoritarian states. But military power will not be sufficient for the United States to achieve its own goals in the next seventy-five years. Nor will the sustainment of U.S. military power be possible if the U.S. does not succeed in other dimensions of competition, including economic growth and technological advantage. There is a risk that the necessary work to defend against the threats posed by authoritarian states consumes not only the attention that goal deserves, but also our surplus attention that ought to be invested in presenting and sustaining an alternative to their model. It is highly likely that much of the coming decades will be characterized by ongoing competition with China, but if we focus too much on who the contest is with and how to counter them, we might lose sight of what that contest is for.

After all, geopolitical success, to be worth caring about, has to have more significance than a football game. The foreign and security policy of the United States is not about "winning" for winning's sake, but about protecting the ability of the people of the United States to pursue a "more perfect union," that is, to make our own decisions about how to manage our society and to continue our uneven, nonlinear progress toward a democratic society that lives up to its principles. That collective mission to make good on the promise encoded in the idea of individual human dignity and written in our founding documents is what gives our foreign policy and our domestic politics meaning. It is a central argument of this book that we will not succeed in defending America's autonomy in the world if we do not renew our social contract at home to make it suitable for the world we now inhabit.

6.

The dimensions of global competition, of what makes one country successful and another country less so, will be different in important ways in the next seventy-five years. Some areas of competition that seem familiar will matter in different ways than they have in the past. And we will face new kinds of competition that will strike some as unusual to think about in the context of international politics. None is independent, and the linkages between them will enhance or detract from U.S. influence in the world. Here are the four dimensions of national strength on which the United States can base a successful strategy to navigate world politics for the next seventy-five years. In each of these is a test for America in the next decade.

Scale. The United States has a population of around 330 million and its population growth, though not as slow as in some other advanced democracies, was slower in the last decade than it had been since the Great Depression. In the last seventy-five years, the United States used the advantages of scale, particularly economic scale, to assert and secure its influence—the dominant role of the U.S. dollar as a reserve currency and in the global financial system, for example, gave the United States significant leverage. In the next seventy-five years, scale will still matter, and will potentially matter even more. Network effects—the phenomenon where something becomes more valuable or useful when more people use it—are more potent in an increasingly digital and data-driven economy. And as countries compete for both strategic and economic edge on emerging technologies like artificial intelligence, being big enough will help countries incubate new applications and shape the rules around them. The United States will continue to represent a significant share of global GDP, but it may not be the largest economy, and its share of the global economy will likely continue to decline as others grow. But that doesn't mean we should turn off the engine and coast—there are steps we can take to ensure healthy population growth, and to invest in the productivity of that population. At the same time, to continue to shape global governance, the U.S. will have to become more invested in—and more creative about—linkages that effectively remove barriers between the United States and its partners and allies so that it can—working together with other countries and pooling their economic, innovative, and political weight—leverage collective scale where once the U.S.'s own heft was sufficient.

Investment. The idea of investment as a predicate for productivity growth is not new. Nor is it novel to suggest that as advanced economies have become more skills-based, the balance of investment needs to shift from traditional capital investments— acquisition of resources, infrastructure, machinery, and the like—toward human capital. If those truths appear to us self-evident, so should the crisis in the American status quo. The United States has failed to marshal an adequate level of public and private investment and is failing to direct it to the areas where it is most crucial. A massive increase in investment in research and development, education, health, and confronting the existential threat of climate change is essential to long-term American competitive success. (The 2021 Bipartisan Infrastructure Bill and the 2022 Inflation Reduction Act and CHIPS Act are a good start.) We need new investment because U.S. success depends ever more upon increasing the productivity of its workers in a world characterized by accelerating technical advancement and global competition. The scientific discoveries that led to the invention of nuclear weapons shaped geopolitics in the second half of the twentieth century; today, new discoveries are poised to give outsized influence in different ways to those who understand them first—and who develop the standards to deploy and control them—in the next seventy-five years.

Fairness. This word is not often used in foreign policy or security policy documents. But progress on fairness will be essential to any version of the U.S. that succeeds in the coming decades. Americans can't compete in a more challenging global landscape if they tolerate the inefficiencies that unfairness precipitates, or the divisions that it engenders. The United States' twin scourges of rising economic inequality and enduring racism impose a tax on U.S. competitiveness by perverting investment allocations and reducing productivity. They erode domestic stability and detract from international authority and influence because they are manifestly unfair. Institutions are also part of the fairness test, because stable expectations of fairness over time require domestic institutions rooted in fairness and the rule of law.

In the United States, arguments for economic policies that reduce inequality and moderate corporate power have often been rooted in social justice claims (which exemplify one aspect of fairness). But the case for fairer competition in our economy, and in our politics, also connects to the practical objectives of attracting and effectively using investment. And as the U.S. and its partners work to establish responsible global guardrails around technology, resources, climate, migration, intellectual property, trade, or a host of other global issues, standards that can be explained with reference to the common good rather than privileging parochial interests of certain companies or certain countries will bolster U.S. influence, while those seen as rigging the system will undermine it.

Identity. Human beings depend upon identity to help us assign meaning to and navigate choices in our lives. The United States' success in the coming decades is dependent on identity in two respects. First, it needs a thin but widely shared sense of national identity, sufficient to knit together Americans in a shared enterprise as the United States navigates a more intense era of global competition. The version of national identity that has historically been privileged in the United States needs renovation and restoration. American national identity has historically been founded in a combination of European heritage and liberal values—and in many ways the choice that we face as a country today is about which of these will be the dominant premise for what it means to be an American. It is essential—not just morally, but *practically*, if we want to secure U.S. influence in the world and the strength of the U.S. economy and political structures—that liberal values win out. Being American must be something that equally includes all Americans, because we are going to need every American's effort to compete.

Second, the U.S. must give its citizens a sufficient sense of stability in the various other aspects of identity, which for most of us are collectively, if not individually, more important sources of meaning and direction in our everyday lives. Being a truck driver or a grandparent or a Jew or an artist is more salient in our daily lives—in our stresses and laughter, as reasons for the actions we take—than being an American. Maintaining a comfortable sense of one's own identity is more difficult in a rapidly changing world. The technological development of the current age, and its impact on advanced economies, has accelerated the pace of changes (and not only economic changes) that have implications for individuals' identities. Identity is core to a sense of security. Few people would say that they want the state to provide, much less determine or dictate, the core of their sense of identity, but when large numbers of individuals feel their identities to be under threat, their responses to this threat tend to undermine political stability and social cohesion.

We need to see ourselves as Americans, and to understand that identity as having implications for how we will work together and how we should see each other. And we need to experience being American, living in the United States, as something that permits and protects all other aspects of our identity that are the stuff of meaningful lives freely and well lived. The challenges surrounding identity are arguably among the most difficult to thoughtfully address through policy tools. But policy matters. Meeting the tests of scale, investment, and fairness will help individual Americans feel more secure in the ways that they understand the world and their place in it. And a thin but relatively common political identity founded on liberal values can knit America together—loosely, but loosely is enough—and be a lodestar to guide the future of our collective enterprise in the coming decades and help buffer the dislocating influences of a complex, ever changing world.

•   •   •

Basically, we need to be big enough, smart enough, good enough, and rooted enough. That's how the United States can succeed in the next half century or more. We have a lot of problems—but instead of playing an increasingly frenetic or despondent game of whack-a-mole, if we focus on ideas that bring us closer to meeting these tests, other solutions and successes will fall into place.

7.

Many of us have become increasingly familiar with that strange sensation of a headline that feels like an attack. Headlines that herald storms, fires, crop failures, diseases, famines, water shortages increasingly attributable to climate change. Ominous op-eds about the rise of China and the Chinese Communist Party's control over an increasingly advanced economy of more than a billion people that is making rapid progress on closing the gap on productivity and innovation. Articles that announce "the end of the American century" and depict the U.S.'s emergence as a major power in world politics with World War I and its acceptance of the limits of its power with the failed wars in Afghanistan and Iraq as bookends of ascendance and decline. The news of yet another Black person dead after an encounter with police. A spike in hate crimes and mass shootings. Charts and graphs that show the failure of the U.S. education system to deliver equal and high-level achievement, and that show rising inequality and decreasing social mobility in a society that still grasps for—but rarely delivers on—the American Dream. And all of this is to say nothing of the images of the fight under way about the future of democratic institutions in the world's longest running democratic experiment—the long tail of January 6. Setting aside the merits of the arguments, it is the fact of the fight—an angry, hateful, heated fight—that is depressing enough.

It is easy to read a lot about what's wrong with America—where we're poorly positioned or where the trend lines are going in the wrong direction. And we can't ignore it: thoughtful analysis and diagnosis is a useful step in addressing problems. But, as we reflect, it's also important to step back and reaffirm the goodness of what we wish for our country. Most Americans—even across geographical divides and partisan acrimony—would say that they want a country where they and their compatriots live free and prosperous lives, and a country that is strong enough in the world to protect its citizens. To make progress, we have to avoid getting lost in, or wallowing in, a list of shortcomings. There's a reason, I suppose, that we speak of health care rather than "disease spotting."

Most of the trends and trajectories that are the sources of our concern are also the products of human behavior and human choices. Different behaviors and different choices are possible. And so are different trajectories.

It can be jarring to realize that there's nothing that says the world must be organized into different countries or sovereign states. Indeed for most of human history the world was not made up of states; the evolution of states in their modern form, as entities defined in international law and with commonly recognized features, is only a few centuries old.

Perhaps the most basic and fundamental question that Americans have to answer is whether, in this century, we will see ourselves as part of a collective enterprise. Will we attempt to navigate the threats and challenges of a changed and changing world together? If not, the tests that this book lays out don't matter. If the answer is yes—as I believe it should be, because I think we have better odds together than apart, and better odds as Americans than as members of any other existing polity—then we have our work cut out for us.

This book is an attempt to answer a question that I've encountered about "the American enterprise" in different forms and different settings over the last five years—in small-group discussions about U.S. politics in rural Colorado; at conferences for educators about tackling equity gaps; on summer evenings eating outside with friends and talking about the state of the world—and in its most basic form the question is this: Given all that's going on, would you still bet on America?

I am bearish about the challenges the United States faces—in many ways, I think they are bigger than we even realize.

But I am still bullish about the future of the United States. So in some sense, this book is an invitation to make that bet with me, and an exploration of the things that we have to do together to make that bet pay off.

2

FROM HEGEMON TO COOPERATOR-IN-CHIEF

THE SCALE TEST

1.

As a child during the last decade of the Cold War, I would look up at the map of the world in my elementary school classroom and ponder the sizes of various countries. I recall examining the United States and the USSR on the map and marveling, with some patriotic jealousy, at the Soviet Union's vast expanse. It seemed obvious that when it came to countries—like presents under the tree—bigger was better.

At some point I asked a question about why the U.S. was so much smaller and my teacher answered that while Soviet territory was much bigger than the United States (over 8 million square miles compared to the United States' almost 4 million), the populations were more similar, with the U.S. only slightly smaller than the Soviet Union—

around 250 million people in America and closer to 300 million in the USSR. But in terms of wealth, of the output of the two economies, the teacher told me, the U.S. was twice the size of the Soviet Union. There followed a nerdy obsession with learning the population of various countries and their GDP per capita figures. Around 1990 I was like a walking Google, as long as what you wanted to know was the population of a NATO member or Warsaw Pact country.

Territory, population, and productivity have been central to international competition in the modern era. Empire was the business model of "successful" powers between the sixteenth and nineteenth centuries—including Spain and Portugal; Russia and Austria-Hungary; France, Holland, and Belgium; Japan and Qing dynasty China; and, of course, Britain. It involved conquest (sometimes aided by innovation in weaponry and transportation, other times aided by population size or disease) and extraction—of human resources, often in the form of enslaved persons, and of natural resources (often with large amounts of subjugated labor). The purported "civilizing" mission of empire was, at its core, a con; it was a thin veneer to cover a violent and exploitative system.

One of the advantages that empire produced (beyond the wealth that accrued to metropoles from using violence to extract value) was scale. It was generally useful to have control over territory that had a lot of people or a lot of resources, or both. Trade networks within empires increased productivity by connecting raw materials like cotton with factories. And empires provided manpower and the ability to put military bases abroad, which was useful for asserting influence vis-à-vis other powers and for defending against their attacks. Empires "overstretched" when the burdens of expanding or defending them, and maintaining systems of subjugation in them, became more than the empire's seat could manage.

In school I learned that one of the unique attributes of the United States was that it was the first modern world power never to have presided over an empire. Yes, it briefly controlled the Philippines and it annexed Puerto Rico and Guam after the War of 1898, and it maintains today several island territories (and a capital city) that have not been fully integrated as U.S. states or parts of states with full political representation, but it never depended on overseas territories it formally controlled as a main source of either labor or resources.

This version of history is a fudge. For of course the United States *began* as part of an empire, as a set of colonies, and long before its founding as an independent nation it had begun to use massive amounts of enslaved labor facilitated by the growing empire of which it was part. Conquest was also essential to America's rise—from the initial European settlers in the seventeenth century to the wars of the nineteenth century, Native Americans were conquered and displaced.

Still, one could say the U.S. was expansionist without being conventionally imperial. And the unusual mode of governance established by the new nation of the United States of America in the late eighteenth century would prove an advantage over time, even if the democratic experiment would likely never have succeeded if the United States hadn't been jump-started and incubated by abundant natural resources and two world oceans that functioned as moats. More recently, in the twentieth century, the United States stepped into the void as the British Empire receded, and—fueled by immigration, resources, and its role in the reconstruction of Europe and industrialization of Asia—became the dominant world power.

For many baby boomers and Gen Xers in the United States, there's a tendency to see the American "moment" in world history as beginning with Allied victory in World War II and the achievements of the Greatest Generation. But while American success in the Cold

War may seem more overdetermined in retrospect than it did in the midst of it, American hegemony wasn't unambiguous until the 1990s. It lasted perhaps only a decade, and certainly less than three.

In any case, the period of America's rapid *relative* ascendance in terms of the scale of its national power is over. Once the United States acknowledges that—and many of the pundits and political leaders who claim to understand this reality nonetheless continue to suggest strategies that betray a stubborn level of denial—the challenges of America's *relative* decline can be managed and addressed so that it does not become an absolute decline. Just because the rise of other countries means that the U.S. is unlikely to represent 40 percent of world economic activity again in the foreseeable future doesn't mean that the U.S. economy cannot continue to grow. Just because the relative dominance of U.S. military power will likely decline over the next half century doesn't mean that the U.S. can't remain powerful enough to defend itself. Just because the U.S. can't reasonably pursue a new era of American hegemony doesn't mean that America can't retain a significant degree of preeminence if it manages to lead in the world. And that has to be the goal if America is to succeed in the coming decades: the U.S. has to be able to protect the interests of its citizens—their life, liberty, and pursuit of happiness, their freedom and prosperity, their security and welfare—without the advantage of being unquestionably the most powerful nation on earth across multiple dimensions.

2.

One challenge that we face is structural. Hegemonic powers—like monopolistic firms—make for lazy strategists. Their surplus of power reduces the incentives for coming up with more efficient or effective ways of achieving their goals. And it can blur their analysis of risk.

For the first fifteen years after the Cold War, from roughly 1990 to 2005, the U.S. did not need a particularly sophisticated strategy because its sole superpower status was so pronounced. One doesn't need to be a savvy poker player if one starts every hand with a full house. In the second chunk of fifteen years after the Cold War, the U.S. struggled to make sense of a new reality precipitated by both its monumental strategic blunder in Iraq and the distinct challenges posed by a revanchist Russia empowered by high oil prices and a rising and increasingly assertive China propelled by two decades of explosive economic growth. To succeed in the next half century, the United States must first acknowledge that while it still has a strong hand to play most of the time, it is no longer guaranteed to have the strongest hand at the table. In the vacuum left by declining relative U.S. power, strategy—a new approach to advancing U.S. interests—must grow.

Declining hegemons have to (re)learn strategy; they also have to adjust what they do to achieve their goals in the world. Therein lies a second challenge: the tools of the hegemon are not the same as the tools of a successful former or future hegemon. The caricature that emerged in the early twentieth century of the U.S. as "the world's policeman" was never wholly accurate, but it is nonetheless fair to say that the United States is losing some of its coercive power. With a smart strategy, it can compensate for this loss by enhancing its political power. There are fewer and fewer situations where the U.S. can achieve its objectives primarily through the international politics equivalent of arm-twisting; consequently, the U.S. will have to get better at persuasion and coalition-building to get what it needs.

The challenge here is one of shifting from being a boss to being a genuine leader. Part of developing the leader's more sophisticated approach is lengthening time horizons. For a hegemon, power becomes a substitute for clear strategic objectives: as long as the hegemon has superior power, it doesn't have to have a particularly clear view of the outcomes it seeks in ten or twenty years because hegemony is a kind of trump card allowing it to influence outcomes as new situations arise. When controlling influence wanes and leadership becomes imperative, the former hegemon needs a clearer sense of what it expects and what it wants in the longer term. The U.S. needs to shape the evolution of international politics and, in a discriminating fashion, apply its more limited power within it rather than expect to dictate outcomes. It needs a more thoughtful strategy. And it needs new ways of implementing that strategy in the world.

As the U.S. navigates a world in which it is no longer the biggest economy, in which its population is not the largest, and in which the other instruments of our national power, while still formidable, are not always as superior as they once were, the first test that the United States faces is the test of scale. It can meet this test with a two-pronged approach: First, make the most of the scale it has and can maintain so that it remains a major world power for the long run. And, second, the U.S. needs to revamp how it exercises power in the world. It needs to treat global politics as a cooperative endeavor that entails working with other countries more than it has since the end of the Cold War. It needs to pool resources and coordinate joint approaches to problems—so that it can create some of the effect and advantages of dominant scale where necessary and prevent other large actors from achieving dangerous outcomes. If we aren't the biggest, can we stay big enough? And, even though we aren't the biggest, can we figure out ways to make it feel like we are bigger than we really are when we need to?

3.

Scale matters for several reasons. In a crude sense, the size of a country's population has some connection to the maximum potential headcount of its military. But military power is—today more than ever before—a proxy for or indicator of other national strengths. The power of the U.S. military depends on the strength of the U.S. economy which funds it, the talent of U.S. innovators who develop its cutting-edge tools, its status as a volunteer force dedicated to defending a democratic society, the history of its development as a professional force under civilian control, and so on. The strength of a military is more a reflection of a society's strength than a determinant of it.

Having a larger population—as long as it's working as a social, political, and economic system—gives a country scale benefits, particularly once it reaches a certain threshold of economic development. It's cheaper to spread the overhead cost of investments—such as high-quality advanced education or an aircraft carrier—over a larger population. And a larger population can make small innovations— such as treatments for uncommon maladies or niche technologies that ultimately become part of a specialized weapons system—more economically viable. Those developing transformative products—such as a computer or alternatives to meat protein—are able to build on the past discoveries of a larger innovation community, find investors in a larger investment community, and find a sufficient number of customers in a larger market.

Scale doesn't guarantee that a country will develop some advantage in international politics, but scale creates the background conditions that make success more likely. Consider the rise of the U.S. as a global power in the first half of the twentieth century. Part of this story is the role the United States' military played in the two world wars. But the story of U.S. preeminence superseding the British was also the story of American industrialization and of energy transition around the rise of oil. The U.S. became an early major exploiter, exporter, and deliverer of oil, which it sold in dollars. And because of this early and sustained role in the oil industry, U.S. naval power became critical to the global economy and the dollar became its currency, augmenting U.S. influence and giving it significant leverage. The early prominence of the United States in the oil industry was not *caused* by the scale of the rapidly growing country, but the sufficient scale of the U.S. was a necessary precondition. The United States wasn't the biggest, but it was big enough.

4.

Population isn't a source of power on its own, but for a country such as the United States, with a high GDP per capita—well above the level needed to meet basic needs—population and productivity are the two components of economic scale. One way of maintaining the benefits of scale is to ensure that the U.S. population continues to be productive, and that it continues to grow at a reasonable rate, or at least that it does not shrink. And there are only two ways to do that: keep having babies in this country or get people from other countries to immigrate to the United States. Procreation and immigration are the only two ways you get new Americans.

The U.S. is not on the list of the twenty countries whose population is expected to decline by 10 percent or more over the next thirty years—a list that includes small countries such as North Macedonia and much larger ones such as Japan and Italy. And even if the United States did see a population decline of 10 percent, from over 330 million to around 300 million, it would still be among the world's largest democracies. (Population decline, however, comes with all sorts of negative consequences, particularly for the economy but also for family life, as aging populations have more care needs that fall to fewer young people.)

The population of the United States is likely to grow more slowly than the world average—birth rates tend to decline as economic development progresses, and especially as women achieve education and more civil equality. But the United States, if it's succeeding, should continue to grow at a rate at or above the average population growth for advanced democracies. In 2020, the U.S. growth rate was less than half of the world average, but about even with the Organization for Economic Co-operation and Development (OECD) average (.4 percent). Healthy population growth is both a contributor to the strength of a democratic society and an outcome of it.

Since 2007, the birth rate in the United States has fallen by about 20 percent according to one of the most common measures used by demographers, which is the number of births per thousand women of childbearing age. In 2007, 69.7 of every 1,000 women of childbearing age (15–44) gave birth. In 2020, that number had fallen to 55.8. Over the same time period, the total fertility rate, which is a statistical estimate of the total number of children each woman will have in her life, fell from 2.12 to 1.64. The rate required for replacement of the current population, without immigration, is approximately 2.1. Americans are choosing to have fewer children. [1]

Setting aside the ongoing battle in the United States over abortion rights, it is clear that in all advanced democracies the decision to have children is, to a much greater extent than it was a few generations ago, a real choice. That parenthood is a choice is a sign of both political and economic development. It is morally good that people are able, as they pursue meaningful and satisfying lives, to choose to have children and also to choose not to. More options on the menu of life—more choices about work, about learning, about where and how to live—add to the individual experience of human freedom.

It's also the case that while for some people the expansion of choices has led them to choose to have fewer children, for others, it's not that they feel empowered to make different choices, it's that the affirmative choice to have children has become a more difficult one for them to make. This distinction is important: it's not just that people are choosing not to have children, they are *not* choosing to have them. From 2018 to 2021, according to the Pew Research Center, the percentage of nonparents aged 18–49 who said that they were "not too likely" or "not likely at all" to ever have children went from 37 percent to 44 percent. That's a huge jump, and given that it included the first year of the pandemic, it's unlikely that more people said they were unlikely to have children because they looked around and saw a bunch of other choices—choices that might preclude having children—as more attractive. The choice to have children itself has declining appeal.

Faced with data that show that fewer Americans are choosing to have children, some argue, in effect, that the way to increase birth rates is to decrease choices, particularly for women. This form of social conservatism is not principled; it is crudely culturally revanchist. It's about turning back time to an era where women had more children and, not coincidentally, fewer choices. It is morally wrong to narrow the freedom and opportunity of some Americans just because we'd like them to have more children. It would also be silly economic policy. Even if a harebrained attempt to re-create the 1950s would increase the birth rate modestly, the other costs of returning to that world—rolling back educational attainment levels and labor force participation by women—would destroy a huge chunk of GDP and set back the entire country, as well as the livelihoods of tens of millions of households. *The Handmaid's Tale* is dystopian fiction, not policy analysis.

And, of course, there is an alternative way to influence the choices that Americans make about whether or not to have children: instead of limiting, through law or culture, their other options with regard to questions like bodily autonomy, education, or workforce participation, we can choose policies that make the prospect of having children a more attractive proposition to those in a position to do so.

When people aged 18 to 49 without kids who say they don't intend to have kids were asked why, a bit more than half of them didn't name a specific reason—they just didn't want kids. But the other half, when given an opportunity to share their reason, gave an interesting list. Medical reasons, not having a partner, age, and a partner who doesn't want kids account for about half of those who gave explanations. Let's call this the no-child-but-not-by-choice group. But a third of those who gave reasons said that their reasons were financial (17 percent), the state of the world (9 percent), or climate change (5 percent).[2] Just to back up a bit and move out of percentages—based on a total population between 18 and 49 of approximately 140 million Americans,[3] and about 62 million who say they won't have kids, we're talking about around 5 million Americans who say they aren't going to have kids specifically because of financial reasons; nearly 3 million because of the state of the world; and 1.5 million because of climate change. (Other polls suggest that the share of those choosing not to have children because of climate change is a larger share of this no-child-by-choice group.) And some of those who declined to specify a particular reason for why they just don't want kids may be people who would want to have kids if it didn't seem so darn hard.

Money, fears about the future state of affairs in the U.S. and the world, and climate change. These reasons are all directly tied to public policy decisions, decisions that we and our representatives make. (Some of the medical reasons are likely affected by policy too.) Financial concerns are arguably the most directly addressable factor influencing the decision not to have children. Before the coronavirus pandemic, approximately one in six children in the United States was living in poverty. The expanded child tax credit, which was passed as part of the American Rescue Plan Act of 2021 (temporarily) made two changes: it increased the amount of the tax credit and it made it "fully refundable," meaning that instead of waiting for annual tax filing time, the credit was paid out monthly to qualified recipients—parents of more than 90 percent of the kids in the U.S. The impact of this policy change was immediate—it effectively cut child poverty in half. (And then it was allowed to expire within a year and child poverty, predictably, spiked.)

Obviously it matters that millions of children were lifted out of poverty by this policy decision, but it also matters that the policy meaningfully changed the experience of parents. Consider a married couple, both 38, with a three-year-old and a six-year-old. Both parents work—say, a cop and a teacher—and they make $100,000 in combined income. For this family, the child tax credit was the biggest tax cut of their lives. If they are thinking about having a third child, it could tilt the balance in making the necessary child care possible. (Three quarters of people who are already parents say they won't have more kids, and of those who gave a reason, a third said financial concerns were the primary reason.) The impact wouldn't be immediate, but the basic point is this: if we chose, as a society, to make parents' lives better financially, it is reasonable to expect that, over time, the tax credit would factor in to the decision-making of some people who hesitate to have children for financial reasons. And before people say "that's ridiculous, no one is going to have a kid just because they get

$300/month!" the point isn't that people would say "oh, I read about the child tax credit and now I am going to have a kid." It's not about a transactional exchange, it's about changing the experience of parenting. If the policy can make general perceptions of what it's like to be a parent in America today a little less stressful and frightening, more people will make the choice to do so.

There are other ways to make parenting easier, many of which are steps we should take and investments we should make for other reasons too, as the next chapter will dig into—support for prekindergarten and preschool, investment in the "care economy," and better public education including higher education. In most cases the strongest arguments for updating the social contract and the way that we invest in people in America have nothing to do with population growth. But those policies can also have positive knock-on effects that help ensure that if Americans choose to not have children, that choice is one that reflects their freedom to craft lives of their own making, and not their perception that parenting in America is too onerous and stressful to contemplate.

The other two nonfinancial reasons—climate change and the state of the world—are more difficult to address in the short term through policy. It's hard to know specifically what folks who said "the state of the world" meant by that, but many feel distraught about the moment we're living in for inchoate and multiple reasons—political polarization, democratic erosion, rising geopolitical competition, the perception that governments and institutions are not equipped to deal with the challenges of our time. Americans—including those who have lived under oppressive laws and social subjugation, who have endured generations of poverty, or who have been dispossessed of land—have still found hope in hard times. It's not that life has to be perfect or easy or that the world has to be free of problems for people to feel hopeful. But in periods of realignment and of shifting paradigms such as the one that we are living through, the social, technological, and political currents that define the context for our lives don't just feel significant and threatening, they feel jumbled and out of control. If you're on a bus and you see a boulder in the highway ahead, that's scary. But if you're on a bus and there's no one driving, that feels scarier.

Climate change is, for an increasing number of people, the most specifiable of their concerns about "the state of the world." When faced with the news that the next decade will determine and reveal whether climate change will be accompanied by existential ecological and biodiversity consequences beyond the catastrophes already witnessed, people look at political leaders and don't want to take the risk that they can be trusted to avert the cliff. This feeling is understandable. And it's addressable. The United States and other countries will not take action on climate change because they want to bolster declining birth rates, but when they do tackle climate change seriously and make real progress in the energy transition, even if it doesn't bring confidence that the worst long-term impacts can be fully averted, it might reduce the sense that we're heading for them apace.

Although a rewinding of the clock is not a defensible or realistic prescription, there is another, more typically conservative, observation about how we might make the choice to have children a more attractive one. It is more cultural and sociological than it is economic: when people say they are concerned about "the state of the world," they may also be expressing an understandable sense of uncertainty about their own place in it. The feeling that so many problems in the world around us creates is often one of dislocation—what am I even doing here?—and *that* question is one that, in previous times, organized religion might have addressed. In many cases, organized religion has also been a mechanism of enforcing social and economic coercion and exclusion; so this view need not invoke an unvarnished expression of nostalgia for times when more Americans were churchgoers. Rather we can acknowledge that it is not only the material circumstances of their own households or the world that may affect individuals' decisions about whether or not to have children. There are more metaphysical considerations, rooted in identity and beliefs about what constitutes a meaningful life that may also affect the confidence of individual members in their sociopolitical community.

Population replacement and growth is one of the ways that the United States can maintain sufficient scale to remain competitive in a globalized world where being big enough to matter still matters. And while it would be incongruous, and ineffective, in the American context for leaders to implore Americans to have more children the way that some leaders in other countries have, the choices of American voters and their leaders can add up to a more inviting or more discouraging environment as people decide whether or not to be parents. Most people who decide to have children do it for personal reasons that reflect their own experience and culture; they don't think about policy questions as part of their decision. But having a child by choice is a vote of confidence in the future. It is a direct contribution to the reproduction of the society of which one is a part. As the United States continues its debates about what forms of adaptation we need to adjust to global competition in an increasingly postindustrial world, we should see those discussions as not only debates about social and economic fairness for members of our society, but also as a pitch to those who might think about bringing new people into the world to join it.

5.

Net migration is the other method by which countries maintain and grow their population. While anti-immigration campaigners malign immigrants as outsiders who absorb resources and take jobs, economists have demonstrated repeatedly that significant levels of managed immigration contribute to economic growth. And, of all the work that immigrants might relieve present-day native-born Americans of, the most significant may be that of bearing and raising children. As Americans choose to have fewer children, managed immigration can help fill the gap and ensure a predictable and stable population with modest, healthy growth.

Without delving into the waxing and waning of immigration through the decades, two notes about the U.S. experience: First, with the exception of Native Americans, all Americans have migration—forced or voluntary—in their family history sometime in the last four centuries, and, for a vast majority, within the last two centuries. Second, the escalating attention paid to migration to the United States—particularly with regard to undocumented migrants from Mexico and Central and South America—is the latest in a series of waves of resistance to immigration, waves that have crested and receded throughout our history. This story is not unique to our times. Resistant reactions appear to be driven less by the contributions or role of immigrants in American society and more by changes in the economic circumstance of other Americans. It is not a coincidence that the Tea Party movement, which included strong anti-immigration positions, followed the 2008 financial crisis. And it is clear that immigrants themselves played little role in precipitating that financial breakdown and the economic toll it took.

One of the most frustrating parts of the way that immigration has been politicized in the United States is that immigration is something that the United States is—especially compared to other countries—excellent at. Over the last century and even before, the U.S. has proven unusually good at taking immigrants and refugees from any part of the world and from a variety of ethnic, religious, and other backgrounds, and, within their own lifetimes, turning them into Americans. Immigration can be accompanied by vile discrimination; racial quotas or religious bans have been used in the twenty-first century as well as in preceding ones. The immigrant story has rarely been an easy one. But beyond the fact that we are "a nation of immigrants," immigration is central to the American story because American communities are good at integrating them.

In the 1990s, St. Louis wasn't in the top ten American cities by population—it wasn't even in the top thirty—but when refugees fleeing the war in Bosnia resettled in the United States, tens of thousands ended up there. The nascent community supported each other and got help—language training, small-business loans, advice on navigating public schools—from local resettlement organizations. And soon there was a "little Bosnia" section of the city with restaurants and shops and hair salons. The community has remained a hub—drawing Bosnians from other cities in the United States—but also has been knit into the fabric of St. Louis.[4] Most people in America would be surprised to learn that there were tens of thousands of predominantly Muslim refugees resettled in a medium-size city in the middle of the country. It has been, by and large, a good-news story that has helped to revitalize a midwestern city—and sometimes good news doesn't travel far. But it should.

The current backlash against immigration in the United States is not only economically misguided and demographically unhelpful in ways that will stymie U.S. national competitiveness, it is a reactionary rejection of a cornerstone of the American political experiment. And while some will say that immigration opponents' real objection is irregular or illegal immigration, and for some individuals that may be an honest expression of concern, this argument is a political red herring. While President Donald Trump's 2017 ban on migration from a collection of predominantly Muslim countries generated outspoken resistance, a large minority of Americans supported it. And if the concern were only illegal immigration, we'd witness a different conversation on refugees, who, by definition, only come legally. Instead, the United States—which has resettled sizable refugee communities multiple times since World War II—has slashed refugee admissions in recent years. Even the Biden administration had to be pressured by outside groups to implement Biden's own campaign promise to restore historically moderate levels of refugee resettlement in the U.S.

No one serious is making an argument for erasing borders or accepting unlimited or unmanaged inward migration. But we can and ought to invert conventional framing of immigration. It is not primarily an act of charity when the United States welcomes immigrants, including refugees; it is a source of national renewal, and particularly so at a time when native-born Americans are choosing to have fewer children. Bringing immigrants into American society, integrating them into the fabric of the country, is not a burden that we endure, it is an expression of strength. Not all polities can integrate outsiders and enlist them in a common project. We can.

The existing U.S. immigration system fails basic tests. It is comprised of outdated laws that are poorly or irregularly enforced. Over recent decades, there have been several efforts at bipartisan comprehensive immigration reform that have foundered on politics. Most elected leaders on the left talk about reform as a social justice issue for immigrants already in the United States, and most on the right talk about it as a law-and-order issue aimed at limiting additional immigration. Those political realities may be the essential components of a deal, but the strategic importance of immigration reform is its capacity to manage significant future immigration, which is something the U.S. will need.

There is little prospect of the U.S. returning to the population growth rates of a century ago, and it's not clear that that level of growth would be good. With the combination of some leadership by national figures and a few specific policy and legal changes, the United States could lay the foundation for modest and steady population growth. And that modest growth in population, through new births and new immigrants, would be an indicator of the success of the United States as a country, just as much as it would also be a contributor to it.

Again, the test of scale is not about being bigger than the rest, it is about being big enough to be significant in international politics and to hold on to many of the benefits that an advanced democracy like the U.S. gets out of being big. While U.S. strategy for the next fifty years needs to accommodate the reality that the United States does not have the largest population and, depending on China's economic trajectory, may not be the largest economy, the United States is well positioned—with smart policies that avert population decline and smart investments to boost productivity and shared prosperity— to maintain a modestly expanding circle of new Americans both native and foreign-born. And that project—of embracing policies that help maintain an America that is big enough to have real weight in the world—will be the foundation for the second part of the scale challenge, which is to think about how we use our influence in the world differently when we can't win just by using our scale alone. The rest of this chapter—and, really, the rest of this book—is not about bolstering the United States' status as the biggest world power. It's about dealing with the relative decline of U.S. scale on some measures, and about what we can do to secure American success even so.

6.

The international system that has been underwritten by the United States and its partners since World War II has been permissive of progress, if not always conducive to it. It has not led to universal and reliable protection of human freedom and dignity in the world as envisioned by early-twentieth-century American leaders such as Woodrow Wilson, Franklin Delano Roosevelt, and Eleanor Roosevelt. But it has provided guardrails; it has reduced violent interstate conflict even as interstate relations have expanded; and, for societies that make progress on democracy and development, it has provided an infrastructure to lean on for support.

For the last seventy-five years, and particularly in the wake of the Cold War, much of the world—authoritarian governments, democratic governments, and those in between—has assumed that the United States would, on a perpetual basis, act as the "long pole in the tent" in the international system. The assumption was that U.S. power, military, political, and economic, would be the backstop. While the United States will remain central, it's no longer tenable that the U.S. can or will do this on its own.

In the context of U.S. politics, this realization can be so jarring to some that it results in knee-jerk isolationism—"we can no longer afford to run the world, so we should just acknowledge that and focus on ourselves" the thinking goes. Depending on who's speaking, if they come from the political left they might add "it's not like we were particularly good at it or deserving of the role anyway," or if they come from the right: "we already spend too much money on foreigners anyway." The core of this argument about America stepping back is understandable but dangerous. It makes untenable assumptions that do not sufficiently appreciate the features and functions of the international system we've got, and that do not sufficiently reflect the likelihood that the alternatives would be much worse for human beings.

The world does not run itself. Shipping lanes on which we depend do not just naturally exist. International agreements about pollution or air traffic or consumer goods standards don't just magically arise and enforce themselves. Borders that we see on maps do not show up as painted lines on the earth and sea. The international system is made up of rules and institutions and platforms for exchange and sharing of technical information, and of political bodies and webs of treaties and regional agreements. It is less visible to most Americans than their local or state government, of course, but it affects all of us in multiple ways. It is flawed. But a world without it would involve less human flourishing and much more human tragedy.

The argument that the United States, because of past behavior and present flaws, does not *deserve* to lead such a system, or is not particularly good at it, misses the point. In its best form this claim uses legitimate criticism of the U.S. track record to obscure the likely consequences of handing over management of the international system to governments that have no meaningful democratic accountability or commitment to liberal principles. It's a tragedy when the United States or other democracies take actions that violate international law or otherwise call into question democratic leaders' commitment to universal principles. The use of torture by the U.S. during the George W. Bush administration was a moral and political mistake. We should condemn such actions and learn from them. However, an obviously flawed democratic superpower is better than a spit-shined autocratic one. To argue otherwise is a morally outrageous indulgence in double standards.

And the argument that American leadership in the world constitutes some kind of optional expense or charity on behalf of non-Americans is similarly misguided. Americans depend on the international system; and not just because we participate in the global economy but because if we are not engaging with the world, the world will visit us at home. As scholar and long-time John McCain advisor Robert Kagan memorably put it in the title of his 2018 book about the disintegration of world order, left untended "the jungle grows back."[5]

The prospect of a new hegemon replacing the United States— potentially an authoritarian state supported by authoritarian partners—is the context for the second element of the test of scale. If such states could rewrite and set the rules for international politics, it would have enormous and intolerable consequences for human dignity, freedom, and prosperity both at home and around the world.

When Britain's period of global primacy ended during the twentieth century, the United States was there to pick up the baton. Today there is no rising democratic actor to take the United States' place, so the U.S. must encourage new cooperative arrangements among responsible states that can tackle global problems. In the absence of an acceptable successor, the U.S. has to work with its partners to build a substitute. This task involves both using power (to support these new cooperatives) and handing over some of the responsibility and burdens of deploying it at the same time—it is practically, politically, and conceptually challenging. The U.S. and its allies in Europe and Asia—who have also depended on American predominance for their own economic and political security—must work together to manage the transition upon us.

7.

Since World War II, and spurred by the emergence of the Cold War, a cornerstone of the United States' security strategy has been a system of treaty-based defense alliances. The North Atlantic Treaty Organization, or NATO, binds the United States and Canada with allies in Europe, and is the largest, most prominent, and most successful example. Less well known is that two years before the signing of the North Atlantic Treaty created NATO in 1949, the U.S. signed a collective defense treaty with countries in South and Central America. And in the years after NATO's founding, the U.S. signed treaties that established ally relationships with Australia and New Zealand (1951), Japan (1951), the Philippines (1951), and the Republic of Korea (1953). The U.S., Australia, New Zealand, Thailand, France, the United Kingdom, the Philippines, and Pakistan—which then included present-day Bangladesh—created the Southeast Asia Treaty Organization, or SEATO, after signing a collective defense treaty in 1954. The organization was disbanded in 1977.

Alliances are difficult to manage. They entail much more than signing a treaty. NATO allies invest a great deal to ensure "interoperability"—so that the various militaries that are part of the alliance can work together. To maximize the benefits of a military alliance like NATO, French tanks need to be able to "talk" to German communications equipment and fit on Greek naval vessels. Even the strongest and most high-functioning alliances, like NATO, are vulnerable to disagreements. A few years ago the French president called NATO "brain dead," provoking alarm in some Allied capitals. Aligning views among allies about what an alliance should do, and what the threats and opportunities are, is essential to making the alliance work. NATO operates on consensus; all allies have to agree on changes to the collective strategy. Some U.S. treaty ally relationships, inside and outside of NATO, are more fraught than others, especially with countries whose domestic politics have taken a troubling turn.

So alliances aren't easy. But they are useful. When defensive treaties work well, they do what they are supposed to do, which is to prevent large-scale wars in part by providing a facsimile of size that makes attacking members of an alliance an unattractive prospect. The preparation, training, and joint exercises that the U.S. military conducts with treaty allies are meant to prevent wars by deterring would-be aggressors. As Ben Hodges, who retired as the commanding general of the U.S. Army in Europe, puts it: "More sweat in training, less blood in combat."

And formal alliances aren't the only way that the U.S. can generate outsized political impact from military cooperation. After Russia's second invasion of Ukraine, in February 2022, the United States went into diplomatic overdrive, setting up the Ukraine Defense Contact Group working with more than fifty partner countries both inside NATO and beyond to coordinate support for Ukraine's self-defense. Before the invasion there were three countries, including the U.S., providing support to Ukraine's military. A month later, there were thirty. Ukrainians had been trained on old Soviet systems. Some U.S. partners had themselves once been Soviet satellites and had extra equipment. Once military planners found the equipment in storage locations, it had to be tested, repaired, packed up, transported, and in some cases backfilled with new purchases and transfers. All of that was more complicated than if the U.S. had just shipped out its own equipment (and it did plenty of that too in the first year of the war), but the internationalization of the support effort increased both the amount of support going to Ukraine and the political message it sent about the scale of the community standing with Ukraine.

In the decade after the Cold War, when U.S. supremacy as the world's only remaining superpower was widely recognized, some questioned the enduring utility of the U.S.'s alliance system. (As late as 2013, when I was serving as a U.S. ambassador in Europe, I had a European counterpart say to me, "But Daniel, don't you think NATO is obsolete? Isn't it time to sunset the Alliance?" That ambassador's government would go on to make a significant investment in new artillery systems in the wake of Putin's first invasion of Ukraine the next year.) The context has changed since the 1990s. Despite enduring military strength, the U.S. cannot, on its own, back and defend the existing international order with military power indefinitely. It must share this burden with other countries, and use their power to augment its own where necessary. Given the rise of nondemocratic powers, the role of alliances in providing a substitute for scale is more important than ever. Alliances are not a "nice-to-have" for the United States in the twenty-first century. And they do not grow stronger and deeper naturally. They require nurturing, investment, and hard work.

Against this backdrop, President Donald Trump's so-called America First foreign policy, which saw him pander to dictators and make repeated rhetorical attacks on NATO and NATO allies, was confounding and damaging. The role of alliances in U.S. strategy is changing—in the post–Cold War decade they were arguably a way for the U.S. to herd (mostly) friendly cats: they were a mechanism by which the United States organized a world of which it was the de facto manager. The situation is shifting. In the years to come, stable sustained alliances will be ever more indispensable as components of the United States' ability to share responsibility for maintaining collective security with others. Alliances are tools for coordinating so that the U.S. can project enough power at scale to deter those who might seek to undermine world peace and prosperity. Working through alliances also sends a political message because doing so is by definition not unilateral.

8.

For now, the U.S. retains significant superiority in terms of military scale. The United States remains by far the most capable military power in the world—representing 38 percent of global spending.[6] And if core U.S. allies are included—NATO, and Japan, South Korea, New Zealand, and Australia—the figure is much larger—61 percent of global military spending.[7] While the Russia-Ukraine war that began in 2022 brought new lessons in asymmetrical fighting—cheap drones proved surprisingly effective—it also underscored some enduring characteristics of conventional interstate warfare: it is expensive, requires logistics and resupply capabilities, and it is incremental and grueling.

President Trump and President Biden have both presided over significant increases in defense spending, often above even what the Pentagon's own budget proposals have requested. The U.S. can manage thoughtful increases, but a habit or trajectory of constant expansion of defense spending faster than GDP growth is unsustainable and risks overstretching the United States. We cannot endlessly spend more; we have to spend smarter (and grow our economy). Constant increases in defense spending reflect both a failure to harvest the benefits of an alliance system, and an anachronistic view of the military as the only instrument of U.S. security policy, rather than as the central component among others.

One of the benefits of military alliances, in theory, is that they spread the burden of defense costs while amplifying the overall military capacity, or "defense benefit," available to any one ally. They are a sort of insurance policy. This burden-sharing aspect is why Barack Obama's administration pressed for inclusion of a floor for each country's own defense budget—2 percent of GDP for all NATO allies—in the commitments made at the NATO summit in Wales in 2014. President Trump vocally continued the pressure on allies (though he never seemed to understand the difference between a country's own defense budget—which is the target of the 2 percent push—and dues paid to NATO, which are relatively small by comparison).

The United States needs its allies to take on a fair share of defense investments because the United States cannot pursue endless expansion of its defense spending and compete in the next half century. Paradoxically, there comes a point at which the scale of a military, or rather of the expenditures required to sustain it, is a strategic drag on a country rather than a strategic advantage. The United States faces the risk that we are trapped—either by our adversaries, by our failure to fully leverage our alliances, by our own outdated frameworks and strategies, or by our failure to spend efficiently—into an endless pursuit of military scale at the expense of other necessary investments to keep the United States competitive.

Any U.S. president with even a modest understanding of the world will prioritize U.S. participation in a robust network of alliances characterized by meaningful and fair burden-sharing. And any U.S. president who has read her or his initial intelligence briefings (or taken the pulse of Congress) will include in her or his national security strategy that the U.S. should retain its status as the world's most significant military power in the coming decades. As the United States declines in relative size and power (with the rise of China and the development of other regional powers), we still want to keep advantages of scale—in this case the scale of our military power—and the advantages that flow from it *for as long as we reasonably can.*

We should not slash the defense budget. We should however adopt three related guiding principles for thinking about defense spending:

1. Here's the hardest one, at least politically speaking: "As long as we reasonably can" does not mean forever. Though we can certainly maintain preeminence for the foreseeable future, it may not be possible for the United States to remain the world's largest defense spender indefinitely. A singular focus on attempting to maintain the most powerful military *at any cost* could undermine the United States' strength in the world and its ability to secure its system of government. It may be appealing to promote a security strategy that entails perpetual U.S. military supremacy, but to do so is either to indulge in jingoism or denial. The reason why military spending, rather than headcount, is the most common proxy for military strength these days is that the productivity of military personnel, like that of workers, can be amplified by training, technology, and equipment. The largest army isn't necessarily the strongest. Indeed, the economic size of a country, especially if it has a diversified economy, is more likely to indicate the ability to invest in and develop the kinds of innovations that make raw person-power decreasingly relevant. Given the highly modernized and technologically enabled military we have, the ability to sustain military strength depends upon the size and sophistication of the U.S. economy. A strategy that pursues military expansion at the expense of general innovation and economic growth (like the one that Russian president Putin has pursued, and the one that, in an earlier era, the Soviet Union pursued in the Cold War), will

lead to a military consuming the future of the country it is meant to defend.

More perilous is the mindset that a goal of permanent preeminence creates, one which encourages kneejerk one-upmanship rather than analytical judgments. Signing up for perpetual military dominance means signing up for an arms race, or a series of arms races, without end. The narrative that the U.S. contest with China will or has become a "new Cold War" is an ahistorical oversimplification. However, it's worth noting that when it is proffered, the implicit assumption in the frame is most often that the role of the United States would once again be played by the United States, and that of the Soviet Union played by China. Why are we so sure that it would be China that eventually bends under the weight of its own defense spending and economic malaise, and not the United States? In whatever contest we may witness between the United States and China, I have confidence in the U.S. in the long run, but I'm skeptical that the U.S. can successfully pursue the current competition in the same way that it pre-vailed in the last geopolitical competition. Outspending in an arms race is not necessarily a replicable strategy.

2. Traditional defense investments and the resultant military power are only one of several sources or potential sources of American strategic advantage. And if the U.S. is likely to be less unambiguously dominant militarily twenty-five or fifty years from now, we ought to be concerned with building out our other sources of power and influence in international pol-itics. I'm not just restating the point about the importance of maintaining an advanced and growing economy, though that is important. It is a recognition that trade and investment,

cutting-edge research, moral legitimacy, reputation as a good-faith actor, regulatory innovation and standard setting, and diplomatic reach and skill, among other assets, already affect U.S. total power on the international stage. We are likely to become more dependent on these factors for projecting power in the coming decades, and there are steps we can take to prepare.

Militaries are meant to deter, neutralize, and destroy threats. The United States and its allies need to maintain military power. But they also need to build up the more constructive elements of national power, and to invest in doing so. And though the U.S. military has a strong record of spurring innovations with general-use applications and training personnel for jobs after military service, if we were going to look to spur innovation or do advanced job training, there are more cost-effective ways to accomplish those objectives than adding tens of billions each year to an $800+ billion a year defense budget.

3. To maintain maximal U.S. strategic advantage from our military for as long as possible, the United States must spend smartly. Scale—and smart alliances—should generate efficiency benefits that allow for the U.S. to get more impact out of a given level of spending than others do. But because of patterns that have emerged in our political system and a collective failure to take the problem of inefficient or wasteful spending seriously, the United States is spending more than necessary to achieve our current level of military capability. There was a time where no other country was capable of coming anywhere near the United States in spending. And while the U.S. is still the biggest spender by a significant margin, it can no longer afford to be blasé about waste. The challenge that the United States faces goes beyond the "military-industrial complex"

that President Dwight Eisenhower presciently predicted. The retired five-star general foresaw that in the midst of a geopolitical struggle, the military and defense contractors and manufacturers would effectively team up to capture decision-making about the public purse. Inefficient military spending is a tax on all citizens—it is a consumption of unnecessary resources raised by either taxation or debt. The U.S. was once so big (or, rather, others were relatively so much smaller) that a failure to spend smart didn't noticeably affect U.S. military competitiveness, but today inefficient allocations aren't just a tax, they are a strategic problem.

In the wake of 9/11 and the invasions of Afghanistan and Iraq, the public lionization of the military has become a salient part of American culture. Servicemembers throwing opening pitches at baseball games, pauses in other sporting events to "thank the troops," discounts at ski resorts, and preferred boarding on airlines. These have all become more common as public ways of acknowledging the service that millions of Americans choose to give in our volunteer military. And their service is worth acknowledging. The ramping up of public praise for the military may also reflect an awareness among political leaders that the continued prosecution of the wars that began at the start of the century was increasingly difficult to justify, and was imposing increasing and disproportionate costs on those Americans most likely to have participated in our volunteer military fighting force. The rituals of public laudation could be seen as a form of—inadequate—compensation over two decades of doubling-down on bad decisions with terrible consequences.

The increase in public praise for the military also

happened against the backdrop of a country that has become more polarized on so many other issues. And so, while it has often been popular to "support the troops," vocal support of the military as a kind of lowest common denominator in American cultural politics has become more prominent as other areas of public consensus have receded in an era of hyper-polarization. And even though defense budgets have grown much faster than the pay for enlisted servicemembers, there is a conflation of military budgets with "supporting the troops." Combine this feature of the cultural moment with the structural financial relationship between private sector defense actors and elected officials and it's no wonder that the budgets keep going up and up.

The United States will spend over $60 billion per year over the next ten years on maintaining and modernizing its nuclear forces.[8] To put that in context, it's the same as the total amount the federal government contributes to K–12 education each year.[9] We know that any nuclear war could bring a catastrophic end to human civilization as we know it. In 2021, President Biden and Russian President Putin restated the principle that "a nuclear war cannot be won and must never be fought," a formulation first used by Ronald Reagan and Mikhail Gorbachev in 1985. It remains the case that any confrontation or contest between the U.S. and other major nuclear powers, most notably Russia or China, would not be "won" by virtue of a larger nuclear arsenal. Amidst the sometimes breathless commentary on geopolitical rivalries, it will take discipline for U.S. policymakers to focus on what the U.S. actually needs in terms of new capabilities and extending the life of existing systems. And although Vladimir Putin's unilateral suspension of New START—the last remaining nuclear arms control agreement between the U.S. and Russia—in early 2023 makes the diplomacy to avert new arms races more difficult, international agreements to limit nuclear weapons remain important. Investing in nuclear arms control should not be seen as the hobbyhorse of peaceniks but rather as a way of managing strategic risks at acceptable cost.

The United States will be more competitive in 2050 if it has a technological and innovation edge, if it achieves the most sustainable internal stability, and if it rallies partners and allies. Future geopolitical contests are more likely to be won by a team of computer coders than by a nuclear strike. Wasteful and other strategically inefficient military spending threatens to undermine U.S. capacity in areas that are likely to be the real source of U.S. comparative advantage in the years to come.

The debate over defense spending needs to be reframed. Right now, members of Congress are politically incentivized to demonstrate that they are "strong on defense" by signing bigger and bigger checks for the Pentagon, as most of them do. Those who oppose increases usually point out other investments that could be made with nondefense spending. Our politics hangs on the idea of a trade-off—we can have strong defense or we can have strong social security or education or health care. But this version of the trade-off obscures the more difficult truths we must face. Yes, wasteful or unnecessary defense spending deprives the U.S. of resources that should be invested in other sources of competitive advantage. But wasteful or excessive spending is also unsustainable, regardless of what other fiscal expenditures it displaces, and it undermines national defense itself. We no longer have a world in which the United States is guaranteed to be forever the biggest; instead, we're in a world in which the U.S. could inadvertently be dangerously overextended. In an era when some measure of *relative* decline of U.S. military power is almost certain given the economic rise of other countries, corporate capture and politicization of defense spending threatens to *accelerate* rather than forestall that decline. We are choosing between a strong defense that includes robust but efficient spending, versus a weaker defense that allows for inefficient and unnecessary spending to continue. As we make the transition from Goliath to David, we can't spend all our money on nice new swords when what we need is the highest-tech slingshot.

9.

In the twenty-first century, military force is necessary but insufficient to defend against security threats. Pandemics and climate change don't care about how many hypersonic missiles a country has. Military power remains the central element of national defense, but it cannot ensure societal resilience on its own. It's a shell, but a permeable one. The point of national defense is defending and protecting a space in which the rest of life—the creating, the teaching, the trading, the debating, the praying, the parenting, the dreaming—takes place. Those are endeavors that give a society strength over the long term, including the strength to muster and supply a military. It's what's inside the shell that matters.

The United States needs to deepen our partnerships with other democracies, going beyond cooperative arrangements on defense and reaching deep into the foundations on which we build vibrant democratic societies. Just as we can amplify the effective scale of our military by working in alliances, we need to aim for a similar kind of facsimile of scale with respect to drivers of societal strength, particularly science, technology, education, and economic relationships that drive productivity. To defend the welfare of Americans in the twenty-first century we need to understand the challenge not as defending the U.S. in its own bubble but rather as building the U.S. into a central node in a network.

Two intertwined shifts since the end of the Cold War have changed how we should think about defending American interests. First, globalization expanded. In 1991, trade was about 37 percent of global GDP; in 2021, it was 57 percent.[10] A big piece of the expansion of trade as a percentage of GDP is attributable to the explosive, export-driven growth of China. And that leads to the second change: whereas during the Cold War the world divided politically into three blocs—U.S.-aligned, Soviet-aligned, and nonaligned countries—and the two blocs affiliated with each of the superpowers had minimal trade between them, the post–Cold War era has seen much more economic integration. Trade within regions has expanded because of the growth of the European Union and other regional economic groupings such as ECOWAS (Economic Community of West African States) as well as trade agreements such as the North American Free Trade Agreement (NAFTA) and its successor, the United States–Mexico–Canada Agreement (USMCA). Globally, trade has expanded with the rise of the shipping container (the role of this relatively low-tech innovation in driving global trade is truly remarkable[11]) and the integration of China and Russia into the WTO and the world economy writ large.

The world is more economically integrated than the world of thirty years ago, the world is also geopolitically more divided than it was in the 1990s. The conventional wisdom, popular a quarter century ago, that economic integration and growth would support a measure of political liberalization has not proved true. Part of the conundrum is attributable to the success of authoritarian leaders like those in the Chinese Communist Party that have split the governance of political and economic spheres: they have taken advantage of the benefits of a global market economy undergirded by a system of rules and institutions expanded in the aftermath of World War II, while eschewing reforms that would advance more liberal political arrangements. They had their economic cake and ate their authoritarian governance too. And Russian president Vladimir Putin, during his first decade of power in the 2000s, used the money Russia gained from selling oil and gas to the West to strike an authoritarian bargain at home, the essence of which was: "You give me control over the political sphere and give up your freedoms in exchange for stability and a rising standard of living."

From the U.S. perspective the current situation is troubling. Though the U.S. economy continues to grow and is likely to remain the world's largest until at least the end of the 2020s, China's economic growth has created a nondemocratic competitor that can use its economic strength for political objectives. China has increasingly leveraged its own scale to seek an edge in particular areas of the economy that are likely to generate political advantage in the coming decades. Chinese leaders have studied the 2008 financial crisis and the sanctions imposed on Russia in 2014 after the illegal annexation of Crimea and first invasion of Ukraine, and again in 2022 after the start of Russia's war on Ukraine.[12] They have sought not only to defend against vulnerabilities that arise from economic interdependence but also to develop asymmetries in China's economic relations with others so that China can continue to use economic relationships for political purposes in the future.

Protecting a U.S. bubble is no longer enough. The United States and its democratic partners are going to remain independent states, but they need to merge their bubbles when it comes to core sources of strength like innovation and research. Achieving this objective is trickier given the history of the last thirty years. The solution cannot be to reverse and replay an alternate path for globalization where we are more attentive to political differences and more careful about extending the benefits of globalization to those who might use them against us. Instead the broad effort should be on where we go from here—and on being more purposeful with deepening relationships grounded in values that allow for intersocietal cooperation and collaboration. There are some specific areas—on particularly sensitive supply chain issues, as one example—where the U.S., Europe, and other democracies will continue to attempt to undo selectively some economic integration with nondemocratic states.[13] But in general there is more value to be gained over the long run from an affirmative focus on deepening partnerships with democratic countries than from undoing relationships with others.

10.

The State Department can generate a list of ways we're "partnering" with almost every country on earth. That kind of general relationship-building is essential, but the kind of deep partnerships I'm talking about take pooled resources, strategy, and people to manage. We can't be everything everywhere all at once. We have to be discriminating. The U.S. should focus its partnership-building energy on two overlapping areas: strategically important segments of the economy, and emerging technologies that provoke both a sense of possibility and a sense of concern. There should be a special concentration on these emerging, potentially transformative technologies—including AI, biotechnology, new energy technologies, geoengineering, advanced robotics, 6G digital wireless communication, new applications of space exploration, and quantum computing—because they are likely to drive economic growth and be a major point of global competition in the coming decades.

Transformative technologies change the way we work and live, the way that we experience the world. They create new forms of power—power that can be used for good or for ill. Power that, when deployed, can have unintended consequences. If not on their own, certainly the combination of the personal computer, the internet, and digital communications technologies has had a transformative effect in the last generation. Even those who understood that the invention of the personal computer was transformative didn't know *how* it would change almost every middle-class job. Even early evangelists of the internet had no idea that it would lead to social media or to new forms of surveillance or propaganda that would challenge existing political and economic structures.

We are in the midst of a next wave of emerging technologies. We don't yet know how these technologies or combinations of them will change the world we live in. But some of these will be transformative, and will present new forms of power that are, at least for a time, untamed by governance.

The intersection of biology and technology is one that promises a range of possibilities to address biological limitations, including disease, but it also raises the prospect of new kinds of societal competition and destructive power. To bolster the leadership of the U.S. and its partners on biotech, the U.S. can build partnerships with likeminded countries in the natural sciences and basic research, the kind of research that is less likely to be conducted by private sector actors because its applications are often unknown. Partnerships between the U.S. and other democracies in Europe and Asia can pool public funding for this kind of research. We could provide incentives for universities in Tokyo, Bangalore, Berlin, and Ann Arbor to collaborate. Streamlining of visas and work permits for scholars doing advanced research would make exchanges easier. Congress and the White House could work together to build on the success of the U.S.'s Defense Advanced Research Projects Agency (DARPA), and create a new entity that would bring together international democratic partners, supported by pooled investment, to work together on the development of innovative applications of biotechnology as well as other emerging technologies. AUKUS, the 2021 joint agreement between the U.S., Australia, and the U.K. to work together on defense in the Indo-Pacific, garnered international attention because it includes a plan for the U.S. to sell nuclear submarines to Australia. More intriguing is the agreement's provisions on collaboration regarding emerging technology, which, if implemented successfully, could be expanded or replicated to include other partners like Canada, Japan, India, and European allies.[14]

Technological innovation and science benefit from scale in education (it's impossible to predict which child will grow up to be her generation's Marie Curie or Albert Einstein—but if you're educating a larger number of people, you're more likely to get a larger number of trailblazers) and research investments (most start-ups fail—but many successes follow first, second, third attempts). And so, in addition to a domestic focus on the early parts of the innovation value chain (including education and basic research), the United States should forge deeper connections with other democracies. The U.S.-India initiative on critical and emerging technologies (ICET), created by President Biden and Prime Minister Modi in 2021, is a case in point.

In the past, the U.S. approach to maintaining a competitive edge has been to protect the sources of our advantage, many of which were rooted in our superior scale, and which included our status as the only tech superpower. An enormous share of the intellectual property attached to the last wave of technological innovation was developed on U.S. soil. But innovation has become more geographically distributed. China has become a tech juggernaut, and other countries like India are developing cutting-edge applications too. To transition to a more durable approach in the future, we're going to have to change the way we think. Instead of hoarding, the U.S. needs to create pathways for what we might call "selective sharing." Because the U.S. military seeks technological advantage, the U.S. maintains a set of restrictions on the export of cutting-edge technological know-how. Many of these restrictions are rooted in Cold War policies aimed at denying technology to the Soviet Union and Warsaw Pact countries. But that U.S. technological dominance is not what it once was both reduces the benefits and raises the costs of these restrictions. It reduces the benefit because, as a practical matter, the diffusion of technological know-how in more places around the world means that the U.S. cannot deny access to information as effectively as it once could when it had something closer to a monopoly on advanced technologies. And it raises costs because these restrictions on sharing knowledge can be obstacles to kinds of collaboration with close partners that the U.S. now needs because of its declining scale. The shift in the costs and benefits associated with them does not mean that export restrictions should be scrapped, but they need to be reconsidered in light of changes in the world and in the U.S. place in it. As former U.S. intelligence officer Martijn Rasser has argued, they should be pursued in partnership with allies to be effective, and restrictions should be more carefully and selectively deployed only when they can deny rivals' ability to compete in areas where the U.S. or its allies have a technological advantage.[15] Broad restrictions on sharing technology made sense for a world in which the U.S. dominated technological innovation and could, when pressed, go it alone.

But we have entered an era when we do more with our friends to compensate for what we used to be able to do on our own.

New frontiers in knowledge also raise major ethical issues that cannot be left to markets. Democracies need to set standards to govern the application of new technologies that are consistent with the principles underlying democratic governance, including a respect for human dignity and autonomy.[16] There may be commercial as well as moral advantage to discipline in this regard: technology is frightening because it is difficult to understand. If democratic societies develop credible, transparent ways to manage its dangerous or frightening aspects, their technology products will be more desirable. The European Union, despite its unwieldiness, has emerged as a kind of regulatory entrepreneur.[17] It hasn't yet figured out the right tools to give consumers and citizens confidence in new technologies while also encouraging the innovation that delivers benefits. But instead of seeking to curb its standard-setting ventures, the U.S. should try to learn from the EU's early efforts, and collaborate with the EU to refine standard-setting in a way that keeps us safe, encourages economic growth, and defends universal values.

The U.S. can function as a node in a network of innovation and of governance—working with partners to incubate transformative technologies, and also to build public trust in them, including with safeguards that counter misuse and abuse of those technologies. The goal is both to maintain a competitive edge and to ensure that the rules that will emerge to govern these technologies are rules that are good for people, not for nefarious actors. The United States and its partners need to retain enough scale around cutting-edge technology to deny authoritarian countries a monopoly over such technologies, and the standards that govern their use. Done right, the U.S. and its partners can use a transparent, good-faith approach to tech governance to win the confidence of consumers and citizens in their own markets and beyond.

11.

As it deepens relationships with close partners to drive innovation and economic growth, the United States also has to change the way it engages in international politics. The United States does not have sufficient scale, or sufficient expectations of its future scale, to assume that others will line up behind U.S. positions. That doesn't mean that the United States should just be one of the gang. But it does mean that the notion of the United States as the natural leader of the so-called free world is eroding, even among the U.S.'s closest allies. Moreover, as a hegemon's ability to determine outcomes declines, other countries begin to hedge; after all, the end of hegemony introduces uncertainty for them too. That's why governments have started to say that they don't want to choose between the U.S. and China. And it's why, in order to retain its leadership in the future, the United States needs to play the role of "cooperator-in-chief" and spend much more energy actually engaging and persuading partners than it does asserting the right path. The era of de facto American dominance has ended. We live now in an era in which American leadership—real leadership that involves rallying partners behind purpose and engaging in the give and take that is part of any group dynamic—is essential.

Such leadership requires real changes in how U.S. officials conceive of and communicate the U.S. position in the world. Paradoxically, by acknowledging that the U.S. is not in a position to give orders by virtue of its superpower status, the U.S. can end up with more enthusiastic partners—on military and defense, technology and research, trade, and so on—than it would if it held on to the pretense of the world being stuck in 1991 or even 2005. An implicit acknowledgment of the changing geopolitical context, and a shift in U.S. approach and behavior, adds to the credibility and influence that the United States has. Denialism detracts from it.

The U.S., for all its challenges, has an enormous amount going for it, and has enough scale that none of the global challenges that other democracies care about can be efficiently addressed without it. Leading in this context might be more challenging than the 1990s but it's potentially richer and more fruitful too; it can result in more resilient solutions where multiple states backstop each other and more meaningful burden-sharing instead of others saying "oh, that problem—we'll let the U.S. handle it."

Effecting this shift requires more than just a change in U.S. understanding of its role in the world, it means a change in how, practically speaking, the U.S. conducts diplomacy and engages in international politics. If the U.S. is going to shift from a pyramid model with the United States at the top to a model where the U.S. is instead playing a leading role in different networks of cooperation, then it is going to have to change the way it does business.

Where American diplomacy was once predominantly conducted in bilateral, country-to-country channels, engaging with groups of countries will need to become a bigger part of the U.S. approach. The U.S. has ramped up its capabilities to establish de facto working groups of priority partners like the new Quad (Quadrilateral Security Dialogue)—comprised of India, Japan, Australia, and the U.S.—that has emerged as a platform for handling certain security and economic issues in the Pacific. Or, to take another example, the Financial Action Task Force (FATF), a group of more than thirty countries, including the U.S. and China, that work together to limit illicit financial transactions and terrorist financing.

A smart U.S. strategy in the next decade will develop many of such "constellations" of cooperation, preferably, but not exclusively, with other democracies. To capture one set of opportunities—say, the development of secure semiconductor supply chains—the U.S. will have to work with one group of countries. To deal with a particular challenge—say, the freedom of navigation and commercial shipping changes caused by the melting of Arctic ice—we need to work with a different (overlapping) group. In each case, the idea is to identify a set of countries that can act as a kind of board of directors or team to tackle a specific problem. And in each case, the goal is for the U.S. to be able to capture an opportunity or deal with a problem without the burdens of acting unilaterally, and for the partnership to help mimic the advantages that come from scale by bringing the entire group's capacities and geopolitical heft to the task. These kinds of tailor-made partnerships are proliferating, and more will emerge.

As the U.S. moves forward, partnerships with other democracies will remain more attractive. Not only because of moral or ideological commitments, but because partnerships based on shared goals and values are more likely to be reliable and fruitful. There is more trust between partners that are seeking the same goals for the same reasons, and these partnerships have a lower cost-benefit ratio. But many issues will continue to require working with nondemocracies. The United States and others that care about human rights and fundamental freedoms cannot present a compelling model for addressing global problems by dividing the world into strict groups and ruling out engagement with nondemocracies. The challenge will be to pursue practical cooperation where necessary in a way that doesn't lend legitimacy to authoritarian models or call into question our own commitment to liberal values.

In a world in which the U.S. is trying to do more with persuasion and politics and can do less with military and economic power, it must increase its influence where international law and norms are endorsed, where standards are set, where force is authorized when necessary. Therefore, the kind of diplomacy that takes place in formal multilateral organizations like the United Nations and various regional and technical bodies is poised to become more important even if those institutions themselves are struggling to adapt to the reality of a new geopolitical context and may require reform for a different set of challenges and a new era.

Former U.S. Secretary of State Madeleine Albright was fond of saying that Americans don't like multilateralism because it has too many syllables and ends in an "ism." But the U.S. needs to get better at multilateral diplomacy—the kind of negotiations with other governments about the common standards that will define important aspects of international politics in the future. We can learn from partners and allies, many of which have had multilateral diplomacy as a central part of their national strategies for much longer. Smaller countries are much more focused on the international system and its institutions because they depend much more upon it. They can't count on scale like the U.S. and other big countries, so they have to appeal to the weight of collectives to address security concerns.

In the State Department, the Bureau of International Organization Affairs has not historically been among the most powerful. It has been possible for foreign service officers (the U.S.'s professional, career diplomatic corps) to make successful careers in the bureaucracy while avoiding ever serving in a multilateral policy position in Washington or in an overseas post at an international organization. But negotiating agreements with fifteen (or fifty or two hundred) other countries is a different skill set than engaging a single government and its populace. In the future, there might be more focus on training diplomats for multilateral engagements. And since they will be working on international agreements about topics ranging from climate to telecoms to artificial intelligence, the next generation of diplomats will need to have more technical literacy in specific areas. When the U.S. was the dominant marketplace for new technologies, much of its domestic standard-setting simply became the basis for international standards. Innovation is increasingly distributed, so more of those standards will be negotiated with international partners.

12.

The U.S. and its partners and allies are in the middle of a transition from an unambiguously U.S.-led international system to one in which the U.S., together with other advanced democracies, must lend both leadership and resources to a much more collaborative approach to what is unappealingly called "global governance." The relative decline of the United States in terms of scale means that others will have to step up and that the U.S. will have to reach out in new ways. From a U.S. perspective, the challenge is to cede some of the responsibility that it has had in the last generation while building a new kind of robust leadership role in the coming generations.

And for that to happen, the U.S. must learn to lead in new ways. Whether the U.S. can rise to that challenge—the challenge of adapting its modes of leadership to a post-hegemonic moment—is at the center of the test of scale. A new era of American global leadership is probably not how most Americans would describe the moment we're living through. There is a great deal of catastrophizing about U.S. decline in the American public sphere today.

There's a lot that still has to go wrong for the United States and its allies and partners and a lot that has to go right for authoritarian leaders in the coming decades for that to be true. It's worth considering the possibility that what we will see is, yes, a significant decline in the United States' relative scale in the world economy and its ability to take unilateral action in international politics, but also that the United States will remain a significant power, and even the most significant global actor, for many decades to come. There are a lot of scenarios short of extremes that are more plausible than drawing straight lines based on the trajectories of the first years of the 2020s. The United States should take seriously the challenges of maintaining its large, economically productive population, but we should take comfort, not fear, from the fact that the challenge in front of the U.S. is not holding on to hegemony, it's to succeed without it.

The test of scale cannot be addressed in isolation. It connects to the tests of investment and fairness. The Obama administration spent years developing the frameworks and drafts for new trade agreements with Europe and Asia. They were not perfect, but they included more robust labor, environmental, and human rights standards than previous generations of trade agreements. From President Obama's perspective, they would have accomplished two strategic objectives. First, they would have knit key partners and their economies more thoroughly to the United States—allowing the United States to achieve greater scale in trade and investment networks based on common standards. Second, they would have sharpened the choices for other countries who weren't part of the agreements: either join the rules-based system and play by the rules, or be excluded in consequential ways. The Obama administration's strategy can be seen as creating economic partnerships that would be like a set of parentheses around the United States in both the Atlantic and Pacific, and, at the same time a kind of pincer that would make it increasingly unattractive for others, particularly in Asia, to contemplate pursuing alternative arrangements.

By the end of the Obama years, a shift in U.S. domestic politics—driven by a failure to reckon with the unequal dividends of previous trade agreements and of globalization more generally—led both candidates in the 2016 U.S. presidential election to announce their opposition to both trade agreements. Shortcomings around fairness in the U.S., particularly with respect to the social and economic dislocation precipitated by globalization, shaped the politics around a strategically important set of policy moves. If the U.S. had invested more in helping Americans adapt to the changing global economy, if the U.S. had better addressed the yawning inequality that an outdated social contract had produced by the early twenty-first century, more Americans and their representatives might have been enthusiastic about new trade deals.

Another lesson from Obama's unsuccessful attempts is that the world won't wait for the U.S. to sort itself out. The Trans-Pacific Partnership draft agreement, of which the United States had been the principal architect, became an agreement without the United States—called the Comprehensive and Progressive Agreement for Trans Pacific–Partnership, or CPTPP. That agreement has taken force and continues to attract new members. Geopolitical competition with China was a catalyst for the drive to develop the TPP. In late 2021, China applied to join the CPTPP. Ironies are often the most interesting evolutions in international politics.

Although the United States must adjust to the end of the brief moment of American unipolar superiority, the prospects are good for the United States to maintain sufficient scale, and thereby enough of the benefits of scale with respect to geopolitics and geoeconomics, to continue to have relatively outsized agency in international politics. The U.S. is indispensable and will remain so.

But the new era, and America's role in it, will require a different set of domestic strengths. The United States has never achieved scale only by having a large population or a large territory or a large alliance system—though each of these has been valuable and true. U.S. influence has derived not only from the scale of its national assets, but also from what one might call their quality. Any given measure of strength or success—economic output, total national power—is a function of both number and quality. And especially in an era where relative number or size is declining on several measures, quality matters more than ever. And the kind of quality needed—particularly superior quality of human capital—will require domestic policy changes. That's where investment comes in.

FROM MONOPOLY TO START-UP

THE INVESTMENT TEST

1.

In 1996, I trained and worked as a cowboy, or "ringer," in the local parlance, in the Northern Territory of Australia. The station, or ranch, I worked on was almost 500,000 acres, about half the size of Rhode Island, and it had sold a year or two earlier for less than half a million dollars. I spent most of my time fixing barbed wire fences in the hot Outback sun, and other than inoculations for the cattle and motorbikes for the station hands, most of the work we did seemed the same as what it might have been a century earlier. More recently, I visited a friend who owns a large family farm in eastern Colorado and spent an afternoon with his son planting corn. I found myself sitting in the cab of a $500,000 tractor that had more touchscreens in its control panels than the cockpit of a jet airliner. The tractor drove itself based on GPS which could be calibrated to less than one inch, planting corn and fertilizing it with precision. The farmer operating it had a master's degree and the mechanical and computer knowledge to operate and troubleshoot in the case of problems. He spent most of the day listening to economics podcasts. This isn't what most of his fellow college graduates living a few hours' drive away in Denver think of when they think of a "farmer."

If you had asked that farmer's dad back in 1996, it probably wasn't what he expected farming to look like in the 2020s either. But now, in retrospect he could see how economic forces beyond their small town had shaped it over the last decades. Technology drives labor productivity gains. Globalization has expanded marketplaces for goods and labor that reward those who are at the top of the value chain on each. My friend and his family had been fortunate—they had been able to invest in the new technology, and they had developed the skills to use that technology effectively, to plant and harvest more crops without additional workers. Some neighbors had not. My friend had grown their family's farm as others were forced to sell. Sometimes the disruptions enabled by globalization are even more unpredictable. The cattle station I worked on all those years ago sold in 2022 for over $20 million—but the buyer wasn't in the cattle business, it was a company that sells carbon credits. Globalization and global challenges are creating businesses that I couldn't have imagined when I was dodging termite mounds and rounding up cattle a quarter century ago.

2.

We are at the intersection of three megatrends. The first is the relative decline in global terms of the U.S. economy's scale, the second is the acceleration and distribution of technological change, and the third is the progress of globalization that—even with policy interventions meant to buy time for adaptation and smooth its effects—will make market forces more and more independent of political borders, so that U.S. workers (and the U.S. economy as a whole) are now irrevocably in a situation of more or less global competition. The combined effects of these megatrends point toward a future in which the United States will need to be more focused and more purposeful about retaining its productivity and innovation edge.

Even if the United States meets the test of scale and finds a new kind of American leadership as a cooperator-in-chief leading within constellations of cooperation with other countries, that model will only work if the United States is also building its advantage in other ways. Charm and good offices aren't sufficient. The U.S. needs to increase the productivity of its workforce and work to be an incubator of innovation. In the coming decades, the United States will need to build power in ideas and skills to make up for some of the influence it once drew from scale.

Someone might reply: "But the U.S. is already a beacon of innovation—look at the inventions and companies of the post–World War II era and what an enormous share of them were made in America. Silicon Valley, one small part of America, has shaped the digital age." Certainly there's an impressive historical track record. But overconfidence grounded in exceptionalism is dangerous. One can believe that the U.S. system has been unusual and has contributed a disproportionate share of global innovation in the last century without believing that it is naturally destined to do so indefinitely. Liberal democratic governance may be necessary but not sufficient to optimize for innovation. A large part of the U.S. innovation advantage in the last century can be attributed to scale, and to the way in which, because the

U.S. was bigger, it had a bigger collection of subnational ecosystems to support innovation and bigger markets to reward it. Scale and innovation are mutually reinforcing. But scale benefits also provide a kind of barrier to entry that lends a competitive advantage distinct from the quality of an idea. Even if the United States didn't focus all that much on generating the largest number of highly qualified computer scientists in the 1970s–1990s, because it was the largest advanced economy in the world, with the largest population of an advanced economy, and the largest number of advanced research universities, it ended up with the talent that shaped the evolution of the internet and the digital economy. One of the benefits of scale is that it generates critical mass around emergent communities and technologies that might not ever germinate in a different context.

Because the United States cannot count on the robust comparative advantage in terms of scale that it used to enjoy, it has to be more focused on developing other points of competitive edge. Like a legacy company that can no longer rely on a monopoly or semi-monopoly status to provide some measure of secure and stable returns, the United States must develop the other foundations for its national economic power.

There is more than a change of focus here. There's a real change in strategy required. It's not just that legacy companies tend to grow complacent as their dominant market share gives them the opportunity to raise prices over time without innovating or raising quality. That kind of strategic laziness is a risk. But there's also a strategic blindness that can afflict those dependent on scale. A friend who used to work for one of the brewing giants reflected to me how hard it is for corporations that have benefited from scale advantages to see the limits of a strategy that is dependent on doing so. Past success engenders a kind of confirmation bias that causes big companies to see their scale as essential to success in their industry. And then something like craft brewing comes out of nowhere and becomes a profitable and nimble disrupter.

Invention and genius drove American prosperity in the last century. But so did massive amounts of low-skilled labor, much of it provided by immigration. In this century, American workers who are highly skilled relative to global peers will be essential to American competitiveness. And what counts as highly skilled has changed. U.S. economic growth in the twentieth century had a lot to do with the man in 1961 shoveling gravel to lay the base for a stretch of highway in the interstate highway system, or the woman who picked vegetables on newly cultivated California farmland. In the coming years, more U.S. economic growth will come from the team of people developing autonomous vehicles or biotechnology innovations that improve agricultural efficiency around the world. Jobs we don't yet know about will exist, and in industries that are recognizable from the last century, the level of technological expertise needed to do many of those jobs will continue to increase. Many who serve in the military, factory employees, construction workers, and farmers are all necessarily advanced computer operators today.

Globalization doesn't come with an opt-out option. Smart industrial policy—where the government provides investment and subsidies to targeted industries and the jobs attached to them—can preserve sensitive supply chains and high-end manufacturing. It can help incubate new technologies and start-ups. But even with concerted efforts to subsidize and incentivize re-onshoring certain advanced manufacturing jobs, the semi-autarky of mid-twentieth-century America is not coming back. Economic integration is difficult to unravel, and the diffusion of technology, and the increased role of technology in the economy, also make much of globalization's impact inescapable.

Trade barriers work better on steel and televisions than they do on code and the human beings that create it.

To secure economic advantage, and the strength and prosperity dependent upon it, the United States must manage the challenges posed by the three megatrends simultaneously. The loss of dominant scale means that the U.S. can't count on being the world's most innovative economy by virtue of its size. Globalization means that the United States *must* be a driver of innovation in order to maintain its prosperity. And the advance of technology has raised the bar on skills, so that the U.S. needs to invest more in research and in workforce training that will give it an economic and strategic edge.

3.

There's a lot to be concerned about when one looks at the economic competition that the United States will face in the coming decades. Not just from China, whose authoritarian system has certain advantages when it comes to devising and implementing a national economic strategy, but also from the EU and rising democracies like India. Just because competition is geopolitically more friendly doesn't mean that it doesn't have implications for the future prosperity of Americans. One of the challenges for the United States in the coming decade will be how it manages to execute strategic investments in key sectors—such as industrial policy aimed at developing U.S. leadership in climate technology—in a manner that complements and catalyzes similar efforts by key partners rather than creating trade tensions that undermine partnerships on which we depend.

There's also an opportunity to use the current inflection point to pursue a renaissance in U.S. competitiveness strategy. In the forty years beginning with Ronald Reagan's administration, majorities in

Congress and U.S. presidents of both parties embraced—with varying degrees of gusto—globalization and deregulation. They relied on the idea that all economic growth was equally good. Generally speaking, the market could be trusted to deliver efficiencies and value; the important thing was not to get in the way. We can see that these policies have not delivered as promised. Though the economy as a whole expanded, the hollowing out of industrial America and the rapid growth of financial services and the financialization of the economy, together with globalization, have left us vulnerable to shocks from abroad and divisions associated with widening inequality at home.[1] A recalibration is in order along with an approach to national competitiveness that can be the foundation for resilience, prosperity, and security in a globalized, digital world. The United States has the assets required to take advantage of the opportunity if we are willing to recognize that the moment demands a shift in our approach. We still have a strong hand; we just have to make up our minds to play it well.

In the next decade, the United States must meet the test of investment—investment at the right levels and in the right areas to build the foundation for shared economic prosperity in the next half century. Doing so will support national security goals and America's ability to lead internationally. And it has the potential to both draw strength from and contribute to a healthier democracy with more promise for its citizens.

If the United States is to function as a coherent and competitive political and economic unit in the world in the coming decades, then it has to get ready for and adapt to a world that will be ever more characterized by deep globalization and accelerating technological advance. To keep up, the United States government needs to ramp up investment, in particular, investment in human capital. I'm talking about something more significant than incremental adjustments to spending dials. American success in the digital age requires different kinds of collective efforts than the American success in the late industrial age required. Successful companies adapt to disruptions by investing in new businesses and new ways of doing business. The United States must adapt to a more competitive world in which Americans are more dependent on each other for success.

The United States should focus its ramped-up public investment on two broad goals: first, bolstering strength in research and development and incubating new industries; second, workforce quality and participation. These goals are complementary and mutually reinforcing, if not completely overlapping. A strategy to achieve these goals must harness the resources and efforts of state and local governments, and of the private sector. However, there is no way for the country as a whole to be successful without the leadership, in terms of both agenda-setting and resource allocation, of the federal government. Private investment has a key role to play, but—especially in a world of quarterly earnings and private equity timelines—the market alone cannot be relied upon to marshal capital in a way that devotes sufficient resources to the generational investments that augur to the strategic benefit of the United States.

The U.S. federal government must lead significant reinvestment in human capital. As the productivity levels of so many others in the world are converging on U.S. workers, the U.S. workforce needs to continuously improve for the United States to retain its edge. Instead, we've become dangerously accustomed to a frustratingly stagnant status quo.

There have been piecemeal approaches to advancing the objectives underlying this test, many of which have been piloted and are compelling. For example, a focus on recruiting science, technology, engineering, and mathematics (STEM) educators, mentoring programs for students, apprenticeships, and so on. These should continue and may become features of a new skills- and innovation-oriented national ecosystem, but as isolated tactics they are massively inadequate to the task in front of us. The transformation of the U.S. workforce that needs to occur cannot be done with tweaks to the current system, which was designed for the post–World War II world. Even if it were fixed, that's not good enough to keep the United States competitive in the future. Thus, the goal cannot be just to raise educational attainment rates and economic participation in the current system; the system itself has to adapt. In order to lead on innovation, the United States has to invest in and transform its approach to human capital that will raise the bar across the board. And in order to take advantage of an expanded skilled workforce, we have to free them up to work.

American economic success is at the core of American power. Public investment aimed at boosting the competitiveness and participation of U.S. workers in the global economy is part of the retooling of our economy, and the renovation of our social contract, that we need to be successful in the political economy of the world in the twenty-first century. Despite its challenges, the U.S. starts in a good position. The United States has the most productive advanced economy in the world. The other countries in the top ten by GDP per capita are mostly havens for banking and financiers; none has a population over 10 million. There is no other large, diversified, advanced economy that is better set up for success.

Spending more will require those who have well-honed neuralgia about increases to the federal government budget to, as they say, examine their priors. Too much of American political discussion about the size of the federal government—to the extent that genuine debate exists—has become captive of syntax that imports decades of baggage from tired political fights. Words like "welfare" and "deficit" and "entitlement" and "balanced" and "taxpayer" trigger emotional responses. We need a new conversation based in today's reality and rooted in the evidence that public investment has often been critical to creating the foundations for growth (and that tax cuts have often failed to deliver their promised impact).

Until the early twentieth century, the majority of government spending in the United States took place at the state and local level. Total government spending was less than 10 percent of GDP. In the wake of the Industrial Revolution and around the time of the First World War, the share of government spending moved toward the federal level, and overall spending began to increase. America's rise as an industrial power and the developments of world politics demanded a shift—a better-coordinated national approach. The Great Depression and the federal responses to it solidified that change, and by the post–World War II decades, total government spending was between a quarter and a third of GDP, with federal spending representing more than half of total government spending, as it does today. Contrary to the narratives of constant government expansion, the share of GDP going to government spending was the same in the last two years of the George H. W. Bush administration as it was in the last two years of the Obama administration, and in the two years of the Trump administration preceding the Covid pandemic.[2] Given that Social Security and Medicare make up a significant portion of federal spending, and that the share of people over sixty-five grew by a third from 1990 to 2019, the consistent level of spending is remarkable.[3]

The increase in government spending, particularly at the federal level, over the course of the twentieth century happened alongside enormous political and economic success for the United States. The life and life prospects of a middle-class American in 2000—in terms of access to healthy food, conveniences like indoor plumbing, avoidance of accidents at work, access to life-extending medical treatments, education, leisure time—were significantly better than an American at a similar percentile on the income distribution a century earlier. The investment test consists of a step change that can allow us to repeat and improve upon this achievement. As in the last century, advances in the world around us mean that we need to commit more resources to the social infrastructure on which we all depend and to expand its reach. Doing so will make the lives of Americans better and more prosperous in this century.

The U.S. can choose to both drive and surf the waves of innovation that will shape the global economy in the coming decades, but not if it reacts passively to the market forces that have wrought unfortunate changes to the American social and economic structure in the last few decades. The United States is rich enough to do this now, but without a renovation for a new era, it won't always be. So the question is not "can it be done?" but "will it be done in time?": Will American leaders be wise enough to make the case to voters that this kind of investment is what will leave their children and grandchildren in good stead?

Stepping up our economy to meet the challenges of our time demands investment in four legs: children, skills, science, and care. The U.S. needs to grow and develop more talent (and waste less talent); it has to channel that talent to lead the world in science and innovation; and it has to ensure that the talent it has invested in is free to participate in the economy. Across each of these necessary areas for investment there is a need not only for policy changes that structure and direct investment, but for deep changes in the political language used to frame a conversation about it. So, Americans don't just need a new approach to investing in children, they need to think about those investments as investments in America's societal strength and future competitiveness—not as handouts or welfare or redistribution. The United States needs a new language of public investment policy, a syntax for this century.

4.

The first area for investment is children. We've become accustomed to hearing the case made for this set of investments on moral grounds. And the moral case seems compelling. We know cost-effective ways of setting kids aged 0–5 up for future success; it seems obvious that it should be a goal that every kid growing up in America gets put on the path to skilled work, and with it, the middle class. But the moral case has not been compelling enough to drive policy changes. The result is a system that fails too many children before they even reach school age, and that leaves talent unharvested that the United States will need to be successful in the future. In a competitive global landscape, failing to develop the potential of millions of American kids isn't just a moral failure, it's a strategic one: other countries will figure out how to develop their talent, and they will seek to outcompete ours.

Abundant research shows that first grade—the first year of compulsory public education in most states—is too late to set kids on a path to success. There is also solid data to show that interventions in the first years of a child's life can positively affect life trajectory, including health outcomes, likelihood of involvement with the criminal justice system, and earnings. Many such investments pay for themselves several times over in averted government spending and recouped government revenues. And so the failure to invest in kids is not just a long-term strategic failure, it's a nearer-term economic one. Investments in children have been demonstrated to have the highest return of any public sector human capital investment.

James Heckman, a Nobel Prize–winning economist at the University of Chicago, has spent years measuring the outcomes and benefits of early childhood education. Heckman and his colleagues' research finds a 13 percent annual return on high-quality early childhood education.[4] Given that the average return of the U.S. stock market in the last thirty years has been about 10 percent, that's a healthy return even by private sector standards. Heckman's research also suggests that when it comes to early childhood investments, the earlier the better—interventions in the first three years of a child's life, when brain formation and the foundations for later learning and skill acquisition are being laid, are the highest-return investments.

The RAND Corporation, a think tank known for its rigorous public policy analysis, including in the national security and defense area, had similar findings when it reviewed a range of education, social, and health interventions in early childhood. While acknowledging the methodological challenges with measuring the benefits, RAND authors assessed that all but one of the programs they examined had positive benefits. Those ranged between $1.25 and $17 for each dollar invested. These positive benefits applied to both high-cost and low-cost interventions.

More recently, a team of economists at Harvard took on the enormous challenge of trying to compare the value achieved by different kinds of policy changes. They took a broad sample of 133 government policy changes in the United States across a range of domains— everything from tax cuts to job training to housing vouchers—over the last fifty years. One of the reasons this project was novel and important is that economists have, for good reason, struggled to compare investments across policy domains because so many outcomes are themselves difficult to compare (how do you value a reduction of homelessness as compared to a tax cut for the middle class?). The economists created a common metric, which they call "marginal value of public funds" (MVPF). It attempts to capture, for all policies examined, the value of the benefit provided to recipients and the cost to the government. Any policy with an MVPF greater than one provides more benefit than it costs, those with MVPFs lower than one cost more than the good they produce.

What they found was not only do investments in early childhood, particularly for low-income kids, have the highest MVPF values, but in many cases those programs had an infinite MVPF. Why? Because these programs paid for themselves through increased revenue from taxes associated with higher incomes and decreased transfer payments. They had a net cost of less than zero to the government, in *addition* to all the benefits they provide to the recipients.[5] The lead authors on this study pointed out that their analysis shows that Heckman's finding of declining returns on investment as targeted individuals get older should not be taken to mean that certain policies, including investments in higher education, don't still offer compelling value further up the care-education-training value chain.

Investing in kids is smart policy. Not only would it lay the groundwork for the future by ensuring that the next generation of Americans has the higher-quality (and more equal) early-in-life support needed to allow them to be maximally prepared for competition in a high-skills world, it would also free up their parents to participate in the economy in the near term. Studies of the impact of early childhood education programs have found that kids' parents, especially single parents, see their earnings rise (and pay more taxes) because early childhood education programs allow them to participate in the formal economy.

Moreover, the impact of investing in kids can be measured in a third generation. A study of the impact of Medicaid expansion in the

1970s and 1980s has allowed a team of public health researchers to demonstrate that high-quality neonatal care for pregnant women corresponds to a measurable positive benefit on the birth weight not only of those mothers' children but also of their daughters' children. (Birth weight has long been an indicator of natal health that corresponds to a range of improved health and economic outcomes later in life.) These researchers report: "the effects of in utero Medicaid access on the second generation's birthweight suggest medical cost savings in the first year of life that are about 60 percent of the costs of providing the *first* generation with in utero coverage."[6] Prenatal care to mothers doesn't just have benefits for their children, it reduces the care needs of their *grandchildren* in the first year of life enough to cover most of the costs of in utero care a generation earlier.

Providing access to infant and toddler care, preschool, and full-day kindergarten would require policy changes at the state and federal levels. According to the Children's Defense Fund, families pay more for child care than for public college tuition in twenty-eight states. Meanwhile, in 2019 child care workers were paid less than half of a living wage for a single parent with one child in forty-two states, making it difficult to recruit, train, and retain a high-quality workforce. Because of funding gaps, existing federal early childhood programs are not reaching their intended targets. Only one in ten eligible infants and toddlers are in Early Head Start and only half of eligible 3–4-year-olds access Head Start.[7]

Educators and caregivers have been the chief advocates for expanding early childhood care and education. They have laid out the compelling case for making investments in early childhood with a focus on the children and the return on investment. Today, against the backdrop of increased international competition in a skills age, early childhood investments are not just a way to make Americans' lives better but an essential element of securing American influence and competitiveness in the world. We all depend on it. The secretary of defense and national security advisor ought to be making the case for investments in children.

5.

In the second half of the twentieth century, the United States had the highest number of high-skilled workers in the world. This was largely thanks to three factors: it had the largest population of any industrialized economy; it had a relatively strong public education system that—even with the enormous wasteful albatross of racism and segregation—was, over time, educating a larger and larger share of Americans; and a high school degree was sufficient to make American workers higher-skilled than most others in the world. Having the largest pool of high-skilled workers drove productivity increases that had positive (though not equal) benefits for other American workers too.

Those three factors now form a shakier foundation for U.S. strength. The U.S. is no longer unambiguously the biggest, and the relative decline in terms of scale of the U.S. among advanced-economy workers leaves it without the guarantee of having the largest pool of talent. And the U.S. is plateauing—at an inadequate level of progress—in educational attainment. While the U.S. made steady progress—from 52 percent of the adult population having a high school degree or equivalent in 1960 to over 90 percent in 2020, according to the U.S. Census Bureau—the world has been progressing too.[8] In 1960, the world literacy rate was just over 40 percent; by 2015 it had more than doubled to 85 percent. As recently as 1990, fewer than four in five Chinese people could read and fewer than half of Indians could. A quarter of a century later, those numbers were 96 percent and 78 percent respectively.[9] A high school degree (and lower levels of globalization) used to give American workers an edge but that edge is fading. As of 2015, looking just at the population of younger workers aged 25–34, China and India together contributed 40 percent of tertiary-educated people in the OECD-G20 (which encompasses most of the world's advanced economies). North America—the U.S., Canada, and Mexico combined—represented just under 15 percent—fewer than one in six.[10]

Primary and secondary education curriculum and teaching methods need to adapt as the world changes. My parents learned in high school how to change typewriter ribbons; soon typing itself may be an obsolete skill. Evolving understanding about how brains develop and retain information, and how to develop analytical abilities and critical thinking is also changing education. The educational reform movement in the United States is a contested field, and questions of race and socioeconomic inequality as well as teacher pay and development are always bubbling underneath. A national commitment to adequately resourced public primary and secondary education systems, and to continuous improvement of K–12 education, is a worthwhile policy. It is also likely to require additional public investment in the coming decades, especially because improving quality will require addressing funding disparities.

Even if the K–12 system (or systems; there are over thirteen thousand school districts in the U.S.) were functioning at near-perfect levels, it would not be enough. Because a K–12 education is not enough. We must expand public education in the United States to cover postsecondary education, including college and other post–high school training programs. Both the political economy of postsecondary education, and what we include in it, need to change.

6.

Since the 1990s, our policy decisions have made higher education increasingly a private good rather than a public one in this country. For reasons of social justice, national security, and economic competitiveness, we should move dramatically toward treating higher education as a public good. Because higher education *is* a public good.

Much of the business model of our current higher education system—particularly the debt and tuition model for financing participation in it—is oriented around a basic assumption that a postsecondary credential is principally a private interest of individuals (and their families), and that the student who receives the credential or degree is not just the primary but more or less the sole beneficiary of higher education. This assumption is false.

There is no question that those who have access to higher education and complete a credential or degree have much better expected outcomes, not just in terms of lifetime income but across a range of quality-of-life measures. There *is* a significant private financial benefit to higher education for most students.[11] But they are not the only beneficiaries. The same combination of globalization and technological advances that have made a post-secondary credential increasingly a prerequisite for individuals who aspire to a middle-class life have also made a well-educated populace increasingly a prerequisite for our nation's economic and strategic competitiveness. We have a postsecondary education and skills training system, if you can call it that, that was built in a time when the United States could be a global power with only a minority of its workers receiving a postsecondary education. That's not the world we live in today. We need more of us—close to *all* of us, really—ready to compete.

Before the coronavirus pandemic and the accompanying economic crisis hit, media reported in 2019 that seven in ten employers said they could not find the talent they need—an increase of threefold from a decade ago.[12] To fuel U.S. economic growth, U.S. employers need workers. And workers need the skills that will allow them to adapt to a progressively more advanced economy. Automation and artificial intelligence threaten to accelerate the elimination of existing jobs in factories and in huge industries like trucking (in 2014 a truck driver was the most common job in more than half of U.S. states).[13] The advent of large language models and the artificial intelligence tools built on them has raised the prospect that large swaths of white-collar jobs are also likely to disappear.[14] There will be new jobs—many of which we can't describe or name yet—but they will require more specialized and complex training and knowledge than the ones they replace.

The 2016 film *Hidden Figures* chronicles Black women mathematicians who worked as human "calculators" for NASA during the space race. In one scene, one of the women sees NASA personnel installing a new room-sized computer that will automate calculations. Recognizing the implications of automation, her reaction is to decide to be the person who learns how to operate the machine. As a society, America needs to decide that we will learn how to use technology, not passively allow technology to happen to us. Advanced economic activity will go to where the workers are, so there is strength in numbers here. Silicon Valley of the 1990s is an instructive microcosm. It attracted more and more tech companies and investors because it had a critical mass of highly trained workers. The United States has to aspire to be a kind of mega–Silicon Valley, or maybe more a conglomerate of Silicon Valleys, with large numbers of high-skilled workers for an assortment of advanced industries.

Our collective economic interests aren't the only reason to invest in higher education. We face a civic crisis too. The increasing complexity and interconnectedness of the world has made the dynamics of global threats—from climate change, to Russian and Chinese disinformation, to pandemics, to trade wars—more difficult to understand. For many, it feels as if the world has grown smaller and is spinning faster. Our democratic institutions depend on informed voices in our debates and informed choices by our populace. Life, liberty, and the pursuit of happiness in the twenty-first century will be possible for an American public equipped to meet the challenges of this century, but an undereducated America will be persistently vulnerable not only to economic hardship but also to the folly and vicissitudes of populism that so predictably follow in its wake.

The good news is that we've been here before. In the wake of the Industrial Revolution Americans recognized that universal elementary and secondary education should be public goods—that they were essential for economic growth and general prosperity—and we created public schools. At that time, we recognized that public primary and secondary education isn't a favor that the public does for individuals. It wasn't a welfare or consumption benefit. It was an investment in the society's success. Effective and expansive postsecondary training and education is likewise an investment in our democracy's strategic competitiveness in the twenty-first century. The individuals who achieve postsecondary training and education are not just advancing their private interests, they are doing something necessary for the public good. We have a shared interest in dramatically expanding the reach of higher education and high-skilled job training.

The system we have is not set up to achieve that goal. It has made getting postsecondary education harder, not easier. The post–World War II history of the American higher education system has been, in important ways, perversely regressive. The G.I. Bill invested in returning servicemembers from World War II, giving them free or near-free college and a path into the middle class, although for many nonwhite GIs the impact of the education benefit was tempered by the fact that many institutions still did not admit them.

Even for those Americans who were not eligible for G.I. Bill benefits, well into the 1980s public investment in community colleges and public universities—including by state governments—remained high enough that tuition was a manageable expense for most students and families without large loans. Meanwhile, there remained plenty of jobs in the American labor market that offered a reasonably secure middle-class life and did not require a postsecondary credential.

In the last thirty years, however, two shifts happened. The first shift was caused by a set of changes to the structure of the higher education economy. A generation ago, public investment in higher education began to wane. It nosedived during and after the 2008 financial crisis as states struggled to balance budgets.[15] With public investment on the decline, schools needed to make up for lost revenue, and so they turned to tuition increases.

Critics of colleges and universities, along with many families and students, decry the fact that tuition has risen faster than inflation in recent decades; but overall budgets on a per student basis for many public colleges and universities have not risen nearly as fast. It's just that they are having to make up the loss of public dollars with private dollars in the form of tuition (in addition to inflation). In Colorado, at public institutions of higher education in the early 2000s, approximately two thirds of the cost of educating a student was covered by public dollars, and one third was covered by tuition. By the middle of the next decade, the share covered by public investment versus tuition had inverted.

To enable students and families to cover the skyrocketing costs of tuition, institutions and the government encouraged students to take on debt, and more of it. As the floodgates opened to debt-financing of higher education, the "customer base" for higher education became less sensitive to price and more demanding of product features—the difference between taking on $95,000 of debt and taking on $80,000 of debt started to seem less important. As long as they were taking on massive amounts of debt, students picked campuses that offered superior (and often more expensive) student experiences.

There is a tendency to villainize institutions themselves for tuition hikes, for exploding student debt, for the rush to offer "luxury" dormitories and other amenities. But the schools were responding to market forces and to the changed political economy of the higher education landscape. Americans collectively de facto privatized much of public higher education in this country over the course of a generation—and now many are outraged and appalled by certain predictable outcomes of that choice.

Another trend that accompanied this substantial privatization of higher education was the rise of for-profit colleges. These institutions still access federal funding for low-income students, so they are far from independent, but between 1995 and 2016 their share of the higher education market doubled. There is a wide range in quality among for-profit schools as measured by student outcomes, and while some fill a useful niche in training for specialized professions like nursing, for-profit schools have an average tuition that is twice the average public four-year institution, and their students who take out loans to pay for school are twice as likely to default on student loans as community college students.[16]

The price of higher education has pushed it out of reach of most Americans without the assistance of mountains of debt, *at precisely the moment* that the second shift became clear: for the first time in our history, economists agree that the vast majority of Americans will need some kind of quality postsecondary credential or degree in order to have any shot at a middle-class life. No wonder today's student generation feels trapped in a catch-22. They can't get into the middle class without that education, but in order to get it, they have to take on burdensome debt that will prevent or delay them from doing other things that we associate with being middle-class—buying a house, starting a business, raising a family, and so on. It can be difficult to find sympathy from the generation in their fifties and sixties because they experienced a different system. They remember a part-time job at the library on campus and a summer job waiting tables to pay tuition and rent without realizing how much harder that is now. From their perspective, the only thing new is overconsumption of avocado toast.

Our current reality reflects and reinforces racial inequality too. For students whose parents or grandparents were able to buy houses in the suburbs in the 1960s, '70s, '80s, and '90s, real estate has often become a savings vehicle, and an asset to borrow against in order for families to help with the rising costs of college. A less-well-remembered feature of the G.I. Bill was that it made home loans available to beneficiaries. However, because of redlining policies that effectively kept minority families from buying homes in suburban areas and near good public schools, these public benefits helped white veterans buy suburban homes that would become a substantial nest egg of family wealth over the ensuing decades while leaving other families out. The U.S. public subsidized investments that built up white families' generational wealth while making Black poverty stickier through redlining. As college has gotten more expensive, family wealth is much less likely to be available to help students of color access the education they need to compete. The gap between median Black family wealth and median white family wealth has remained stubbornly persistent over the last half century and has grown in real terms in the last thirty years.[17]

The necessary shift back from a private luxury to a public good also implies a shift in the content of what a postsecondary education—at least a public one—entails. The distortions in the higher ed market have led to a situation where too many people are pursuing postsecondary education programs that give them skills that—while potentially personally fulfilling—have neither a personal nor public economic benefit. Too many people are getting expensive degrees that don't prepare them for good jobs.

There are two different problems here. One is a quality problem. Some institutions and programs don't impart the knowledge and skills that they purport to. The federal government tries to identify and shame these schools or programs through "gainful employment" rules that measure whether the debt students incur to pay tuition can be repaid by their income after finishing. Recent proposals suggest that the government add a high school earnings benchmark, which measures whether or not a program's graduates earn more than similar workers with only a high school degree, to identify low-quality programs.[18] There is also a selection problem. Some programs really *should* be seen as a luxury and as a form of consumption rather than as an *investment* in education per se. I'm not saying that there should only be degrees and programs offered in subjects that offer a minimum standard of economic utility—people can have all kinds of reasons for pursuing learning. But students and families shouldn't be led to believe that any college degree in any subject will set them in good stead to get a well-paid job.

Indeed there are many cases in which a four-year college degree is an inefficient and expensive way to prepare learners for high-skilled jobs. Two promising dynamics are under way in postsecondary education that could make American investment in higher education more effective in enhancing U.S. competitiveness. The first is the evolution of alternative pathways like high-skill apprenticeships, certificates, and other credentials that take less time than a four-year degree but can prepare workers for good jobs. The second is an effort to get employers to free themselves from the use of four-year degrees as an (imperfect) proxy in their hiring processes when a skills-based approach rather than a degree-based approach would help them better identify employees that are a good fit for their jobs. These trends face headwinds—not least the halo that American society attaches to a traditional degree and stigma associated with technical education—but these shifts could significantly help enlarge the middle class by enabling a more effective investment in America's human capital. Again, it's not that colleges and universities will go away, but if the United States needs to go from having around half of adults with a postsecondary credential to having three fourths or more, that increase should not be just pushing more people through the existing pipes, it should be expanding the number of pipes that can lead to high-skilled jobs.

One impulse might be to say that the public should only subsidize certain programs, ones for which there is a known public utility. And we already do use grants and loan forgiveness to make some choices more affordable to students by offering incentives, for example, for certain programs that lead to public service careers. But rather than saying that a modern dance program is off limits, it would be better to increase the transparency to prospective students. Students may choose to take out loans to fund the pursuit of a program that doesn't promise a high-paying job, but they shouldn't be surprised by a predictable set of personal financial outcomes. Transparency will give students and families a much better understanding of the choices that they face. An investment in data and analysis would allow students and families (and state legislatures) to make better decisions about where to invest in postsecondary education.

There are efficiencies to be gained and improvements to be made, but getting to 70 or 80 percent of Americans with a quality postsecondary credential or degree is going to take more public investment. It's an investment that will pay dividends, for individuals and for the society as a whole, but it will require an up-front commitment to put more money into higher education, broadly construed, in the coming decade.

The investment test can only be met if we also meet the fairness test. Because an investment in expanding the supply of high-skill workers will only work if we also address the historic failure of the public education system to achieve similar outcomes across different racial and ethnic groups. The achievement gaps between white Americans and Black and Latino Americans are not just a social justice issue, they are an economic issue and a security issue. Because the numbers are clear: there is no way to reach the levels of attainment that America needs to compete without focusing attention on making sure that the public education system—early childhood through post–high school—is serving all Americans and producing results.

7.

Science is the next leg in the investment test. The United States has funded basic research that has led to innovations that have transformed every domain of human life, from what we eat, to how we communicate, to the medical treatments for our ailments, to the way that we fight wars. Investment in public research funding complemented and reinforced private research and development carried out by companies and produced an economic juggernaut that underpinned the United States' superpower status. It's not just entrepreneurs that built the success stories of the twentieth-century American industrial economy, and it wasn't just the militaries of the U.S. and its allies that liberated Europe and defeated the Axis powers in World War II. In both cases, the scientists and researchers behind new products (and new weapons) played a role. Indeed, behind every great businessperson and every brave servicemember is a nerd. The United States needs to be purposeful about investing in and building a new and expanding generation of nerds. Part of the reason that we need to invest in early childhood and renovate the way that we fund and structure college is that we need more nerds, and that means not letting any potential ones slip through the cracks.

In discussions on science and technology in geopolitics, there tends to be an overwhelming focus on the strategic advantages that accrue to the first country to happen on particularly powerful new coercive technologies like nuclear weapons or mass surveillance. While these breakthroughs matter, particularly at key moments, they tend to overshadow the innovations that actually drive the bulk of economic growth, job creation, and improvements in people's everyday lives. Science and technology have too often been seen primarily in the context of a kind of digital arms race—and there's a danger in obscuring the other, more affirmative reasons for wanting to see the United States remain a leader in cutting-edge research and invention. In the same way that an exclusive focus on building up the strongest military can counterproductively distract from building the foundation for societal strength at home, a disproportionate focus on the weaponization of technological advances can distract from using technological progress to make people's lives better and retain an economic edge.

Cutting-edge R&D has been a source of American advantage, and the United States continues to have the legal, economic, and physical infrastructure to support it; it must be a matter of national priority not to lose this edge. Our overall level of national investment has mostly held steady at a moment when we need to ramp up. Holding steady is not sufficient. At the beginning of the current century, the United States accounted for well over one third of R&D globally, while China represented less than 5 percent. By 2020, the U.S. was responsible for 27 percent of R&D spending while China reached 23 percent of world R&D investment.[19] Between 2000 and 2010 alone—in part because of the 2008 economic crisis—there was a major convergence as the U.S. share dropped by nearly a fourth, while China's share tripled.

The mix of R&D has also shifted. In the last fifty years, the share of overall R&D done by corporations has increased as government spending on R&D as a percentage of GDP has declined significantly. This shift is significant because government R&D tends to focus more on the "R" and corporate R&D spend is more focused on the "D"— development of new products and bringing them to market. Basic research, much of which is conducted without a known application, can take decades to have an impact on the economy. The discovery of a new biological process or material capacity might not appear in a medical application or a new consumer product for thirty or forty years or more. But it might then be transformational.

The combination of long timelines and the interaction between discoveries and diffusion of ideas make it difficult to prove an economic advantage that comes from more public R&D spending. Countries don't have Tarot cards or fortune-tellers, but for countries with advanced economies, where growth is likely to be particularly driven by innovation, a country's R&D level functions as a kind of intuitive leading indicator—those who invested in discovery twenty years ago are likely to be seeing benefits today. Moreover, research is a group endeavor—it's collaborative and depends on networks—and inventions are rarely the product of a single brain in which a light bulb just magically goes off. That's why R&D tends to benefit from scale as it creates communities of innovation in which individuals amplify their collaborators' efforts.

The United States should seek to maintain and expand its relatively high levels of public and private R&D investment. Public investment in R&D predominantly involves spending money on salaries of middle-class and upper-middle-class workers, the kind of people who work at universities and national laboratories—those workers have an average effective federal tax rate of 15–20 percent, so the effective immediate cost of that spending is 85 cents on the dollar, without taking into account positive spillover effects. And federal R&D spending can also seize opportunities to invest in ways that seed new geographies of innovation (or boost nascent ones) in parts of the country that have not been hubs in the past.[20] Especially if states are investing in their own systems of secondary and higher education, federal research money could help reward state-level investment and multiply its impact. Private sector research and development is geographically concentrated in the United States—over 60 percent of private R&D takes place in ten metropolitan statistical areas (MSAs)—eight of which are on the coasts. Fully a quarter of it takes place in two adjacent MSAs in Northern California.[21]

Some of the investment attached to the 2022 CHIPS Act and Inflation Reduction Act can be implemented with a focus on incubating innovation ecosystems between the coasts. These two pieces of legislation provide tens of billions of dollars per year for investment in semiconductors and clean energy technologies in the coming decade. These public investments have the potential to create new-innovation ecosystems because of the network effects of technology innovation. A computer programmer benefits from being connected to other computer programmers working on related challenges—they are each more likely to create value as part of a community (or network) of innovation. And the U.S. should want to seed these communities because the best jobs that come out of innovative applications of technology are likely to stay close to where they are invented.

A team of economists conducted an analysis of innovation over several decades in the United States, looking at the patents that went into twenty-nine technologies that disrupted existing industries. The patents in their study accounted for over a fifth of all patents awarded in the U.S. between 1992 and 2016.[22] They found that the innovations overwhelmingly happened in a few geographic "super clusters," and the addition of high-skilled jobs in those locations lingers for decades. Meanwhile, though all of the disruptive technologies spread across the country (and elsewhere around the world), and added jobs in places away from the innovation hubs, these jobs were mainly lower-skill and lower-paid jobs.

Consider rideshare technology—the majority of employment that was created by this disruption of the taxi and chauffeur industry has happened in cities across America. But the overwhelming majority of high-skill jobs associated with that innovation remain in San Francisco where rideshare companies are headquartered. Consumers in the United States will benefit from technological advances wherever they are made—they'll get better health care or entertainment or cars—but the skilled jobs created by innovation are likely to be geographically "sticky."

In addition to the economic and direct strategic benefits that may accrue to the United States because of an innovation edge, there is a reputational advantage at stake. In a world in which the United States needs to accomplish more through persuasive influence and cooperation and less through leveraging absolute scale and coercion, that reputational advantage is an increasingly central and strategic one.

The race to find a vaccine during the coronavirus pandemic was, in the first case, a race to mitigate the extraordinary human costs of a deadly disease, but it was also a geopolitical race. As the Chinese government attempted to distract from the virus's initial spread among humans in Wuhan, public relations campaigns around its contributions to virus response became part of its diplomatic playbook. Russia, too, engaged in vaccine diplomacy and vaccine vanity—rushing to develop its own vaccine in a bid to demonstrate strength. Both Russia and China, even though their indigenously developed vaccines were medically less effective, have tried to leverage those vaccines for geopolitical influence.

The capacity to translate scientific excellence into useful technologies for confronting global challenges is an enormous source of potential political advantage. That the three most effective vaccines were developed by Euro-American companies and researchers may have included an element of good fortune, but the countries where mRNA vaccines were developed feature an environment of intellectual freedom and superior research capacity. Although the effective rollout of vaccines in the United States in the early months of 2021 was heralded as a demonstration of American capabilities,[23] the United States and its partners failed to capture international political dividends of their vaccine innovation as effectively as they might have. Even though there have been billions of doses delivered to poorer countries, this was seen in much of the world as belated. In the U.S. an inclination to be attentive to domestic politics—and to the optics of getting Americans vaccinated before sending doses elsewhere—trumped the need to distribute effective vaccines to the world quickly and affordably, and to broadcast a commitment to do so.

The U.S. and its wealthy country partners may get a rerun with a future pandemic. Or there may be other global challenges that present opportunities to marry innovation and magnanimity in a way that generates political power. Climate change is already having disastrous effects, including on communities across the United States, but scientists warn that what we've seen so far will be dwarfed by the catastrophic impact of human-caused climate change in the coming decades. Given the political realities and technological assets available to the world today, it is impossible to point to a realistic path to meet the commitments governments and major private sector actors have made with respect to decarbonization timelines.

Even after the United States adopted the Inflation Reduction Act, we are nowhere near close to what will be needed to adapt to climate change and mitigate its worst effects. Knowing what we know now, the world is failing at the collective action problem in front of it. Instead, political leaders are making an enormous mostly unspoken bet that technology will solve the decarbonization problem. In 2022, global consulting firm McKinsey released a report that suggested that meeting the decarbonization and emissions reduction goals already made by governments with jurisdiction over 80 percent of the world's emissions would require an average investment of around 7.6 percent of global GDP in energy infrastructure every year for the next three decades. And in the medium term—during the years 2026–2030—that number would have to be closer to 8.9 percent.[24] (To put that in context, the entire U.S. defense spending budget is about 3.5–4 percent of U.S. GDP.) There is no conceivable version of political evolution of advanced democracies in the near term that includes those spending levels.

We are effectively taking a gamble, whether or not we admit it. We are gambling that something is going to change the underlying challenge in such a way as to reset our sense of the possible. As the effects of the climate crisis are felt in more communities across America and around the world, concern about addressing climate change is likely to become even more mainstream—among both voters in democratic countries and citizens of authoritarian ones. There is going to be a political dividend that accrues to the countries whose research communities are responsible for devising new technological solutions to address facets of climate change. Colloquially, what we call climate change is not really one thing so much as a basket of connected systemic trends, and the complexity of those interacting systems means that the chances of a discovery that—presto change-o!—solves the climate crisis are much lower than those of several such innovations that offer meaningful but incremental progress. Technological innovation to address the climate crisis is likely to come in a collection of brass bullets, not a single silver bullet.

The Inflation Reduction Act, if implemented effectively, could generate significant innovation and scaling of new technologies. Perhaps its most important aspect is the fact that it commits spending—more than $35 billion a year—for a decade, which gives a long enough timeline to generate new ecosystems of private sector activity. There should be a parallel effort to coordinate and link up with international investments. The influence that the United States and its allies would harvest from addressing this existential physical threat would be difficult to quantify. This is especially true because the current approach to the climate crisis, which is focused on curbing emissions, has serious implications for the economic development of less developed countries and for poor people in all countries who will be affected by higher prices, especially for energy and food. Internalizing externalities is expensive. Elected leaders are going to be in an unenviable place with their constituents, having to tell them: you get less for more. The impacts of climate action in slowing climate change will not be felt for years, and that makes the sales pitch harder. There's a dividend to be harnessed not just from generating the innovation but from leading and contributing to the cooperative approaches that will develop and distribute it.

Democracy earns the faith and respect of citizens because of its dividends. The United States has an enormous amount to gain if its democratic system helps to deliver a global public good in the face of the climate crisis. In the twentieth century the U.S. was called the world's policeman. That aspiration is no longer compatible with a reasonable U.S. national strategy, but to be the world's indispensable and indefatigable problem-solver is an aspiration that the U.S. is well suited to.

Whether it seeks innovation and technological advance to address global challenges or to spur domestic economic growth, the United States retains enormous societal advantages. Technology and science are not self-actualizing. A discovery about how to create synthetic proteins or how to make smaller semiconductor chips or about how to allow computation without sharing data does not magically become a new product or tool. The development part of R&D traditionally includes the additional research and practical work needed to transform a discovery into an applied technology—turning a discovery about synthetic proteins into meat substitutes, for example. But, on a broader view, development also includes the social, political, legal, and economic factors that have to come together to enable that transformation and make it possible to distribute the end product. Financing for entrepreneurs, credible testing regimes to ensure product safety, public relations efforts to answer questions of possible consumers, public discussion of ethical issues or unintended consequences of the introduction of a new product or tool. Particularly with the technological advances that are likely to transform the way we live and introduce step-changes in productivity, the combination of efficient allocation of capital with a governance approach that builds public trust amplifies the impact of innovation. Open societies, with institutions subject to scrutiny, with public debate and democratic oversight, have advantages in animating the potential of new discoveries.

In a recent discussion with a senior U.S. official working on artificial intelligence, the official, a scientist by training himself, remarked that technological teams don't typically include anthropologists and ethicists. With AI, however, some of the biggest concerns are about how AI can be deployed to foment mistrust and social breakdown using tactics such as deep fakes. And some of the greatest potential benefits of AI, such as improved early diagnosis of breast cancer and other diseases, require public trust in the way that data is handled and processed. Developing a holistic approach that integrates technological knowledge with understandings of human behavior and ethical considerations will make it easier to mitigate risks and to harness potential benefits of AI. Two consequent observations: Open societies that tolerate dissent and disruption excel at cross-pollination of domains of expertise, so the United States should have an advantage over more closed or authoritarian societies, even if their top-down management of directed research appears to have short-term efficiency benefits. Second, the humanities and liberal arts still matter, and it is the integration of those spheres of knowledge with science and technology that can be a basis for comparative advantage in the years to come. Scientific and technical expertise can develop in an authoritarian society. Free inquiry about history, power structures, and ethics requires a liberal environment. And, in addition to helping us manage the advent of new technologies, it is those areas of study that anchor us in humanity so that technology remains a tool to serve human ends, not a logic to determine them.

8.

Like factories and machines, human capital has maintenance costs too, and care is the last leg of the investment test. Because the United States depends ever more on a highly skilled workforce and on the full participation of Americans in the workforce in order to ensure economic strength against a backdrop of decreasing relative scale, the costs of failing to care for that workforce or of having highly trained workers drop out of the formal workforce are increasing. By the 2030s, the Boston Consulting Group estimates that the U.S. stands to lose $290 billion *a year* in GDP if it doesn't address the shortage in care employees and the related phenomenon of productive workers leaving the workforce for care duties whether they want to or not.[25]

As with investments in education and other attempts to strengthen U.S. advantage in terms of human capital, getting investment in the "care economy" right requires a rethink of the way that such investments have historically been seen in the U.S. political discourse. Child care and health care, to the extent that Americans have seen the U.S. government as having a role to play at all, have been seen as entitlements or social benefits aimed at particular populations. And elder care—an exploding need because longer lives are not necessarily independent ones—has historically been considered mainly a family responsibility for all but the wealthy.

The historian and sociologist Theda Skocpol shows how the progenitors of today's social safety net policies (such as they are) emerged in the late nineteenth century and were focused on the veterans of the Civil War and their spouses and children.[26] This is in contrast, according to Skocpol, to the European context where welfare benefits arose to protect workers. Social policy took another major step forward during the Great Depression with the establishment of Social Security, and then with Medicare and Medicaid in the 1960s. And while the context for each of these was different, it has been a consistent thread in the history of the United States that the most common frame for understanding things like supports for low-income families or government-provided or subsidized health care for veterans, seniors, or low-income children is a rubric of public charity, magnanimity, or social justice. It is about attention to the vulnerable and the unfortunate, or recompense for a sacrifice. It is, in this reckoning, public *spending* on care. It is not a public *investment* in the economy.

That perspective is a limiting one that can obscure the ways in which, as harnessing human potential has become ever more strategically important, publicly funded care is not only an expression of compassion or gratitude or minimum standards of decency (though it can be and is each of these), but also an essential piece of social infrastructure that supports a twenty-first-century economy. President Eisenhower's investment in the interstate highway system transformed the American business environment by making it easier to transport goods (and for families to pursue interstate tourism). A national investment in the care economy can unleash existing talent into the formal economy, including the care economy itself, by freeing up some of those now delivering care in the nonformal economy. It can secure the longevity of investments in training and skills by keeping workers healthy. And it can remove barriers to entrepreneurialism and competition by decoupling health care from specific jobs so that people can respond to market forces.

•   •   •

There will continue to be millions of words written each year on the problems inherent in the U.S. health care system. Whatever the details of those arguments, two simple truths remain: First, the U.S. pays more—way more—for health care but gets measurably worse outcomes than other advanced democracies. And second, there are multiple available models for alternative approaches that have lower costs and better outcomes. In terms of U.S. competitiveness, the current U.S. health care system is both a drag—because its inefficient system is spending more and getting less than other advanced economy competitors—and a missed opportunity, because better outcomes would not only mean healthier and presumably happier lives for more Americans, it would also increase the return on other social and educational investments in those Americans—the value of two more years of productive work from a healthier citizen is an enormous benefit to harvest from better health care.

About half of Americans have health care through their employers (or a spouse's or parent's employer). Our lack of a universal health care system makes the U.S. labor market more sticky and less efficient—because people hesitate to leave a job to search for a better one even if they are underemployed. Workers are also less likely to create start-ups because the cost of private health care makes leaving a job to start a business even more expensive and risky. Making progress toward universal care, for example, by creating a public option, so that all Americans can buy into Medicare coverage at an affordable price, is an investment that would advance American competitiveness.

Americans are living longer, but not always healthier, lives. Many will require care for extended periods later in their lives. Like child care, elder care has historically been—for everyone except the wealthy—a service provided by family. A societal investment focused on shifting elder care from the informal economy to the formal, and professionalizing the field, would enhance health and life outcomes, free up family members to work in the formal economy and in a capacity that matches their skills, and create new jobs for trained home health and elder care workers.

Women and people of color make up the majority of care workers, including those who provide child care, elder care, home health care, and nursing. This is true in both the formal and informal care economies. That these workers continue to fail to capture the value of their work in economic terms is both a product of and reinforcement of racism and sexism in American society. Put another way: if white men were running day cares, or eschewing other work in order to care for their mother-in-law, these care jobs would be paid more. There is a reinforcing loop that needs to be shattered. Care jobs have been underpaid because they have been held by those with less power in U.S. society; and because they are underpaid, they are taken up by those who have fewer options. But in an era in which investment in human beings and their capacities is essential to the U.S. competitiveness, the United States can't afford the structural racism and sexism that produces this outcome. Instead of the doom loop that keeps America from investing properly in care, there is a benefits loop available: by investing in the care economy, we'd be freeing up more Americans to work in high-skilled jobs and prepare more Americans for a future in which doing so will be essential. We'd also make meaningful progress on addressing gender- and race-based wage gaps, and turn more low wage jobs into good jobs. A City University of New York study looked at public investment to raise care wages in New York state from the current median of $22,000 to $40,000. The investment would produce better care and pay for itself in additional tax revenue, reduced public outlays in other areas, and spillover effects.[27] Addressing inequality would have not only economic benefits but social and political ones.

9.

The need for new social structures and investments to adapt to economic progress and accompanying societal and global shifts is not new. We've encountered this need for evolution, and responded to it, before. It is a curious phenomenon that those in the public sphere who appear most committed to American individualism, to the idea of self-reliance being core to the American ethos, are also often the same people (politicians and pundits) who wax nostalgic about the first few decades after World War II. There is no question that, especially for white Americans, those decades were an era of unprecedented growth of the middle class, of expanding homeownership, and the democratization of access to automobiles and to college education. Middle-class people were able to pursue lives of their own design to a much greater extent than they had been in the interwar years, or, before that in the unregulated industrial landscape at the turn of the twentieth century. But these decades were also characterized by massive subsidies of the key features of the middle-class life, and of laws that supported collective bargaining and union wages and benefits. The reason why politicians can speak of their parents' generation working hard to provide a middle-class life, or to talk about "working my way through college," is that it was possible for them to earn a middle-class wage at a union job and because as late as the 1970s someone could pay for a year's worth of tuition at a public university on a summer job at minimum wage. The 1950s and 1960s may have been a golden age for the (white) middle class, but that's not because they were characterized by some kind of libertarian society driven by individualism. The golden age for individuals wasn't an age of individualism and radical self-reliance, it was a golden age of collective social investment.

The United States is not only a territorially demarcated entity that we can look at on a map. It is not just a sovereign political government whose marble-columned institutional homes in Washington we can recognize on TV screens. It is a collective enterprise—one which can defend and advance the ability of individuals to lead free lives, but it can only do that if the collective is strong enough to compete in and shape the world of the twenty-first century.

We need to spend more than we have in the past on developing human potential. It's more expensive to build a country where the vast majority of the population have a postsecondary credential than it was to build a country where the vast majority stopped at high school. It takes resources to make it possible for highly skilled Americans to have and raise families and also contribute their skills in the formal economy. It's more expensive to ensure that we maintain an edge not just in natural resources and geography but also in innovation and ideas. It's more expensive to have a higher-quality enterprise, but it is also more productive and will produce a healthier, more prosperous democracy. And there is no reasonable alternative to the federal government as the focal point for coordination of that investment. Who else can reliably do it? That doesn't mean that the U.S. government has to be the only mechanism for investment—indeed free markets will continue to ensure that the private sector invests in development of new ideas into products and services, and states and cities can also increase resources channeled toward the development of human potential. But the U.S. government must be the principal architect and general contractor of the investment in people and ideas that will keep the United States strong in the decades to come.

In the U.S. political context, narratives of "fiscal responsibility" have been hijacked by ideological commitments to "small government." The resulting skewed perspective, common to a number of mainstream political narratives, threatens the strategic interests of the U.S. in the medium term. The United States remains the richest country in the world. As a society it can afford to make the necessary investments in human capital to facilitate adaptation to the postindustrial, globalized, advanced economy of the digital age. Indeed, it is fiscally *responsible* for the United States to make such smart investments because the long-term fiscal health of the government depends on the economic progress of the citizens who support it with their productivity.

The market alone cannot be relied upon to direct the necessary investments, and a blind commitment to "small government" will leave the United States at a disadvantage. Instead, the United States should embrace the comparative advantage that its relative prosperity offers it today: it can borrow to make the investments that its future comparative advantage requires. To fail to make use of this advantage would be a strategic blunder. The U.S. can make up for diminished relative scale with superior technological expertise and invention. Investment is the principal material lever in driving an increase in productivity, and in securing American workers' edge, so that they are more likely to have good, high-paying jobs.

Investment also has a reciprocal relationship with the fairness of American social and political structures. An investment in care and education will drive better future economic outcomes for all Americans and can aid in eroding some of the stubborn disparities along racial, ethnic, and gender lines in health and economic outcomes. A significant portion of the gains from the public investments the U.S. needs will be harvested in the form of improved outcomes for those who have been historically left out of America's promise.

At the same time, the U.S. will only be able to seize the benefits of the investments that it needs to make if it addresses the structural unfairness of the way that public investments have been made in the past.

If discrimination continues to significantly pervert the way we direct necessary investments, and if some groups of Americans are left out of the effort to develop and nurture America's human capital assets, we may invest significant resources and miss harvesting the outcomes we need from those investments. The test of fairness is, in part, about removing existing unfairness in America that acts as both an obstacle to marshaling proper levels of investment and to maximizing the impact of such investments.

4

RIGHT MAKES MIGHT

THE FAIRNESS TEST

1.

Historically, the dominant national origin narrative of the United
States has been that of immigrants coming to a new land. As Ronald
Reagan memorably put it in his farewell address, hearkening back to
Governor Winthrop of the Massachusetts Bay Colony, America has
been a "city on a hill" and, in Reagan's words, a beacon "for all the
pilgrims from all the lost places who are hurtling through the dark-
ness, toward home." In the rhetoric of Reagan and other American
political leaders, most of whom are descended from European immigrants, this narrative has been centered on their own ancestors. The
United States is depicted as a place of freedom from the European
Old World, freedom from a continent crowded with countries and
cultures and churches and history and power structures and elites

all of which imposed their own kinds of constraints. In this retelling, arrival in America, regardless of station, is understood as arrival to a place devoid of the Old World's baggage and restrictions, to a land of vast expanse with an unwritten story.

In recent decades important historical corrections to this narrative have become mainstream. Responsible public figures acknowledge that this telling of history doesn't describe the experience of those who were enslaved and brought to the U.S., nor that of the indigenous inhabitants of the continent, nor, indeed, that of many of the poor immigrants from Europe or refugees from around the world who have arrived here.

But in addition to the *historical* corrective and admission that this idealized encounter with America is a kind of collective nostalgia for an experience of America that never existed, there needs to be a *moral* corrective too. It's not just that a kind of proto-libertarian idyll wasn't really how most people who came to the United States in the last four centuries experienced it; the mythologized version also isn't a reasonable version of freedom to pine for in the twenty-first century. The ideal is not ideal.

It may well be that for immigrants fleeing religious or other persecution from illiberal and monarchical powers in Europe in the seventeenth century, or for peasants escaping famine in the nineteenth century, or for refugees in the wake of society-destroying wars in Asia and Europe in the twentieth century, America offered a kind of escape or solace, if a complicated one. But the kind of freedom defined by the absence of constraints—rather than by the ability to live a secure and autonomous life—was always thin, and attractive because of the severe unattractiveness of the alternatives.

The United States needs something more—some more attractive and more reliable basis for social, political, and economic relationships. And to secure the futures of its inhabitants in a way that allows them the freedom of making lives of their own choosing, the United States must be able to function effectively as a collective enterprise in a competitive world.

The third test that the United States faces is the test of fairness. An unfair America will not be as stable or as productive, will not invest where it should and at the right levels, and will not earn the moral legitimacy that can bolster U.S. influence as the era of U.S. hegemony recedes. If the U.S. is not going to be the biggest world power it must be the best, and if it is going to be best then it has to invest, particularly in people and ideas, and if it is going to maximize the potential of people and the generation of innovative ideas, it must become more fair. And if the United States meets the fairness test, the fairness with which it treats its citizens will enhance America's social cohesion and bolster U.S. influence and leadership in the world.

2.

A word on that word, "fairness." I use fairness here to talk about a quality that can be seen in varying degrees in any society. Constitutional democracy is, as Winston Churchill quipped, the worst form of government except for all the others, in part because its institutions make it most likely to achieve a modicum of sustained fairness in its internal arrangements and to find paths to reform other than revolution. Constitutional democracies themselves vary in their legal and institutional approaches. Some achieve similar levels of fairness with different institutional structures, some achieve different levels of fairness with substantially similar structures. And some nondemocracies or deeply flawed ones can nonetheless provide a modicum of fairness on certain dimensions.

In moral or political philosophy courses at college, this sense of fairness might be presented as the concept of justice. Like justice, fairness can adhere both to particular outcomes and to processes or arrangements for arriving at outcomes. In the way that I use the word, the idea at the end of the U.S. Pledge of Allegiance of "liberty and justice for all" might be understood as "liberty and fairness for all." I have chosen fairness in part because it has fewer legal connotations than the word "justice" and is, to my mind, more accessible in its meaning and less likely to be associated with particular political systems and their respective vocabularies (like human rights and rule of law). Fairness is relevant everywhere.

Most genuine political debates have, at their core, a discussion about fairness: in the tax code, in the social welfare system, in criminal law, in health care, in rights protections. And these debates are seen as matters of domestic concern. Even when other countries are used as a point of comparison, the relevance of the comparison is usually to identify good (or bad) examples—the British health care system, the South Korean workweek, the Nordic social welfare state—for how the U.S. might organize itself domestically, not to make a point about international competition. The quest for a "more perfect union" is understood as an effort toward national self-actualization in accordance with democratic values, rather than an imperative driven by geopolitics.

As the United States declines in relative scale, and as other countries converge economically with the United States, the inefficiency and division caused by unfair aspects of law and social systems become a strategic albatross. Fairness deficits distort social investments in education and in the development of human and intellectual capital. Unfairness, when it distorts access to opportunity, is an efficiency drag on the entire society. Unfairness predictably causes resentment between individuals and among groups, and so undermines the goal of social cohesion. The push for fairness is not just a push for a more perfect union; it's an effort to make the United States a more powerful one.

The principal argument behind the fairness test is a practical one, not a moral one. Many of us find moral arguments for improving America's fairness persuasive. That said, moral arguments sometimes provoke defensiveness and indignation, even when made without an intent to blame or shame. As with the case for investing in closing the achievement gaps in our education system, the political, social, and economic justice reasons for addressing fairness are not essential to my case for urgency—they're good reasons for action, but they're not my primary reasons. Though I would like it if there were more Americans on the political left and right who agreed on the moral value of fairness, we can't wait for that alignment. We have to get fairer if we're going to succeed in the world in the coming decades. Because if we don't make progress on fairness, given the backdrop of international competition, we're going to fall behind or fall apart.

Progress on fairness in fact and in reputation can add to U.S. influence as it seeks to manage and deploy power in international politics in a world where U.S. coercive power is substantial but no longer hegemonic. In the 1950s and 1960s the Soviet Union shone a spotlight on Jim Crow and racist segregation to diminish the United States' standing. Two generations later, many citizens of fellow democracies continue to get news of racist application of the death penalty (a punishment that has increasingly isolated the U.S. in the community of liberal democracies), or of police killings, of homelessness, of health care failures, or of disparate economic outcomes.[1] These shortcomings detract from the moral authority of the United States in international politics.

Elements of the fairness test can be found across several intertwined dimensions of American life. Making progress toward fairness in our *economic arrangements* will give Americans more reason to have faith in the U.S.'s ability to deliver shared prosperity for future generations, and contribute to social cohesion. Addressing fairness gaps in our *political system* will make political decisions—including about where to make social investments and how to distribute responsibility for funding them—better and more legitimate, and counter the cynicism and erratic swings that currently afflict us. And successfully tackling long-standing manifestations of unfairness in our broader *society*, including racism, would remedy perversions in the way that we invest today, unlock economic gains, and open up a new level of social cooperation that would be the envy of other countries.

3.

There is a tendency in American politics to reject policy responses that could be seen as contributing to addressing economic aspects of the fairness test as anticompetitive or, yes, "socialist." (Most of these accusations are themselves arguments for greater investment in public education in the United States as they evidence a pervasive ignorance about what socialism is.) To the contrary, meeting the fairness test is in part about salvaging and preserving (fair) competition as a basis and driving force for our economic relations, not abandoning it.

We don't have markets because they are essentially good in some way; we have them because we believe that they are an organizing mechanism for efficiently and effectively channeling effort and resources toward meeting human needs, especially in a system made up of thousands or millions or billions of people. They aren't perfect, but we haven't identified better systems that function in practice to do this work as efficiently and effectively. Markets and competition are not holy goods, they are a means to an end; they are valuable because they help satisfy human needs. It is consistent with a general commitment to markets to be willing to impose guardrails on them and make adjustments to the way they function to achieve a better outcome. We will *need* to make such adjustments because of the way that unconstrained markets work over time to deliver market power to certain participants such that markets themselves become uncompetitive and lose that special power behind their efficient function. Judicious, effective regulation and other corrective responses to markets not performing as we'd like should be seen not as "antimarket" or "socialist" policies, but rather as tools for making markets perform better for people.

Recent polling has suggested that millennials and Gen Z Americans are significantly more disenchanted with capitalism (and less persuaded of the superiority of democracy as a system of government) than older Americans. But for a generation that has seen the postindustrial hollowing out of the middle class; massive and disproportionate inflation in the cost of education, health care, and housing; flatlining wages; and a political system where outcomes are increasingly driven by money and therefore controlled by those who have it, that millennials are skeptical about capitalism and democracy may be understood as skepticism about the increasingly unattractive and unfair versions of capitalism and democracy that have prevailed during their lives rather than a rejection of the premises of market economics and democratic governance. As Carroll Doherty of the Pew Research Center wrote for the George W. Bush Institute in 2019, "the data suggest that Millennials are not clamoring for socialism. Instead, what they mostly want is an economy that works better—and more fairly—for them."[2]

Americans, and most citizens of advanced economies in the

world, are committed to the basic ideas underlying a market economy. Even if their encounters with the realities of contemporary capitalism have left them disillusioned, they understand how the principles behind a market economy link to foundational ideas of liberal governance. Regulated market competition has proven itself as a driver of productivity. And democratic societies have shown that it is possible to generate policy and governance responses to major technological and economic shifts, to market inefficiencies that undermine productivity and competitiveness, or to evolving understandings about what should and should not be left to market forces. These policy responses have enabled democratic societies to harness competition and markets as (regulated) engines for economic growth, even as the economy changes.

Efforts to aim market forces at specific challenges or to protect people from market forces they can't control have often also come under attack as they have been proposed and implemented. The creation of Social Security in the United States in the late 1930s effectively established that even if the market didn't value old people, the United States was committed to the idea that workers shouldn't be indigent in old age.[3] Frances Perkins, the nation's first woman cabinet secretary, endured accusations of socialism for her efforts to negotiate the creation of a social protection program that has since become sacrosanct in American politics.

When syntax gets bound up with politics, it becomes more difficult to know what people really think. When "socialist" is used to describe anyone who believes in universal health care (or "capitalist" is assumed to mean opposed to universal health care), terms start to lose their value. Being in favor of a social safety net that includes subsidies for family farms, or thinking that there are some indispensable goods or institutions (like, say, the military) that shouldn't be left to the market to provide, doesn't make someone a socialist who believes that the state should control the means of production and distribution. And being in favor of introducing more competition in parts of the market for health care or education doesn't mean that someone wants to return to the era of robber barons or see children working in factories.

Starting around 1980, we've run an experiment with a set of policies—often grouped under the mantle neoliberalism—for four decades. These policies have been the backdrop for the technological transformation of advanced economies and a significant acceleration globalization and they have defined our responses to these shifts. While there has been significant economic growth overall, huge imbalances have developed that threaten the sustainability of our economy and of our politics. As we look to the future, we have to learn the lessons from the experiment. We need to refocus and reinforce competition as a driving force for productivity. And we need to ensure that opportunity and prosperity are more widespread because we are going to need a bigger, more productive, more competitive middle class to ensure that America can compete.

4.

In the market, scale begets power (even when economic means aren't used to buy that power directly in the political system). Since 1980, and especially in the first two decades of this millennium, economic activity has been consolidating. Three quarters of industries in the U.S. have seen significant consolidation, with fewer and fewer firms competing against each other. At the beginning of this century, the revenue of the *Fortune 500* was 58 percent of U.S. GDP. By 2021 that had risen to 70 percent.[4] In the three decades from 1982 to 2012, the top four firms in each of the six major sectors of the U.S. economy—

retail, wholesale, utilities, finance, transportation, and services—all saw their share of total sector revenue increase; in the retail sector the top four firms' share doubled.[5] Economic activity has consolidated in fewer actors over the course of several decades.

Consolidation doesn't necessarily mean that industries have become less competitive, but the evidence suggests that this is true. From 1960 to the mid-1980s, corporate profits were between 5 and 8 percent of GDP. Since 2010 (with the exception of the first year of the pandemic when they dipped back below 8 percent), they have been over 9 percent of GDP. In mid-2022, they were over 12 percent.[6] That's a 50 percent increase in the share of GDP going to corporate profit from where it was during the halcyon days of the American middle class.

The decrease in competition can be seen in the higher prices that consumers pay, the lower wages that workers get, and in decreasing numbers of start-ups. This last datapoint is particularly concerning given that the United States needs to remain a center for innovation in the coming decades. There was a 30 percent drop in the number of employees working for young firms between the late 1980s and the late 2010s. And while the overall number of start-ups (firm entries into the marketplace) decreased over this period, the number of business failures (firm exits from the marketplace) stayed constant, meaning that a greater proportion of start-ups were likely failing amidst a less competitive marketplace characterized by significant market power in entrenched big firms.[7]

Antitrust measures are meant in part to guard against that power becoming so deleterious to the driving force behind the market—competition—that the rationale for the market is undermined. Enforcing rules that protect competition, by curbing excess market power, spreads out economic benefits among different participants in an economic system. That means antitrust rules have an equalizing effect without requiring taxation and redistribution. While rich people consume more than poor people, they spend a lower share of their income and wealth than poor people do. At the same time, the richest 10 percent of Americans hold a lot more investments in corporations than the bottom 90 percent. And so, as Yale economist Fiona M. Scott Morton writes, "if a dollar of monopoly profit is transferred to lower prices, most of that dollar moves from benefitting the top 10 percent through the value of their stock or dividends to instead benefitting the bottom 90 percent through lower costs of purchases."[8] Those who don't like the idea of redistributing economic gains after the fact should support better ways to make the game of the U.S. economy more fair as it is played.

Congress and the federal government, including not only the antitrust division at the Department of Justice and the Federal Trade Commission but other government agencies like the Federal Communications Commission and those responsible for federal contracting, can do more to enforce antitrust regulations in a way that benefits consumers and workers and preserves a fairer economy.

Another way to make the American economy more fair by creating more competition is to address anticompetitive measures in the labor market. Almost one in five American workers, approximately 30 million people, have signed a "noncompete" agreement with their employer that prohibits them from working for another company in the same industry or from starting their own company for a period of time. Popular perception associates such agreements with senior executive jobs, but many in the middle class, and many hourly wage workers are also subject to them. These agreements distort the function of the labor market. Workers who might be a better fit for another company and be more productive there don't move, and workers who might otherwise be able to use an offer from another company to negotiate a raise at their employer don't have the opportunity to do so. They also obstruct entrepreneurialism because workers can't leave to start their own businesses when they see a way to innovate (and they'd struggle to hire people if they did). The net effect is lower wages for those workers and higher prices for consumers who would benefit from more competition from new firms. Several states have banned non-compete agreements in recent decades, giving economists a chance to study the before-and-after impact of these bans. As Evan Starr from the University of Maryland summarizes, these studies "tend to find similar results: when you ban non-compete agreements, wages rise, job mobility rises, entrepreneurship rises."[9] The Federal Trade Commission estimates that barring noncompete agreements for employees would raise wages for American workers by nearly $300 billion.[10]

5.

In addition to addressing anticompetitive unfairness in the way that our economy works, we need a reset of the fairness that we demand with respect to the outcomes that our economy produces. This, in turn, means deciding that there are certain things that we will not leave up to the marketplace because doing so is damaging to the longer-term interests of American society.

The United States needs a fairer deal when it comes to minimum standards of economic welfare. The level of poverty in America is unnecessary, unjustifiable, and corrosive to the United States' social fabric, self-confidence, and power in the world. Policies such as minimum wage laws are not just a way of compensating for power disjuncts between workers and their employers, they are a statement about how poor someone who works *should be* in America. They are statements of fairness.

Acceptance of one in six children in America growing up in poverty (one in three Black children), or of one fifth of households living with food insecurity, is acceptance of an unfair outcome for an economy that produces as much wealth as America's does. This failing corrodes the respect that we have for our own society. When walking by a homeless encampment in the shadow of the White House, one rightly flinches for one's patriotism.

We know that growing up in poverty has predictable effects on future life incomes, including educational levels, employment, and involvement with the criminal justice system. Tolerating child poverty today is accepting that large numbers of Americans will not reach their full potential tomorrow. That's sad in its own right. It's also a cost to other Americans who need their compatriots to be ready to compete to manage in a world where the United States is relatively smaller than it once was.

We need to establish an economic floor under Americans. We also need guardrails and investments that will more fairly distribute the dividends of the U.S. economy to Americans above that floor. Anyone who has read a newspaper in recent years is familiar with the facts of rising inequality in the United States, and the fact that the incomes of most Americans were decoupled from economic growth more than a generation ago, and have failed to keep pace ever since. Since 1979, average incomes have risen in real terms by about 1 percent per year. However, that growth has gone disproportionately to the top. Earnings for the top 1 percent of Americans have increased 2.7 percent annually (4.2 percent for the top 0.1 percent of Americans). For the bottom 90 percent—the vast majority of Americans—that number is just 0.6 percent. The result is historically unprecedented—with the top 1 percent of Americans taking a record-high share of overall earnings in America and the bottom 90 percent a record-low.[11] Other statistics tell a similar story. The upshot is that data about growth in the economy overall in the last generation obscures the fact that, for most Americans, real incomes have stagnated.

Behind our widening inequality is the decline of the middle class, the decline in social mobility, and the stagnation in educational attainment. Each of these reduces the number of Americans ready to compete in the technologically advanced, highly globalized economy of our age. And individuals don't experience statistics—they experience pressures, disappointments, feelings of powerlessness in their daily lives and their economic encounters as consumers and workers. Too many American workers are alienated from the economic system in which they participate. It's not delivering for them, or giving them confidence in the future. This pessimism has negative effects on social cohesion, and on individual choices about whether to invest to prepare for that future.

Widening inequality can be traced to structural factors, but it's not an unavoidable reality. It's the result of policy choices. The choice to not raise the minimum wage. Monetary policy choices that prioritize low inflation over low unemployment. Regulatory policy that encouraged the financialization of the U.S. economy at the expense of industries that create things.[12] Choices about whether to enforce protections against wage theft or discrimination. The choice to disincentivize or weaken labor unions. We can make other choices to rebalance the economy so that its benefits are better shared, and so that the incentives to invest in its future are shared too. The American Dream was a compelling national narrative not because it was about a lottery that would make a few people filthy rich but because it was meant to describe a society characterized by broad opportunity—accessible to the vast majority of people—to achieve a good life.

In its original incarnation in Western political thought, the idea of a social contract referred to the implicit political bargain between a government that exercises authority and the people who make up the governed. Crudely put: a measure of security was exchanged for a measure of obedience. More recently it has come to be seen also as a kind of economic pact between citizens that entails certain kinds of mutual responsibility. Both of these views examine the relevant society in a vacuum of sorts. But a social contract can also be seen as the framework that organizes a society's collective efforts in the context of a competitive and intertwined world. There are ethical reasons for thinking that the United States' social contract needs updating in the first two senses because of the economic and political consequences of the digital age. But even those who are unpersuaded by the idea that technological and digital transformations have changed and will change the moral and ethical relationships between governments and citizens, and among citizens themselves, can nonetheless sign up to the idea that the United States needs to be organized internally to compete in the twenty-first century. One can support renovating the U.S. social contract to make it more fair with an eye toward national competitiveness without getting too deep in a discussion about social, economic, and political justice in a globalized, digital age.

The world we face is new, but many of the solutions are familiar in their form. A more active role by the federal government in defining the playing field for competition and enforcing its rules. A prioritization of education and training as public goods because they have economic value. More purposeful investment by the government in key industries or the public infrastructure that can support them in order to create good jobs, drive growth, and enhance security. The American social contract has evolved significantly before.

In U.S. high schools, many students read Upton Sinclair's *The Jungle*, a novel in which the celebrated muckraker exposed the hellish working conditions of meatpacking workers (and the disgusting hygienic standards) in the factories in which Americans' food was made at the turn of the twentieth century. The Industrial Revolution changed the power dynamics between different actors in the economy; it introduced new issues around supply chains and product safety. In the years and decades that followed, the government established new regulatory standards and bodies to protect consumers and businesses. And Congress passed new laws to support the wages and bargaining power of workers whose labor had been commoditized in the marketplace by industrialization. As the economy became more complex and integrated, the need for guardrails to protect its competitive nature—part of its fairness and its function—also grew.

The United States didn't have an income tax until 1913 and it took two decades of legal battles and a constitutional amendment to make it possible. In the preceding century the economy had changed and increased labor's relative share of GDP generation (and its lesser, but still augmented, share of income). The policies around revenue generation for the federal government changed likewise.

A quarter century later, the emergence of social welfare programs provided part of the foundation for mid-twentieth-century American economic growth. It's not a coincidence that the idyll for which American conservatives so often pine—the great postwar boom of the 1950s and 1960s—also followed the establishment of new social programs, expansion of public education, investment in infrastructure and public works, regulations of banking and other key industries, rising numbers of women in the workforce, and laws that enabled collective bargaining. The recalibration of the economy, and of the government's role in creating an enabling environment for it, laid the groundwork for an historically unprecedented era of shared prosperity. Our own time demands another update to the social contract, so that investment, fairness, and future success mutually reinforce each other.

6.

In order to achieve a fairer and more advanced and competitive economy, the United States needs to make greater social investments. And in order to make these investments, the United States needs to raise revenues. It should do that in a way that contributes to, rather than undermines, fairness. There are two sources of funds for government investments—taxation and debt. Assuming that the United States continues to use debt as a routine way to underwrite government expenditures (and there's nothing wrong with smart use of debt to finance genuine investments), it will also need to raise more revenue from taxes. Tax revenues in the United States are among the lowest as a share of GDP among advanced economies. One could reasonably expect scale benefits to reduce the percentage of GDP that the U.S. needs to raise in order to achieve similar outcomes—but the U.S. is also the most advanced of the large advanced economies, with a higher GDP per capita than its peers. Sustaining this level of economic sophistication requires ongoing investment.

The U.S. is in the bottom fifth of OECD countries in terms of total tax revenue (including federal, state, and local taxes) as a share of GDP.[13] If it moved modestly from the 18th percentile to the 33rd percentile, or bottom third, and matched Japan, the second lowest of the G7 large industrialized economies, this would generate an additional $1.3 trillion annually. I'm not proposing here a specific level of taxation but rather pointing out that the U.S. has scope to maneuver. Over time, it's possible for the United States to move toward dedicating more of its GDP to investment, including investments in human capital. And those investments would themselves increase GDP in the long run.

Overall, we can afford to dedicate more resources to investment, but generating those resources through taxation is getting harder and harder to do, both because of increases in economic inequality and because of the role that economic elites play in shaping outputs of the political system, including tax policy.

The first problem here is math: the hollowing out of the middle class has eliminated tens of millions of potential taxpayers from the group for which a modest increase in taxation to fund investments for future generations could be levied without unacceptable reductions in consumption. There aren't enough of the people that my parents used to refer to as "comfortable" to make up an adequate individual income tax base. The United States needs to tax the rich, but not because of some sort of twenty-first-century class warfare. It needs to tax the rich—people and corporations—to be able to make more of them.

The investments needed to create a new American middle class will require a greater contribution from the wealthy and corporations. Regressive options, like a Value-Added Tax (VAT)—essentially a national sales tax—may end up as part of an overall compromise to raise revenue, but a VAT on its own would make the United States less fair, and put more of the tax burden on the poor and the middle class. Instead, the U.S. should tackle the necessary recalibration of the tax system to raise more revenue with an eye toward making its tax system more fair. The federal income tax system is already progressive—meaning that wealthy families pay a greater share of their earned income than others—but it has regressive elements in it that could be adjusted to provide more revenue and improve its fairness.

Amendments to the federal tax code could reduce the role of taxes that are imposed on the income generated from individuals' own work, reduce tax advantages that accrue disproportionately to the wealthy, and increase the share of taxes that are derived from income and windfalls that are not connected to individuals' labor. The government could also do more to simply collect the taxes that are owed, which would both advance fairness and raise revenue. And Congress can make taxes more fair by using taxes to assign appropriate costs to those whose economic activities create them—like taxes on polluters.

Tax rates on capital gains—the income made from selling appreciated stocks, for example—are about half of what they are on income earned as wages for work for high earners. Most Americans earn the majority of their income by labor; only a relatively rich few make their income principally from buying and selling investments. But these few pay a lower level of federal taxes on the income they make passively than many workers do on the marginal income they make putting in overtime after a forty-hour workweek. Narrowing the gap between these two taxes, especially in a progressive manner, would make the tax system more fair and could be done in a way that retains incentives for working people to save.

There are also a number of tax deductions that could be removed for the wealthiest Americans. One of the only progressive parts of the significantly regressive tax reform enacted under President Trump was the capping of the state and local tax (SALT) deduction. Reinstating the deduction, as Democrats have proposed to do, would cost tens of billions in lost revenue, and 96 percent of that money would go to the top fifth of earners—and most goes to the very top: 57 percent of the tax cut to the top 1 percent, and 25 percent to just the top 0.1 percent (who would get an average tax cut of nearly $145,000).[14] A better way to incentivize states to set their own tax levels so as to fully fund key public services would be to expand the use of federal matching funds, so that states that raise revenue for education and other public goods get a direct subsidy.

The mortgage interest deduction is another tax law that disproportionately benefits the wealthy. It could be adjusted to continue to provide a tax break for the middle class while excluding the top earners. Additionally, one of the greatest tax breaks for the wealthy is the "stepped up" cost basis at death. Under current law, if I buy a stock at $10 and its price rises to $100 and I die without selling it, my heirs inherit it with a "stepped up" cost basis of $100. If they sell it the next day they never have to pay taxes on the $90 of profit (and neither did I). This loophole means that huge amounts of capital gains go untaxed, and it creates distortions in the market and inefficient allocations of capital because people hold stocks longer than they otherwise would in order to evade taxes.

The relative roles of income taxes and estate taxes could also be rebalanced. Until now, federal tax law has treated estate taxes as a tax on the person who dies. The rhetorical strategy of calling the tax on transfers from one generation to the next a "death tax" is effective but it's not true: dead people don't pay taxes; and if they did, surely it would be better to tax them than the living!

It is a peculiarity that when a diner waitress wins the lottery in America and scores a $10 million prize, she pays income taxes on the whole of it, but when the scion of a wealthy family wins the lottery of birth and inherits $20 million from his parents, he pays no taxes at all. There is a public policy interest—with respect to social mobility, equality of opportunity, and fair competition—in preventing a permanent, entrenched, economic elite. And, philosophically, for a society that wants to reward people for working for themselves, the taxation of inheritance should be preferable to the taxation of earned income or income earned from disciplined savings and investment by individuals.

As New York University law professor (and Assistant Secretary of the Treasury) Lily Batchelder has observed, inheritances are taxed at roughly one seventh the rate of earnings from labor and savings. To fix this, Americans should reframe the policy question to focus not on those who make the bequest, but rather on those who receive it—the inheritors, who are, after all, the ones who pay any tax that is imposed. There shouldn't be an estate tax; there should be an inheritance tax. From a standpoint of public policy, and of fairness, it is different for a couple to leave $20 million to their only child than it is for them to leave $500,000 each to forty children and great-grandchildren. It is the inheritance which becomes a form of income to the recipient.

So how would this work? Batchelder proposes reforms that would abolish the estate tax and its attendant peculiarities and instead integrate inheritances into existing transfer taxes. It would allow Americans to receive gifts, including inheritances, of a certain amount over their lifetimes, and then tax amounts above that threshold as income. What's a reasonable amount? The median price of a three-bedroom home plus the price of a college education? Enough to generate the median national income in perpetuity? Either would give a significant advantage to its recipients, and both of these would recommend thresholds below $1 million. If the threshold were set at $1 million, the taxes on inheritance income over that amount would raise approximately $1 trillion in the next decade.[15] And remember, that $1 trillion would be collected only as a portion of cumulative inheritances *over* $1 million per heir. It's a tax paid only by literal millionaires who have luck, not work, to thank. (Batchelder's proposal envisions a tax deferral system for family farms and small businesses.)

Another way to raise new revenue from those who can most afford it is a wealth tax. In addition to logistical challenges around the periodic assessment of individuals' net worths, the idea of a wealth tax unsurprisingly finds fewer advocates in an environment in which the political ambitions of most elected leaders are substantially funded by those who might find themselves subject to such a tax. Nonetheless, it remains true that most Americans do pay some kind of wealth tax in the form of property taxes on their home, or, indirectly, through rent. (The median house price and the median net worth of homeowners are both around $250,000 in the U.S., meaning that someone near the median on both is paying property tax on an asset about equal to her or his net worth.) An argument of wealth tax proponents is: middle-class homeowners already pay a tax on the asset that represents the majority of their wealth, the very wealthy should too.

Enforcement of existing tax law is a way to raise revenue without raising taxes at all on law-abiding taxpayers. The U.S. Treasury Department estimates that the tax gap—the difference between taxes owed and taxes collected—in the U.S. is some $600 billion *annually*. To put that in context, it's about half of the total Social Security payments made to 70 million retired, disabled, and widowed Americans and their children. It's four times the total federal expenditure on education at all levels. It's twelve times what we spend on the State Department and U.S. Agency for International Development, including foreign assistance.

The gap between taxes owed and taxes paid is disproportionately prevalent among the wealthiest Americans. If your income is entirely or mostly derived from a wage or salary, as it is for most working people, you discharge the majority of your tax liability as you get your paycheck when your employer withholds taxes. The investment income that wealthy people make tends to be more opaque and is only reported at the end of the year. In a recent National Bureau of Economic Research (NBER) paper, a team of economists and statisticians using random samples estimated that 36 percent of unpaid federal income taxes are owed by the top 1 percent, and that collecting taxes owed from this group—just the top 1 percent—would yield $175 billion annually.[16] The Inflation Reduction Act included provisions to help backfill the expected retirement of thousands of Internal Revenue Service (IRS) employees, and to boost staffing levels aimed at enforcing tax laws on high earners.

When I led the Department of Higher Education in Colorado, about a third of families applying for federal financial aid for college were "flagged" for verification based on their applications, whereas the IRS audits fewer than 1 percent of income tax returns. Rates of auditing have been declining for over a decade, and went from about 1 percent in 2010 to .4 percent in 2021. But according to researchers and analysts at Syracuse University's TRAC Center, those at the lowest income levels—below $25,000—have been five times *more* likely to be audited than other taxpayers.[17] And although audit rates rise again at higher levels of income, the audit rate for those earning over $1 million was still less than 2 percent. The unpaid taxes of the super wealthy are less likely to be discovered even if they are audited, since many of the methods that they use to hide income, including offshore accounts and complicated business pass-through arrangements, are less likely to be discovered by a standard audit and require more thorough investigation.[18]

There are a number of reasons for the failure to collect taxes owed. A decades-long decline in staffing at the IRS, including a precipitous drop in the number of experienced employees who have the skills to evaluate complex tax returns, is one. Over the course of the decade starting in 2010, the number of these "revenue agents" at the IRS declined 40 percent even as the number of Americans submitting returns with over $1 million of reported income doubled. Everyone should not have to go through their tax returns with an IRS agent each year, but when enforcement becomes very unlikely, more people see the benefits of bending the law as worth the small risk of getting caught. Awareness of enforcement tends to conduce to voluntary compliance.

Not all of the $600 billion gap in uncollected taxes is recoverable, but even if the part that could be recovered by more robust enforcement amounts to just 5–10 percent of the lost receipts, that's still a huge source of revenue. The Biden administration, which had proposed expanding IRS enforcement capacities, estimated that this enhancement could yield a net benefit of $400 billion over ten years.[19] The Congressional Budget Office projects provisions in the Inflation Reduction Act to net over $120 billion in the same period.[20] More could be done.

Taxation can contribute to fairness not only by assigning responsibility for shared social costs in a manner that reflects people's differing capacities to contribute, but also by assigning specific social costs incurred by specific companies or people. Because of the global nature of the decarbonization challenge, the global consequences of climate change, and the role of historical emissions, carbon taxes are difficult to calibrate both technically and from a substantive fairness perspective. But these taxes would force those whose economic activities impose costs on all of us to incorporate some of those activities' social and environmental costs into their balance sheets. This is more fair than allowing a subgroup of people (say, shareholders in an oil company or frequent fliers) to enjoy the benefits of an activity with significant negative externalities but pay no differentiated cost for that externality. Politically speaking, it may be useful to make such taxes revenue neutral—that is to say to offset any increase in taxation generated by a carbon tax with cuts to other taxes. The purpose of such taxes is not to reduce overall consumption, it is to more accurately price the consumption of certain goods with significant negative externalities.

Better accounting for the true cost of carbon, like other policies that make the United States more fair, will also give the United States more political influence internationally when we negotiate for fair deals for American workers, consumers, and companies.

Making the case for standards consistent with American interests and values for trade and investment, for technology, for land use, for labor standards, for climate and ecological impact, for weapons use, and so on, will be easier if the United States' own example is more obviously one worth emulating. A United States with lower levels of poverty, with a robust middle class, with less extreme economic inequality would be a better example for the world, and a more credible and persuasive voice able to serve as cooperator-in-chief in international political debates about how to manage a globalized world. Workers in the United States will be able to compete more successfully in an integrated global economy if other countries uphold minimum standards in their labor and environmental laws. Families will feel more secure if there are standards on technology. American entrepreneurs and companies will continue to depend on trade and investment agreements and intellectual property protections. We will all benefit from coordination that averts the worst consequences of climate change. And these outcomes are all going to be products of deal-making, not dictates.

7.

One of the principal obstacles to building a fairer American economy is the unfairness in American politics. No one likes to play a rigged

game. Public confidence in the fairness of the U.S. democratic process has eroded in recent years because of a perfect storm of factors:
the hyper-charging of the role of money in U.S. politics; failures of
leadership and the consequent erosion of democratic norms; and
evolution of the media that has increased awareness of both new and
long-standing unfair aspects of the political system. This last one is
somewhat paradoxical. In some important ways, U.S. governance
has become more democratic even as its institutions have not. The
internet, social media, and, yes, even cable news have eroded elite
dominance of the public sphere and have given platforms to a much
broader range of voices, and compelled responsiveness from elected
leaders to issues that in an earlier time might have been silenced or
swept aside. These media have also, of course, proven a fertile ground
for conspiracy theories and radicalization.

In 2010 and then in 2013, the U.S. Supreme Court made two
decisions that, in different ways, were each body blows to the fairness
of the American democratic political process. The first was the decision in the case known colloquially as *Citizens United* that opened the
floodgates to unlimited spending in American politics. The second
was the decision to strike down key requirements of the Voting Rights
Act of 1965 and the overture to a new era of restrictions on voting,
that basic procedural right of a citizen within the democratic process.

8.

In 2020, Americans spent almost $15 billion on federal elections,
almost double the 2016 total. For non-Americans who live in democracies, the role of money in American campaigns is one of the
most confounding aspects of U.S. politics. What has become normal
to Americans makes no sense to observers from overseas and seems

obviously and egregiously corrupt. I had a brief and undistinguished personal encounter with the reality of money in politics when I ran for U.S. Senate in Colorado in 2019 (my half-year run ended when my former boss, Governor John Hickenlooper, entered the primary). As I geared up to launch, multiple people warned me that all that mattered was money. One Democratic political consultant told me that in every Democratic Party primary for governor, U.S. Congress, or U.S. Senate in Colorado since 1976, the candidate with the most money had prevailed. Candidates spend the better part of two years raising the money they will need to "communicate" (run ads) in the last month of a campaign.

The fundraising imperative means that candidates spend a disproportionate amount of time with rich people (the minimum contribution for most of my fundraisers was $250, and the maximum contribution was $11,200 for a couple; it would be higher today). So candidates spend hours every day listening to the concerns of rich people, responding to their ideas. Hey, rich people are people too, but they aren't representative, and their ideas are no better or worse, no more or less deserving of attention, than those of others. And it's not just rich people, it's rich legal "persons"—remember when former presidential candidate and now Republican senator Mitt Romney was pilloried for saying that "corporations are people, my friend" in response to a heckler at the Iowa State Fair in 2011? Well, he wasn't, legally speaking, wrong. Especially for incumbents of both parties, corporate political action committees (corporate PACs) become an easy way to advance fundraising goals, and an easy way for corporations to ensure they'll get access to elected representatives in a pinch.

What's more, the rise of small-dollar or grassroots fundraising is not the unmitigated good that some might have you believe. Small-dollar fundraising only makes a dent in campaign goals when it happens at scale. For every $11,200 donor couple a competitor picks up a check from, a candidate has to find more than one thousand $10 donors. And that kind of small-dollar scale is only achievable if the candidate is already famous or already deep into a campaign that has probably been funded by rich people in its early months. Even with the explosive growth of grassroots fundraising, "small" donations (less than $200) still supported only 22 percent of campaign expenditures in 2020 (compared to 42 percent for donations from large individual donors).

While candidates are less likely to pay special attention to the particular views of the $10 donor than the $10,000 one, the thirst for grassroots donations has had a polarizing effect on campaign messaging, and likely on voters themselves. Anyone who has found themselves on a campaign email or text list has probably noticed that the messages they receive are not thoughtful or nuanced. They are written to provoke emotion, particularly outrage or anxiety, and they often oversimplify complex stories, misrepresent polling, and take headlines out of context. They are, after all, not intended as contributions to political discourse; they are advertising that is trying to get readers to "buy" support for the candidate. And campaigns in both parties have learned that the most successful of these messages are those that provoke strong reactions from a subset of supporters who make repeated donations. (In 2020, Donald Trump became the first presidential candidate in history to have contributions of less than $200 make up a majority of individual fundraising.[21]) The grassroots donors aren't representative of the majority of voters, and campaign communication with them feeds indignation and hostility in party foot soldiers that doesn't go away when the campaign ends.

Money has long mattered in U.S. politics, but it matters more and there is more of it now than ever before. When Gary Hart won the

U.S. Senate seat from Colorado in the 1970s he raised $300,000 for the whole race, primary and general election. When I ran, I raised $300,000 in my first week. After Hickenloooper entered the race, he raised over $30 million over the course of the campaign (he won). To put it in context, that's $7 for every voter in the state, and $20 for every vote he received. That's crazy.

And that's only on the so-called official side. *Citizens United* opened up the world of super PACs, entities to which contributions are unlimited and which can spend unlimited amounts alongside campaigns. Officially they are not allowed to coordinate with the candidates' campaigns themselves. But both parties use a series of practices to work around this restriction. A campaign will post extra video footage to little trafficked corners of YouTube so that super PACs can use it. Or they may post opposition research (dirt on an opponent) on a Facebook page. The super PAC ad makers know where to find these treasures, and when they cut their attack ad, the campaign says "we don't run attack ads, and we can't control what independent organizations do."

Citizens United has corrupted American politics. It has given substantial control of U.S. politics to economic elites. The largest donors in 2020 were the late conservative casino magnate Sheldon Adelson and his wife, Miriam Adelson. Together they gave over $3 million to campaign and political action committees—so-called hard money contributions that are subject to limits. But that $3 million looks tiny next to the $215 million they contributed in "soft" money to super PAC groups.[22] The top one hundred donors in America were responsible for about one of every ten dollars spent in American politics in the 2020 elections.

Politicians of both parties depend on these contributors. Senators are especially dependent because they have expensive races that almost always cover multiple media markets across entire states, but they are less likely to garner the kind of national attention that results in saturation on cable news and an army of small donors as presidential campaigns do. As a result, the balance of the Senate depends on super PACs and their megadonors. Unsurprisingly, Republican Mitch McConnell's super PAC was the biggest super PAC spender in 2020, and Democratic leader Chuck Schumer's was the second largest. Together they poured half a billion dollars into competitive Senate races.

Swing voters—or rather persuadable ones—and voter turnout decide elections. Persuadable voters and voter turnout are demonstrably affected by advertising. Advertising costs money. And determinant amounts of money are coming from a subset of the wealthiest individuals, robbing individual voters of the significance of their voice and their votes in the democratic process. The composition of the U.S. Senate is, to a significant degree, chosen by megadonors. And those megadonors are not shy about communicating their policy preferences to lawmakers. Even when those preferences are substantively unobjectionable, the process is not. And much of the time the preferences represent a short-circuiting of policy debates that advances corporate and elite interests. And it's not just the unfairness of tax codes or hesitancy to regulate key industries that results. I had a conversation with a Republican U.S. senator before the 2016 election who told me about a megadonor who called him and said, "I'm just making sure you're ready to hold up any of Hillary's judicial nominees." And the senator replied, "Well, for how long are you thinking that's possible?" and the megadonor said, "Four years." The implication was clear: you want my check, you have to sell your vote and jam up the proper function of two of the three branches of government.

American democracy is meant to be a process that reconciles the interests and values of its population of 330 million. A battlefield for the richest 1 percent does not produce good or fair outcomes on substance. It also is not a system that we can point to and say, "Even if you don't like the outcome, you can see that it treats everyone equally as a matter of process."

When I worked in the human rights bureau at the State Department, I used to talk about Russia, China, and other countries as facing a "dictator's dilemma." As these and other regimes tighten the screws of repression, they create tensions and dissatisfaction which require still more repression to suppress. The only way to preserve a certain level of unjust deprivation of rights is to escalate the deprivation of rights in the face of complaints. When the legitimacy of fairness in process is lost, the exposure of unfairness in outcomes becomes an existential risk to a regime or government.

Political corruption has a similar dynamic to political repression. It creates structural incentives for a downward spiral. As corruption rigs the political system, ever more corruption is needed to continue the rigging in the face of obvious popular consequences. As popular dissatisfaction with high drug prices or low wages or a tax system that favors the wealthy rises, it costs more money to distract voters from the power that has been taken from them, and what is being done with it.

There can be no unilateral disarmament on super PACs—if one party or one candidate took the principled stand of rejecting them, they would lose elections. (Though it ought to be possible for candidates of one party to agree to eschew super PACs in *primaries* for certain posts—even if they need the soft money for the general election.) The only solution in the long term is to seek to overturn the disastrous decision in *Citizens United*, and the best way to reliably and permanently do that is through a constitutional amendment, which would necessarily have to be a bipartisan project.[23] This process would take years, but it is achievable. Even if elected officials benefit from super PACs, that doesn't mean they like them. Politics attracts people with robust egos. They don't necessarily like being dependent on the whim of a few rich people. Popular support for reducing the role of money, and of big donors in particular, in politics exists: recent polling suggests that 88 percent of voters in both very red and very blue districts agree on the importance of reducing the influence of big campaign donors. [24]

Incidentally, corporate and economic elites would and will always have disproportionate power—they are more likely to have their voices picked up in media, they are more likely to move in similar social networks to political leaders, they hire lobbyists to inform lawmaking, and employ lawyers to minimize the costs of compliance. A constitutional amendment to reverse *Citizens United*, like campaign finance and voting reforms, would not put them on a level with ordinary people, it would just remove some antidemocratic features of the current system that corrupt fair process and conduce to unfair and suboptimal outcomes.

9.

In addition to *Citizens United*, in the 2013 case *Shelby County v. Holder*, the Supreme Court struck down key aspects of the Voting Rights Act. The process of voting in the United States is managed at the state and local levels, and the Voting Rights Act had established safeguards aimed at preventing discrimination in the process. The direct impact of *Shelby* was that states and localities that had a history of racist disenfranchisement were released from the Voting Rights Act's requirement for "preclearance"—or federal approval of changes to voting practices. In the three years following the decision, state and local election authorities closed over eight hundred polling places, and these were disproportionately in Black and other minority communities.[25] Indeed, the bipartisan U.S. Commission on Civil Rights submitted a report to President Trump in 2018 that outlined its findings about discrimination in voting. In their report, the commission wrote that in the wake of *Shelby*, "the narrowness of the remaining mechanisms to halt discriminatory election procedures before they are instituted has resulted in elections with discriminatory voting measures in place."[26] And the problem is particularly pernicious because the elected officials charged with setting the rules for and overseeing the administration of elections—to whom one might otherwise appeal for change—are among those that benefit from such discriminatory measures.

Shelby catalyzed a new era of highly politicized pitched battles over voting rights. The same bipartisan commission noted that:

> In states across the country, voting procedures that wrongly prevent some citizens from voting have been enacted and have a disparate impact on voters of color and poor citizens, including but not limited to: restrictive voter ID laws, voter roll purges, proof of citizenship measures, challenges to voter eligibility, and polling places moves or closings.[27]

Over the course of more than two centuries, the story of voting rights in the United States has been neither unidirectional nor linear. Voting has always been contested because of its impact on who holds power. In 1856, North Carolina became the last state to drop the property ownership requirement maintained by most states at the founding. But even as states removed requirements for white men, they imposed new restrictions on others: New Jersey and Pennsylvania both enacted laws to *remove* Black men from the ranks of eligible voters in the early 1800s. The end of Reconstruction in the wake of the contested 1876 presidential election and the rise of Jim Crow in the South represented a period of significant voting rights contraction as poll taxes, literacy tests, and other obstacles were implemented to prevent Black men from voting. Around the same time, Native Americans were barred from voting by an 1876 Supreme Court decision that denied them citizenship, and the Chinese Exclusion Act of 1882 that blocked most immigration from China also barred Chinese American immigrants already in the U.S. from becoming citizens and therefore from voting.

In the wake of the First World War, a half century of voting expansion began. The Nineteenth Amendment, ratified in 1920, expanded the franchise to women (though many women were prevented from exercising their rights by other enduring barriers). And the Voting Rights Act of 1965 established an imperfect but effective legal framework for meaningful progress at eroding the legacy of Jim Crow and boosting equal access to the vote for all Americans. The *Shelby* decision and the backsliding that has followed represent a new period of contraction. American history has shown that this trend can be reversed. The future of America demands that it must be.

There is perhaps no other institutional principle so self-evidently core to the fairness of democratic governance as that of "one person, one vote." The act of voting in a free and fair election is a citizen's direct participation in self-governance, essential to the liberty that a democratic system of government offers. Representative democracy entails a tolerance for the indirectness introduced by representation— voters of both parties understand that not all Democrats will have a Democratic congressperson or Democratic senators, and not all Republicans will have Republicans representing them. But gerrymandering practiced by both parties stretches the reasonable tolerance that citizens have for the end result of the process.

New efforts to undermine voting rights aren't the only challenge. Old institutions that entrench unfairness also demand remedy. Critics sometimes depict the Electoral College as a kind of semisecret plot or scheme. Most Americans don't understand it, but it's not a secret plot: it was always overtly a departure from the idea of genuine popular election. While the nonrepresentative nature of the U.S. Senate was the product of extensive negotiation at the Constitutional Convention, the process of allocating electors was more a product of exhaustion and time pressure than of careful consideration. The delegates devising it opportunistically seized on the compromise of a proportionally representative House (where state delegations corresponded to population) and a Senate that allocated two seats to every state. While the 2000 election focused some new attention on the Electoral College, the 2016 and 2020 elections supercharged it. In 2016, Clinton won the popular vote but lost in the Electoral College. And in 2020, Biden won the popular vote by 7 million votes but only secured the Electoral College by fewer than 50,000 votes spread across three states (Wisconsin, Arizona, and Georgia). As many have observed, in addition to creating situations where electoral outcomes don't accord with the popular vote, which challenges basic intuitions about fair elections, the Electoral College system creates an incentive for candidates to focus their attention on a narrow group of swing states.

Because one party will always benefit from the unfairness that the Electoral College creates, a constitutional amendment to abolish it is unlikely. Another way to address the Electoral College is to get states representing a majority of electoral votes to pass state laws that mandate that their electors be assigned to the winner of the national popular vote. These laws, which have been adopted in fifteen states representing 195 electoral votes, are written to only take effect when enough states have passed similar laws so that they could ensure the selection of the president by popular vote, enough states to generate more than 270 electoral votes.

Still another way would entail expanding the House of Representatives, which has not happened for over a century. Members of Congress represent four times as many people as they did when the size of the House was set at its current level, and they represent far more people than their counterparts in other advanced democracies.[28] Doubling or even tripling the House of Representatives would pose logistical challenges around office space in Washington. But it could have salutary effects in making the House and U.S. presidential elections more democratic. Smaller districts make individual communities more likely to get representation from their representatives and make it more possible for retail politics, rather than big money, to sway enough voters. And adding to the number of representatives in the House would dilute the distorting effect of Senate seats in the allocation of electors in the Electoral College, making it far more likely that Electoral College outcomes are consistent with the popular vote.

In a world of increasing competition, including with authoritarian states, the United States needs its democracy to be a source of comparative advantage. Participation in the democratic process is part of the foundation for tolerance of outcomes of that process that one does not like, including bad outcomes that are objectively unfair. Loss of confidence in the fairness of the process undermines the legitimacy of its outcomes and the stability of democratic governance. To succeed in the coming decades the United States cannot afford to be moving toward political arrangements that exclude more Americans from the political process and undermine their confidence in it. Even if such moves incite no rebellions or popular movements against them, they divide Americans in a moment of world history and mounting international competition when harvesting democracy's practical fruits is as urgent as its enduring moral appeal. The struggle within the U.S. to improve our democracy's function and fairness isn't just a domestic affair for those who care about freedom and equality, it's part of shoring up the U.S. to compete in the coming century. The corruption of legislative and executive branch priorities perverts substantive outcomes. And both of these factors undermine the United States' capacity to deliver sustained commitments both in governance at home and in its foreign policy abroad.

10.

Social anthropologists have posited that the role of fairness in fostering commitment from participants to a social arrangement might be explained by practical self-regarding considerations or by more relational and identity-connected reasons. On the first explanation, people commit to fair systems because they expect that over time things will work out fairly and so the outcomes will be good for them. On the second, we like fair systems because they say something about our own worth, and our connection to those with whom we participate in such a system. When examining contemporary democracies and their politics, both explanations for the attraction of fairness resonate. And the pervasiveness of unfairness undermines both kinds of benefits.

Cynicism is a virus that feeds on itself. The perception that nothing good can come of government, that all politicians are self-serving and bought-and-paid-for by elites, that the judiciary has been irretrievably politicized, that elections are rigged—all of these attack citizens' confidence that the political process incorporates their voice, all of these erode their commitment to live by that process's outcomes. When citizens lose confidence in the overall fairness of the system, they lose confidence in their significance within it. They disengage or give up; or opt out, not only of voting, but of any kind of constructive discussion of issues with fellow citizens. In a democratic society, cynicism is self-perpetuating: the feeling that nothing any individual does matters in the face of special interests or in the context of a rigged game leads to apathy and diminished democratic accountability, which enable more of the practices that empower the purveyors of cynicism in the first place.

And the abandonment of the behaviors of a citizen leads to the relinquishment of core aspects of one's identity as citizen. If the rules don't matter or aren't fair or enforced, why would I want to think of myself as a citizen? Better to look elsewhere for the aspects of shared identity that bind me to others. After all, citizen is not the only social construct that people have come up with as a basis for shared identity; there are other options: nationalism, race, religion, gender. Cynicism creates a vacuum of genuine political participation and discourse between citizens that is filled by other, cruder forms of politics based on in-group and out-group loyalties and material spoils. The fairness test is connected to the identity test too.

Stanford classicist and political scientist Josiah Ober set out to answer the question of why ancient Athens was so much more successful than dozens of its contemporary city-state peers, as measured by criteria such as its wealth and the reach of its currency, its legacy of cultural capital, and its record of military victories. The ordinary factors—particularly geography and resources—did not explain it. Ober traced the Athenian advantage to its mode of governance. Athens was hardly a democratic idyll—enslaved people, women, foreigners, and others were barred from citizenship and therefore from participation in the polity. But it did have some of the characteristics that democratic governance achieves, including what might be called "cross-pollination" of knowledge and expertise, facilitated by citizen participation in governing institutions.[29] A farmer taking his turn in a representative body could bring unique knowledge about when to attack a rival power based on the timing of the harvest. And he could bring the knowledge derived from his discussion with other farmers to explain why a road or a port made sense, and where it could be built to encourage new production.

Even authoritarian societies that do not institutionalize citizen participation or input into governance have sometimes figured out how to harness the kind of experimentation that decentralized or bottom-up engagement allows. China's post-Mao nationwide economic reforms in the late 1970s under Deng Xiaoping didn't start with a central planner, they started with an experiment on land reforms in Sichuan and Anhui provinces.[30] That experiment, when adopted nationally, became an essential step in an explosive four decades of economic growth. And despite the lack of democratic process, the Chinese Communist Party has successfully continued to seek to leverage subnational experiments to drive policy innovation. As one political scientist put it, "experimentation under hierarchy is the key to understanding the emergence of an unexpectedly adaptive authoritarianism in China."[31]

The perversions of fairness in the democratic process in the United States reduce the potential for innovation in governance by reducing the number of perspectives brought to the policymaking process. But like friendships or ideas or futures that could have been, the loss of good, innovative ideas is an ephemeral counterfactual. Much more real and tangible is the fact that the unfairness in the U.S. system produces bad governance decisions. Decisions not to impose taxes fairly or to enforce tax liabilities equally. Decisions about government spending that drive waste. Decisions about financial regulation that decrease resilience at the expense of working people while relying on bailouts that effectively socialize risks taken by the wealthy. Decisions about health care that are optimized for corporate profits at the expense of health outcomes. These are all connected to the power that economic elites have over elected officials, and the current role of money in the electoral system, which maintains and consolidates that power. Purposeful efforts to bar or discourage certain voters from participating further skew democratic outcomes.

The systematic disempowerment of certain communities of Americans leads to disinvestment in those communities, even as the future of American success depends on them. Voting rights restrictions are problematic because disenfranchisement runs counter to bedrock democratic principles, but also because a system that excludes certain ones of its participants from decision-making is denying them inclusion in other ways too. This point is not abstract. It has practical impacts. Look at school funding for rich versus poor communities or for predominately white versus predominately Black communities. Look at the speed at which broadband reached rural communities as compared to urban ones. Or consider public assistance in the wake of natural disasters—an ever more important function of the state in a world of climate change. One of the biggest budget lines for disaster assistance is often aid to homeowners. It makes sense that rebuilding a town or city means rebuilding homes, and homeowners are easy to identify and verify in public records. But this approach rewards those who had the most before the disaster, and leaves out those most vulnerable before an event, and who are likely to be devastated afterward. Low-income people are disproportionately renters, not owners. Their recovery—getting back to work, getting back to school—is important to long-term economic growth and community sustainability. When voters who would be most likely to surface concerns about assistance approaches that send the lion's share of resources to those who own property are excluded from the democratic process, the efficacy of assistance in supporting broad-based recovery is reduced, and the divisions within communities are exacerbated.[32]

Bad substantive decisions lead to other problems. The ugly lurching of American democracy in the last decades is a product of the cynicism and suboptimal outcomes engendered by unfairnesses in its democratic process. When groups within a society believe that government will only consider their ideas and interests when members of a subgroup to which they belong have control, it creates perverse incentives that reinforce these perceptions. It creates a contest of identities rather than ideas, and rewards politicians for advancing that model. As journalist Michela Wrong showed in her history of contemporary Kenyan politics, *It's Our Turn to Eat*, clannish politics, even when competitive, devolves so that elected leaders serve their own material interests and those of "their" voters rather than those of the whole of the population.[33] The contemporary United States is increasingly subject to similar dynamics. In this situation laws themselves, instead of safeguarding principles and reflecting compromises based on shared norms, become an instrument of power used by one side to target the other.

And such laws, because they are not seen as a product of compromise that emerges from a fair process, have less durability, and are targets of reversal when control of government changes. Democracy's advantage comes from permitting change without revolution, but also from an inherent conservatism toward genuine products of fair democratic process, conservatism based on respect for the citizens whose will is supposed to be reflected in that process. It's not only the judiciary in which a principle of generally letting what's been decided stand, or stare decisis, might have both principled and pragmatic appeal. We don't think laws should be adopted and then repealed every few years—and not just because of the chaotic governance that would result. Laws, once duly passed through Congress and signed by the president, should be accorded a measure of respect as products of a democratic process. When, in 2017, John McCain cast the decisive vote against repealing the Affordable Care Act (a law which he had voted against adopting when it was in front of the Senate in late 2009), he was, in part, demonstrating that kind of conservatism—a sense that democracy can't function well if it becomes tribes that repeal each other's laws every time power shifts. But when democracy is manifestly unfair, its participants split into these kinds of political tribes, and each prioritizes serving its own. Over time, members of one tribe don't accord much respect to the decisions that flow from the other's period of control.

Contemporary dynamics in U.S. politics punish acceptance of anything the other party has done while in power. If not for John McCain's one vote, the effort to reverse the Affordable Care Act would have been successful. By 2017, companies, states and hospitals had all already spent money to adapt to the ACA, and it had proven successful at its main goal of expanding medical coverage to more Americans. Repeal would have meant the adaptation costs would have been in vain, and would have generated a new round of costs to get back to the way things were before. Repeal, and the end of the marketplaces that it created, would have resulted in a spike in the number of Americans without health care. Among these would have been people who had used the availability of insurance from exchanges to start small businesses, go back to school to pursue a better job, or even leave a bad marriage.

The push by some Democrats to reverse the Trump era elimination of the state and local tax (SALT) deduction is another case in point. It's fair to say that Trump supported the elimination in part because of political vindictiveness: he saw it as a way of punishing blue states on the coasts that generally have higher state and local taxes because they spend more on schools and other state-level priorities. His motives were tribal. But just because he championed the move for bad reasons doesn't mean that Democrats should, in a knee-jerk fashion, support reversing it. Repealing major legislation is sometimes necessary, but it's hugely disruptive. When decisions taken or laws passed by another party are seen as automatically and for that reason deserving of reversal, domestic governance is disjointed.

The vicissitudes of political swings have infected U.S foreign policy too, as we witnessed with President Trump's decisions to pull out of the Paris Agreement on climate change and the Iran deal, and more recently with the significant number of Trump-supporting Republicans questioning the U.S.'s principled support for Ukraine's resistance in the face of Russian invasion. Our status as a trusted actor has more of a significant impact on the strategic outlook for the U.S. than it did in an era of U.S. relative hegemony. Reversing the decisions that the United States has taken, tearing up the commitments it has made, sending a message that the United States may dramatically change its engagement with the world with each new election, reduces the United States' credibility as a partner. It also harms our ability to make future deals. And we will need more deals in a world where we have less ability to dictate outcomes. The United States' success requires generating the advantages of scale through alliances and partnerships rather than only through its own coercive ability; the loss of U.S. credibility is a strategic loss, it is the loss of an aspect of American power. An international politics that dissolves into transactionalism—where there are no stable expectations of good-faith cooperation over time, and where each interaction must be treated in isolation—is zero-sum. That describes a world that favors coercion over cooperation.

The United States faces enormous governance challenges—the need to overhaul the education and skills training system for the digital age, the ability to refocus a defense strategy on Asia and better leverage alliances, the imperative to lead the world in tackling climate change and investing in energy transition—all of which require the United States to take complex policy and legislative decisions that last more than a couple years. The cynicism and lack of confidence that unfairness in our economy and our politics engenders weakens our ability to do big things together.

11.

To meet the fairness test, the United States must continue to address the centuries-long national impairment of race. The historical accounts of how race became a defining structure of our society, the sociological accounts of how it continues to shape our economy and politics, the ethical exploration of how it corrupts the conscience and undermines the moral dignity of all Americans—these are all worthy of our engagement and reflection. My argument has nothing significant to add to the work that others have done and continue to do in this regard.[34] Race is a central part of the fairness test because it affects our national competitiveness. For as long as race retains its explanatory power as a key social factor in the political economy of the United States, the United States will fail to meet its practical (and moral) potential.

Addressing the negative effects of race is essential if we're going to strengthen U.S. competitiveness by leveraging the talent of every American. It would be an enormous boost to the legitimacy of American democracy both domestically and in the eyes of the world. And it would give the United States a more potent version of an old advantage—the ability to integrate people into a political project as genuine co-citizens, regardless of race or origin. The United States has drawn strength from the integration of outsiders in the past; it will need to perfect these capacities in the future in order to maintain a competitive edge. The U.S. is, for all its challenges, better positioned than most democracies—and far better positioned than national- ist autocracies—to seize this potential source of strength. Tackling America's race problem is part of a mission to make America more influential and more powerful in the world.

It would strengthen the U.S. economically too. Recall that around two thirds of jobs in the U.S. require some postsecondary training, and that share will grow as automation increases and new technology-related careers emerge. In 2020 the rate of postsecondary attainment for white American adults was about 50 percent. For Black Americans it was 38 percent. And for Hispanic Americans it was 30 percent. Also in 2020, the majority of people under age sixteen in the United States identify as nonwhite.[35]

The Georgetown University Center on Education and the Work- force assesses that the U.S. economy currently misses out on $956 bil- lion per year because of attainment gaps in education between white and nonwhite populations.[36] Almost a trillion dollars, including $300 billion a year of increased tax revenue and more than $500 billion of additional consumer spending. You don't have to care about social and racial justice to see that education systems that don't effectively serve nonwhite populations are a problem. You just have to believe in addition and multiplication. Structural racism is expensive.

But there's another less-appreciated but significant economic benefit to be harvested. The problem is not only that racial inequalities continue to lead to untapped potential among people of color in the United States. It's also that racism has consequences—economic consequences, not just moral ones—for its perpetrators as well as its victims.

Heather McGhee, in *The Sum of Us*, her eloquent and hopeful examination of how race has shaped American social policy, tells the story of the beautiful public swimming pools that were built in many American cities by the Works Progress Administration (WPA) during the Great Depression. These pools became centers of community, they were architecturally impressive, crystalline jewels bedecking parks in city centers at the middle of the last century. Then, desegregation set off a sad turn of events: rather than implement integration orders, white communities chose to fill the pools with dirt and cement. Rather than share a public good with Black compatriots and neighbors, they decided to deny themselves. It's not the behavior of a healthy or mature society to destroy something of economic value— something which isn't even meaningfully depleted by individual use!—just to deny some other group of people the enjoyment of it.[37]

The same logic has infected American political debates and decision-making about a range of other public goods, investments that need to be made to strengthen the country's ability to compete in the coming generation. Those who oppose social investments in early childhood, health care, and higher education and skills training have made arguments —sometimes cynical, sometimes misguided— targeted to low- and middle-income white American voters that play on preexisting prejudices and falsely suggest that social programs are principally for the benefit of nonwhite Americans. Elected representatives use this insinuation to justify damaging votes against expanding investments in higher education and health care.

There are actors in American politics who capitalize on one kind of cultural and structural unfairness—racism—to perpetuate another one: an insufficiently regulated economy that fails to offer a fair deal to workers, exacerbates economic inequality, and eschews necessary investments for a strong future. As McGhee explains, racism produces a conditional definition of who counts in the public, where public goods "are only for the public we perceive to be good." When faced with a choice between sharing benefits with others or giving up benefits altogether, those with power choose the latter. "It's often unconscious, but their perception of the Other as undeserving is so important to their perceptions of themselves as deserving that they'll tear apart the web that supports everyone, including them."[38]

Most white Americans do not know that a plurality of recipients of food stamps are white. As are a plurality of recipients of public education. Same with Medicaid. Same with Pell Grants for low-income college students. The majority of white voters have backed elected leaders who have resisted expansion of social programs or even cut their funding. Caricatures like Ronald Reagan's depiction of a "welfare queen" driving a Cadillac have persuaded them that these programs involve sharing social benefits with people of color. In order to deny such benefits to fellow Americans they support politicians who eliminate programs from which they themselves and their families would benefit. They impair their own ability to be healthy enough and well-educated enough to compete in a global economy in order to deny their fellow Americans the same achievements.

There is an argument made by some, sometimes in good faith, sometimes not, and often in the context of particular policy debates, that to talk about race is to reinforce its power in social and political structures. The argument is attractive because it appeals to our ideals. Certainly we should all embrace a vision of a future where we can talk only of high liberal principles, not of crude categories. But we can't get there from here without admitting where we are. The effects of race on American society and the individual lives of Americans remain so significant that the only way to make progress is to admit the reality and to address it. It should be a national strategic goal to have the middle class grow, to have educational attainment rise, to achieve per capita GDP growth, to expand life expectancy and quality of life measures, and to do all these while—and by—halving, and then halving again and again the gaps between people of color and white Americans on these and other measures. They are not separate goals. They are components of the same imperative.

We tend to see racism and discrimination as domestic issues. But from a geopolitical perspective, because racism is an unfairness that stains the democratic legitimacy of the American republic, because it distorts political decision-making about how to prepare the whole of society to compete, because it continues to be reflected in societal outcomes, the enduring power of the race-based caste system that was encoded in law for the majority of American history constitutes more than an immoral denial of the full humanity of American citizens. It is a self-imposed, self-policed, self-impairment of the United States' competitive strength in a challenging world.

Bias remains part of the cultural software of America—one doesn't have to see individual people as evil or to see America itself as irreparably flawed to acknowledge this fact. The hardware of the human brain and its immutable psychological proclivities may make overcoming bias particularly challenging; we like to divide people up into groups, it's part of how we organize our understandings of the world and of our place in it. One of the lessons from the example of the swimming pools above is that caste systems are not just about a dominant group's hoarding of wealth and power, or denial of society's material spoils to the lower caste; caste systems are also about defining and preserving identity. After all, their exclusive privilege, and the sense of superiority that it gave them, is the only thing that white people stood to lose through integration of a swimming pool. The fight against racism must include an effort to replace the role that race has played in defining Americans' sense of self. In this respect, antiracism is not fundamentally a claim for redress. It's a metaphysical transformation.

12.

Many Americans feel regret for the polarization, especially along political lines, that afflicts the United States today. While nostalgia for earlier times is fraught (my marriage would not have been legal just a decade ago) and our present divisions are overdetermined (the reasons for acrimony are multiple and diverse), accumulating deficits of fairness have played a significant role in fomenting the kind of social dissatisfaction that leads to recrimination and polarization. The fairness of a society, especially a free society, has implications not only for its efficiency but also for its durability. Fairness affects social cohesion. The years that followed the 2008 financial crisis brought rising perceptions of two kinds of unfairness. First that no one punished the culprits for the financial collapse, and second that the consequences of the recession fell mainly on the middle and working class, and that its hardships lasted longer for them than for the wealthy. In the fetid ground of a slow, uneven recovery, illiberal political weeds grew. In the 2010s, a wave of populism rose within the span of a few years in constitutional democracies in North America and Europe.

It's not just that people felt the pinch on so-called kitchen-table issues, it's that they saw that hardship as a result of unfairness. Social psychological research suggests that fairness affects individuals' attitudes toward particular arrangements and toward the other people associated with that arrangement—independent of outcomes. UCLA psychologists Golnaz Tabibnia, Ajay Satpute, and Matthew Lieberman conducted a series of experiments that replicated a basic setup. Two players are in a game in which there is a pot of specified value— say $20. Player 1 gets to offer Player 2 a division of the pot. Player 2 cannot negotiate, they can only accept or reject the allocation. If it is accepted, the pot is divided according to Player 1's proposal. And if the allocation is rejected, neither gets to keep any money.

Most Americans' intuition might be to split the $20 down the middle. Or perhaps they would argue that Player 1 can skew the offer slightly in their favor, given the asymmetry in the two players' power (life's not fair). Of course, in the setup of the experiment, no matter how skewed an offer Player 1 presents to Player 2, it makes economic sense for Player 2 to accept anything that Player 1 offers, as long as it is greater than zero. But most people aren't surprised to learn that a number of players, when presented with what they perceive to be an unfair split, reject it. And, what's more, those that do decide to accept skewed allocations harbor negative feelings toward the other player. The negative response is neurological—it is visible on a brain scan, and unfair arrangements trigger activity in a region of the brain that has been shown in other experiments to be associated with moral disgust.[39]

To isolate the effects of the perceived unfairness, rather than the amount that Player 2 received, the psychologists repeated the experiment with different monetary prizes, and demonstrated that receiving only $2 in an unfair split was associated with negative feelings while receiving $2 in a fair split was not. The experimenters concluded that it was not the nominal prize that affected satisfaction of players, it was the fairness of the system.

Furthermore: not only did the researchers find that negative associations attached to the players who proposed unfair divisions, they found that fair divisions engendered positive feelings. These reactions were also visible in brain scans of another part of the brain. That humans don't just recoil from unfairness but are attracted to fairness may sound obvious, but it's not necessarily the case. That fairness has an affirmative psychological attractiveness for most people is an essential insight into why fairness—rather than, or at least distinct from, absolute equality or some particular minimum level of wealth—might be a powerful social adhesive that attracts people to a particular set of social arrangements. The psychologists noted that the positive response to fairness exists across cultures, and they posit that it connects to the evolutionary value of social cooperation. We like fair arrangements, they theorize, because fair arrangements indicate a measure of in-group acceptance.[40] We like fairness because it means that our fellow humans respect us.

The point here is not that psychology demonstrates that particular societal arrangements are superior, but rather that there is scientific evidence that accords with an intuition that most of us have: that collective arrangements that are fair are likely to have more durable and voluntary commitments from their participants.

That commitment has the potential to deliver comparative advantages. Consider a business whose employees perceive their arrangements to be fair and who get asked, occasionally, to work late or scramble for an extraordinary challenge. Or think about the morale advantage of soldiers who believe in the essential fairness or goodness of their society. The extra benefit that each of us might perceive from participating in a fair arrangement or set of arrangements is a kind of "fairness dividend" that gets added on to whatever other benefits we might accrue from the arrangements themselves. In a game where two players split $4 evenly, they each get $2. But they also get something else: the satisfaction of participating in a fair interaction.

The fairness dividend, by engendering good feelings about a system of social organization, can also play a role in helping a society's members to see interactions with each other outside a zero-sum paradigm. Repeated experiences of fairness can give members confidence that in the long run outcomes work out more or less fairly, and that allows them to not worry as much about individual interactions—which could be especially valuable in times of need or emergency. The fairness dividend engenders the kind of trust that allows for more optimal and sustained commitment to a collective entity, and more resilience in extraordinary times.

13.

There are plenty of reasons to despair about the state of fairness in America. The loss of the middle class in the postindustrial, postglobalization digital age is a hollowing out not only of the present for many American workers but also of the future for their children. Enormous racial wealth gaps persist and are growing larger. The corruption of the political system by money and the persistent use of racism to drive a wedge between groups of Americans is preventing us from making the adjustments needed for an effective state underwritten by an updated social contract for the globalized, digital age. And, perhaps most disappointingly, too many political leaders have themselves chosen cynicism over leadership, surfing the waves of populist sentiments that are anathema to the cooperative citizenship that a successful shift in strategy appropriate to the exigencies of the coming decades demands.

The deficits of fairness across American political and economic systems are inefficient and damaging—but, on the flip side, because closing those deficits would drive growth and power, there is opportunity in our failings. We're nowhere near our ceiling. The sinner can be better, the angel can't. And the United States has already shown that this is possible as it has harvested the benefits of addressing instances of unfairness. Although it is incomplete, the progress already made on improving the allocation of Black people's and women's talent in the U.S. economy was responsible for as much as 40 percent of U.S. per capita economic growth in the half century from 1960 to 2010. Economists from the San Francisco Federal Reserve estimate that persistent economic discrimination with respect to race and gender reduced U.S. GDP by $2.6 trillion in 2019.[41] On the one hand, that's a high price to pay for the ongoing effects of racism and sexism; on the other, there's a real prize to win from tackling it. In work funded by the W. K. Kellogg foundation, Ani Turner estimates that the benefits of closing racial equity gaps could add $8 trillion to the U.S. GDP by 2050.[42]

Policies to kick-start growth are likely to prove ephemeral in their impact if a country lacks long-term institutional arrangements needed to sustain the economy in the face of inevitable shocks.[43] The United States is not a developing economy, but the resilience of the economy will be more important in the decades to come. The progress of globalization means that there are more opportunities for regional economic crises to become global ones. And noneconomic events that have economic impacts, like pandemics and climate or biodiversity disasters, increase the likelihood of external crises causing unexpected shocks to the U.S. economy and other aspects of its security.

One of the ways that citizens—reasonably—evaluate the quality of their government and of elected leaders is by the way that they manage and mitigate threats from phenomena that citizens are unable to address on their own, including things like pandemics or forest fires or global supply chain problems or financial crises. And while part of managing such shocks will always be moving to marshal resources and capabilities to mitigate their impacts, another way to reduce their downside risks is to have a society that is more resilient in the first place. A more fair America would be a more resilient one. If everyone had health care, the United States would be better prepared for the next pandemic and for ensuring that whole communities did not get left out of health responses. If there are fewer people living paycheck to paycheck, there will be fewer people who are one paycheck away from being homeless when the next economic downturn comes. If universities and other postsecondary training programs are more affordable, there will be fewer students who drop out of their programs leaving the U.S. with deficits in its skilled labor pipeline.

As we look to the coming decades, we can expect more shocks, not fewer. And a fairer society will be more resilient to these shocks, less likely to suffer collapse or dramatic setbacks, more likely to avert the worst of human suffering that might come from them, and to escape the corresponding political upheavals. A fairer society will be more stable because it will weather bad times better than one where huge numbers of citizens are perpetually on the cusp of disaster, and because it will be primed for equitable recovery. A fair society includes not only investments in human capital but also social insurance schemes to help smooth consumption for the poor and help small businesses recover from shocks. It's not only that these kinds of programs result in better outcomes for many of the most vulnerable in the society and low-income workers, it also produces better overall outcomes because of the interdependent nature of actors in modern economies. Systems that are finely tuned for maximum "efficiency," including by minimizing expenditures on social insurance schemes, may not be efficient at all because they do not sufficiently integrate the negative impacts of systemic shocks and longer recoveries in the way that they measure efficiency. They are only efficient in a single snapshot of "normal" conditions—and they can't handle deviations from the norm. But we live in a world where deviations are normal. And it's not a world of snapshots because each frame in the story depends on the previous one; resilience matters in the moment and for what comes next.

The United States possesses the assets necessary to seize the opportunity of tackling unfairness. It has democratic institutions. It has high-quality educational institutions. It is wealthy—like really wealthy. (None of the fourteen countries that have a higher GDP/capita than the U.S. has a population greater than 10 million. According to the International Monetary Fund's 2022 figures, U.S. GDP per capita adjusted for purchasing power is 20 percent higher than Australia's or Germany's, 30 percent higher than Canada's, 35 percent higher than the United Kingdom's, and still more than three times the size of China's.[44]) It has a free press. It has a judiciary that has at times played a fundamental role in moving the country toward more fairness, according to liberal principles, and notwithstanding popular opinion. The challenge is not to build the institutional foundations of a fair society from scratch—which is the challenge in so many other places in the world. The institutional equipment that the United States needs doesn't have to be invented, it just has to be used.

And meeting the fairness test does not mean addressing every unfair arrangement. Though all unfairness is worthy of redress, to distort a commonly cited aphorism: practically speaking, every injustice anywhere is not, in fact, a threat to justice everywhere. America will meet or miss the fairness test by addressing obstacles to giving its inhabitants a fair shot and fair competition, fair process, and fair consideration of their common humanity. Momentum and direction of travel matter for generating confidence in this respect—every injustice does not have to be remedied for people to believe in the legitimacy of their social arrangements and for them to be committed to the future of their society—but things need to move in the right direction.

The economist Thomas Piketty wrote a 2013 book, *Capital in the Twenty-First Century*, that made the argument that, for structural reasons, returns on capital grow faster than the economy, and therefore inequality will tend to grow worse because the wealthy derive a disproportionate amount of their wealth from the former, whereas wages correlate more to the latter. One might have expected Piketty to be a pessimist, if not a revolutionary, given that he diagnosed a seemingly inescapable force accelerating inequality that has dominated most of the last half century in advanced European and American market economies. He is not. In an interview, when asked why he's optimistic that the United States and others will achieve a greater measure of fairness in the decades to come, he argued for taking a long view: "The key in history is not the big catastrophes but the positive political construction of an alternative, and this process started with the French Revolution, the U.S. revolution. This process toward more equality is more deeply rooted in our modern ethos and modern political cultures than most people believe." Democracies get off-track—in the wake of the last major wave of globalization and industrialization at the end of the nineteenth and beginning of the twentieth century the U.S. also had an enormous concentration of wealth. The Depression and the policies that followed it reset the course. There's another reset coming, Piketty predicts, if only because exacerbated concentrations aren't just bad for fairness, they are bad for prosperity too.[45]

Yes, the U.S. can't continue on the path it is on and achieve a more fair society, the kind of society that can preserve sufficient U.S.

influence and leadership in world politics in the coming decades. But it can change course. It has done it before. It can do it again. There are no guarantees—a fairer society is not written, of course, and there are many short-term interests that conspire against achieving it. We could fail. But that failure will be a choice, not a fulfillment of destiny.

TAKE A CHANCE ON WE

THE IDENTITY TEST

1.

Of the four tests, the test of identity is the toughest. It also unlocks the most difficult-to-emulate strategic benefits. If the United States meets this test it will achieve a comparative advantage in international politics that will give it outsized influence and power in the world, and the ability to secure the futures of its citizens. And as difficult as the test of identity is, the United States has a better chance of meeting the test than any other advanced democracy. The prize would be moral and strategic exceptionalism.

It is an oversimplification to reduce expectations about geopolitics in the twenty-first century to a contest between the U.S. and China. That paradigm excludes other democratic states, especially in Asia and Europe, and entities, such as the EU, that cannot be bystanders in such a contest. It excludes the majority of the world's population, which now lives in middle- and low-income countries outside of China and North America. Many of these people don't see either China or the U.S. as a primary concern, and their chances for a decent future depend on a different geopolitical narrative emerging. The U.S.-China contest is an oversimplification, and so is the contest between democracy and autocracy. Not only do these heuristics gloss over complexities, they suggest questionable approaches. The U.S. will not outcompete China because it wins an arms race. Democracy is not going to beat out authoritarianism by winning over hearts and minds in a philosophical assessment of competing political ideologies. Both frames suggest one side will succeed by besting the other. The most trenchant question is not whether democracy will beat authoritarianism but rather whether democracy will beat itself.

As the dominant example of a state purveyor of an alternative to democracy, and as a growing power, China represents a genuine geopolitical challenge to the United States and the world's other democracies. The Chinese leadership's geopolitical strategy with respect to the United States is premised not only on China's expanding economic and military power and leverage, but also on U.S. decline. American decline is an assumption built into their plan. One way to upend the Chinese strategy, then, is to not decline.

To prevail in the geopolitical contest, or contests, of the coming decades, the United States needs to maximize its assets—particularly its human capital—internally, and its partnerships with other liberal societies externally. To do that, it has to invest, substantially, and without the perversions of caste, waste, or the disruptions of justified discontent, which means it has to be organized fairly, and deliver fair (not perfect, but fair) results. And to protect the interests and rights of its citizens, the United States must function reliably as a shared enterprise in a challenging world. To renew, fuel, and sustain that shared enterprise, it must meet the test of identity.

2.

For the U.S. to succeed it has to solve a challenge that is fundamentally different from any it has ever faced: the basis for American national identity has to be upgraded, and that has to be done without complete democratic collapse in the process. For the hardware of American power to work, the software has to be updated to better reflect the liberal values on which the country was founded. And that doesn't require a restoration of some real or imagined past, it requires building something new that has never existed before. Whatever stories we tell ourselves, we've never truly had the kind of sufficiently shared political identity—rooted in liberal values and not in race or religion or other divisions—that can be a foundation for making a pluralistic liberal democracy work. To be maximally competitive in the coming decades, the citizens of the United States will need to develop such a political identity. It can remain relatively thin compared to other aspects of identity, but it needs to ground a more robust commitment to a collective enterprise than it has for most American history.

One question is whether the United States can—with its population of over 330 million people drawn from all corners and cultures of the world, and spread across an expansive country and connected in a complex, vast, domestic economy—develop a foundational layer of identity, one that need not be among the most important features of most people's sense of self, but is, nonetheless and more or less, common to all.

And smuggled into that question is a second question: Can the thin layer of common identity be based at least in part on a shared commitment to democratic values—the equal dignity of persons, the inherent value of human freedom, the possibility of just self-governance through principled deliberative process? The reason that I say this question is "smuggled into" is that, given the United States' existing diversity, it is difficult to imagine the content of any national identity which could be *common* and *not* be liberal.[1] Any identity based on ethnicity or race or religion or gender or country of origin would automatically fail the test of universality; it would not be a common identity accessible to all Americans.

3.

Identity isn't a standard subject matter for discussions of geopolitical strategy, at least not overtly so, and it's worth thinking through what identity means in this context and why it matters. Identity is a psychological phenomenon, a construction of the self, that helps people make sense of their experience of the world.

Identity is personal but also inherently relational—the way that we understand who we are is principally in relation to other people. We derive and confirm understandings of our identity through our interactions with others. Not only explicitly through information that they might share or teach us about language, culture, and knowledge, but also implicitly through the cues that are part of the relationships themselves. Being a son is part of my identity not only because my parents told me "you are our son" and explained how that came to pass, but also because of the interactions that I have had with my parents, and the interactions I have witnessed between others and their parents, that help me to form a composite sense of what son-ness is. I know that this relationship is a loving one not only because my mom tells me she loves me but also because we treat each other in a loving way.

Our identities help us navigate the world because they function as a set of cognitive shortcuts. They give us information about how to "be" in different contexts, not only suggesting modes of behavior but also understandings of situations, especially with respect to our interactions with other people. And it is not only our own identities but our understandings or judgments about the people we interact with and their presumed identities that shape these encounters.

Because they help us move through the world and make sense of it, our identities also help us find and make meaning in it. They are a mooring point for judgments we make about ethics, for discerning right and wrong action. They are a prism through which we regard our own experience, our thoughts, and the world around us. And although our identities act as a kind of crutch for our brains, helping us to process our experiences, and in some ways constraining our interpretations, they are also reasons to act and essential to our sense of autonomy. When we act in ways that are consistent with our sense of self, we feel the fulfillment that comes with having exercised a kind of freedom, that twenty-first-century virtue of "authenticity."

As we depend on identity, identity is deeply connected to an individual's sense of well-being. Our identities can change over time, but they are as essential to our psychological existence as our hearts are to our biological one. Major threats to or disruptions of our identities are experienced as existential. A reasonably stable sense of identity is, for this reason, part of an individual's sense of security. And, inasmuch as people count on political structures to deliver security, in moments when they feel their identities, their understandings of themselves through which they perceive and make sense of the world, to be under threat, they can respond in ways that echo the behaviors that people exhibit when experiencing other kinds of threat.

•   •   •

Because identities are relational, individual identities turn in significant measure on our membership in groups. These groups can be formal and informal, clearly delineated and less so, small and large. Our family. Mrs. Johnson's kindergarten class. The cool kids. English speakers. Christians. Democrats.

Our existence under the authority of certain political entities is for most of us an acknowledged part of our identity—even if we don't think about it all that much, even if it isn't that important to us, even if it doesn't primarily signify for us some expressly political identity. "Are you a Coloradan?" or "Are you an American?" are questions we understand in a way that we wouldn't understand "Are you a Northern Hemispherer?"

And when someone asks about being a Coloradan or an American, the category is probably recognizable enough that both the asker and the answerer have some ideas about what it means to see oneself as such. These imputed meanings might not be explicitly political. When asked, "What does it mean to be a Coloradan?" my first answer is not "it means that I live under the jurisdiction of the government of the State of Colorado and that every four years I have a right to vote in the election of its executive officers." Instead, the first ideas that most people would have about their identities as Americans or as residents of their states might revolve around tendencies to have certain interests, shared experiences, or values. ("I'm a Coloradan, I'm outdoorsy, I'm chill.") Being an American or from some U.S. state could, for some people, also connote membership in certain other groups—like ethnic or racial groups, or political parties. When we answer questions about the nature of our own identities, we are also expressing views about what we believe to be true about others who share that particular identity, and about what other kinds of identity might determine who is eligible to share in this particular one.

4.

The United States is facing two related crises of identity. First, millions of Americans who enjoyed privileged status in the sociopolitical hierarchy of the United States since its founding have found their identities within that hierarchy challenged. The second crisis—in part because a large number of Americans experiencing the first kind of identity crisis have reacted by turning toward the false security of a more tribalistic form of politics—is that too many people are prepared to jettison or reject liberal values as a nonnegotiable part of what it means to be an American. Without the second crisis, the first would be transitory. Democracy would force an adaptation. But the second problem is existential. Political scientist Francis Fukuyama has observed "successful liberal societies have their own culture and their own understanding of the good life, even if that vision may be thinner than those offered by societies bound by a single doctrine. They cannot be neutral with regard to the values that are necessary to sustain themselves as liberal societies."[2]

These twin crises are animating a political era that threatens to make impossible the commitment to liberal values that must underlie the political identity of Americans in order for American democracy to function and thrive in the coming century.

Starting in the months leading up to the 2016 U.S. election, established mainstream media began what seemed like an unending set of explorations of the experiences of mostly white, mostly working-class people in what we might call noncoastal America. (The apotheosis of this line of inquiry may have coincided with the publication of now U.S. senator J. D. Vance's *Hillbilly Elegy*, which it seemed like every "coastal liberal elite" was reading in early 2017 as they sought to make sense of their shock at the outcome of the 2016 election.) These stories were increasingly parodied and greeted with derision in certain parts of the American left. It seemed a grave misplacement of concern to focus on the pain of white people in the wake of the election of a leader who had used racist rhetoric. Critics accused journalists of exonerating Americans for their illiberalism on account of their difficult and deteriorating economic circumstances and encounters with addiction.

The criticism is understandable. Why should the hardships of formerly middle-class white people in America be any more deserving of our attention than the significant indignities and deprivations endured by generations of Black people or the challenges faced by millions of immigrants to the United States? Why did the opioid addiction epidemic produce so many more sympathetic human-interest stories than the crack cocaine one that began two decades earlier? One answer is racism. Another, not mutually exclusive, answer is that while these people's lives didn't matter more *morally*, they did matter more *politically*.

These stories excavated the narratives of millions of Americans who, over the course of years and decades, experienced a sense of accumulating and serious threat to core aspects of their identities. Their response to that experience—rejection of liberal democratic principles—had national political repercussions. Some threats to their identity—like the economic degradation of their communities that undermined the ability of blue-collar workers to sustain middle-class life—provoked sympathy. For large numbers of Americans, other events—like the election of a Black man as president of the United States, or the prospect of a woman president—also triggered additional perceptions of threat to their identity. The coincidence of these threat perceptions—of dislocating economic change and of women and people of color in positions of prominence—caused them to be associated with one another in some people's minds.

It's not just working-class white people from the Midwest or South who feel challenged. It's also those who remain part of the establishment: those who went to Ivy League schools, who have become partners in law firms or started companies, whose sense of earned satisfaction at their own accomplishments, whose identities as successful participants in a meritocracy, are called into question by efforts to interrogate how structural racism or sexism may have affected their own life outcomes. For them, too, efforts to remediate systemic unfairness skewed in their favor can feel like an affront. As my friend Franklin Leonard memorably put it in a recurringly viral tweet: "When you're accustomed to privilege, equality feels like oppression."

White people in the middle of the country have been disempowered by the role of money in U.S. politics in the same way as other "ordinary Americans" have. Millions of them have lost out in an economy that lacks guardrails and seen their livelihoods changed by the unmitigated effects of globalization. Many feel dislocated, insecure, and emasculated by economic changes; they feel a loss of dignity. But they have not lost their votes. Their votes have become more powerful because of the gradual nature of reapportionment of congressional representation, gerrymandering, and the purposeful nonrepresentativeness of the U.S. Senate; they have retained sufficient political power to respond to threats to their identity. One of the through lines of U.S. politics in the twenty-first century has been the grievances of white men. But white men, white people, are not the only ones who are going through monumental, dislocating changes and enduring economic shocks. The experience may be novel *for them*, but it is not novel.[3]

In the late nineteenth and early twentieth centuries, the French sociologist Émile Durkheim observed that industrialization had been accompanied by a form of social dislocation. He used the term *anomie* to describe the condition of individuals who had been alienated from society by the combination of significant social changes and the division of labor that followed from industrial capitalism. Increasing economic complexity made people more dependent on one another, yet it also made the experiences of individuals in the economic system more different from one another, challenging their capacity to understand each other's realities. Individuals were prone to become alienated from society and its norms; they ceased to feel themselves a part of a shared moral universe, one which presented them with meaningful and achievable standards of success. Separated in this way from others in their society, people pursued fulfillment of their individual needs unconstrained by social conceptions of what was good or worthwhile, but also unable to be fulfilled by living a life recognizably so.

Durkheim's exploration of anomie was part of his sociological examination of the economy in *The Division of Labor in Society*, but also, perhaps more poignantly, of his sociological examination of suicide, in which he posited that—contra conventional wisdom—suicide was not only a manifestation of individuals' independent struggles with mental health and depression but a social phenomenon connected to the anomie inherent to modern industrial societies.

For observers of contemporary America, there is much from Durkheim's inquiry into the alienation and dislocation that individuals feel in the wake of massive economic changes that resonates. The rate of suicide in the United States rose by more than a third in the first two decades of this century, and rose fastest among young people.[4] As scholar Juliet Schor has argued, contemporary American consumerism is driven in part by the way that growing economic inequality makes people feel their position in society is precarious. "We have a society which is structured so that social esteem or value is connected to what we can consume. And so the inability to consume affects the kind of social value that we have," Schor explains.[5] Americans' self-reported feelings of loneliness—which more than three in five reported in a survey conducted in the months before the start of the Covid-19 epidemic—also suggest an erosion of the kind of social connectedness that we associate with feeling secure and "knitted in" to a community or society.[6]

There may be many factors contributing to this reality—the rise of inequality, the emergence of social media as a principal mode of interpersonal interaction, the decline of participation in organized religion and other community and social associations—though many of these trends could be explained as examples of correlation, not causation. Whatever the explanations for it, it seems reasonable to say that large numbers of Americans are experiencing modernity in ways that lead them to question their place in it. This twenty-first-century anomie, this societal identity crisis is real, and it has implications for the kind of society and politics we might seek to create and for the prospects for our being able to improve upon the one we've got.

5.

Every American schoolchild learns these words from the United States Declaration of Independence: "We hold these truths to be self-evident, that all men are created equal, that they are endowed by their Creator with certain unalienable rights, that among these are Life, Liberty and the pursuit of Happiness." But while the Founders may have seen these truths as self-evident, the nature of these rights— what they entail, what they entitle us to, what they demand—is far from it, and has been the basis for debate within the liberal tradition for centuries.

The triad of asserted unalienable rights proceeds from most obvious and least abstract in meaning to most obscure and most unusual. "The pursuit of happiness" is the most intriguing of the three, and the most uniquely American: it finds few analogues in other founding texts or constitutions. The French Déclaration des Droits de l'Homme et du Citoyen of 1789 also delineates certain natural rights, but these are, in French reckoning, liberty, property, safety, and resistance against oppression.

The intervening centuries may have given rise to some confusion about what Thomas Jefferson intended by the use of the term "the pursuit of happiness," and scholars have debated the reasons why the Declaration's author chose the words he did. Some have suggested that he intentionally departed from the list of "life, liberty, and property" put forward by John Locke in his influential *Second Treatise on Government*, because of misgivings about the institution of slavery. Jefferson, they suggest, did not want to put *that* kind of property on a moral pedestal, but meant nonetheless to nod at property as the means to achieving satisfaction of human needs. Others have suggested that it was a mere rhetorical flourish, a bauble in prose, and a demonstrably effective one. Given what we know of Jefferson as a slave owner and as an intellect, the first explanation gives him too much credit, and the second too little. And both imply that, to Jefferson, the words—whether for purposes of obfuscation or entertainment—were part of a sleight of hand.

The happiness to which Jefferson appealed was neither a synonym of the emotional state of joy nor some sort of material satisfaction of human needs. It seems much more likely that Jefferson was suggesting something closer to what we might today call fulfillment or meaning. What is asserted as a natural right is not happiness itself, of course, but the pursuit thereof—the quest for fulfillment, the search for meaning. The state or society could not reasonably guarantee ful-fillment itself. And the humanistic ideal that Jefferson studied in life and embedded in his prose held the act of crafting a life of one's own choosing as good in and of itself. In this his words recall the Aristote-lean concept of *eudaimonia*—that of a state of satisfaction attached to living a good life—as well as the writing of Jeffersonian contemporar-ies like William Blackstone.[7]

Whatever it meant to Jefferson, the idea of the pursuit of happi-ness has meant something to America. Though the Constitution—in the Fifth and later in the Fourteenth Amendments—reverts to "life, liberty, or property," the concept of "the pursuit of happiness" has been invoked in nearly one hundred Supreme Court cases as a basis for litigants' claims and justices' decisions.[8] More than two centuries after the Declaration, Ronald Reagan's first inaugural address in-voked it.[9]

And the idea remains pervasive today. We see it in the language of religion—we're all sinners, it's about working to be closer to God—and hear its secular echoes in the words of self-help gurus. The idea that the pursuit of happiness is what matters is not only a moral proposition but also a comforting reassurance for those who have not reached their goals. Look around, and it's everywhere in popular culture. When I was in high school, my mom gave me one of those framed inspirational posters for my bedroom wall. "Success is a jour-ney, not a destination," it said. ("Success is a rowboat on the side of a lake," I used to muse to myself while staring at the cheesy sunset scene behind the text on angsty teenage nights.)

The notion of the pursuit of happiness is, I think, particularly helpful for thinking about what we can each hope for in whatever time we have on earth, what we ought to wish for ourselves and for others, and for imagining the kind of society that liberal governance should aim at. I offer this observation not as some kind of ethical originalism—some claim that Americans must go back to basics and understand the Declaration drafter's specific intent in order to refind our way—but rather because I think the poetic turn of phrase, even if it was indeed only that, captures well what it is that we ought to value and protect in our engagement with fellow citizens, and is consistent with contemporary intuitions about what makes a society good.

What then would taking "the pursuit of happiness" seriously as a basis for a shared American political identity in the twenty-first century mean? What would it require from Americans? What would something closer to an ideal civic identity look like? It would mean that Americans subscribe to the proposition that a successful America would be one in which one of the common experiences that citizens share is an opportunity to pursue lives of their own choosing, and thereby to seek their own happiness.

This vision does not imply a life of monastic philosophical reflection about autonomy and agency and identity. As philosopher and ethicist K. Anthony Appiah puts it, "People don't, as a rule, imagine themselves as having arrived at their own conception of the good life." Quite to the contrary, he continues, "their conception of the good or well-lived life would be undermined by their imagining it to be a wholly volitional affair, chosen among equally qualified candidates."[10] The good life, the pursuit of happiness, is for most of us a simpler endeavor. Rather than looking to philosophers' tomes, we might hear chords of the pursuit of happiness when a political leader says that "everyone should have a fair shot at having a middle-class life." Middle-class in this sense isn't just about an income level or a particular kind of job. For most Americans it connotes a potpourri of other experiences too—maybe a garden, or a church group or book club, family barbecues, hikes in the outdoors, or playing in a garage band. A middle-class life is implicitly one in which the individual has enough space to make choices about how they want to live.

If there were a thin consensus that a society that both allows and enables individuals to pursue happiness is the kind of society that is good, then to support and perpetuate such a society, Americans would have to identify as citizens—as bound with other Americans in this polity. And they would see that identity as both a reason to act and a way to understand their relationship to compatriots. They would recognize their paradoxically interdependent-independence: their own life and liberty, the conditions in which they can pursue their version of a good life, are made more secure by their membership in the common endeavor.

But the citizens of an America that protects their equal and individual rights to pursue happiness need more than the shared commitment to value the pursuit of happiness. They need ways of working—of sorting out how the collective endeavor will be run—that are consistent with this idea of everyone getting to make a life of their own choosing. The basic tenets of what is known as political liberalism flow from this idea: that there should be rules, under which citizens are equal, and that these rules should not violate principles underlying ethical individualism. The rules should permit individuals to define for themselves the good life as much as is possible while not jeopardizing the rights of other individuals to do the same. In other words, the state, like its citizens, should be committed to both fundamental rights inherent to human beings (life, liberty), and to broad tolerance with respect to the various ways in which people pursue happiness.

To be an American, then, must be to recognize oneself as an equal part of a political project with other Americans that aims at protecting the conditions for the expression of human dignity that is bound up with each person's capacity to make a life. And being an American must also be to see that identity as reason to accept the basic principles of liberal democratic governance. What about aspects of their own and others' identities *other* than this elementary political one of being an American? Those other aspects of identity can be recognized and embraced as sources of meaning and self- (and other-) understanding, but *not* sources of entitlement to pursue happiness more freely or fully than co-citizens.

One of the reasons I find the pursuit of happiness compelling as a candidate for the cornerstone of American civic identity is that, although it is an abstraction, it allows us to think about and define what would make America successful: the measure of whether or not our society is succeeding is whether or not it is creating an environment in which its participants can engage in the pursuit of happiness, can build recognizably fulfilling lives.

Successful societies will not be static, because while the principles that underlie the pursuit of happiness are timeless, what is necessary to create and sustain conditions for it may change over time. Citizens can and should recognize that as systems of economic interdependence become more complex, people need more than just liberty in the sense of absence of physical constraint in order to be truly free to pursue happiness. Participation in the U.S. economy of the nineteenth century didn't require a high school diploma. Participation in the economy of the twentieth century didn't require more than one. What people need to be able to meaningfully pursue happiness changes over time. It is much easier to defend libertarianism in the context of a feudal agrarian society where every family practiced subsistence farming, and where their pursuit of the good life was most likely to be undermined by a marauding horde or a repressive monarch, than it is in a society where access to knowledge and technology significantly affect individuals' power in a complex and interdependent economic system. Not only is no person an island, we are all nodes in a network.

In defining our mutual commitment to compatriots, we can acknowledge that this circle is morally arbitrary. There is no reason, other than accidents of history, geography, and birth, that the people who count as Americans are the particular 330 million people they are, and not other people. We must define being American as being a participant in this common project, and not with reference to other identities. There can be rules around how new members might sign up to be co-participants, to take on the identity, but there cannot be, at the outset, a proscription of their participation based on any other aspect of their identity. As an identity, Americanness can be practically exclusive, but must be morally inclusive in the sense that it is, in theory, possible for anyone to be as American as any other person.

So, what does this version of American political identity look like in sum? And how would it interact with other aspects of Americans' identities? On the one hand, what I've described is an affirmative identity—that Americans recognize themselves as, well, Americans, and that they understand that that means that they are part of a society, inclusive of all Americans equally, and also that the society in question has both a general goal—the pursuit of happiness by each of us—and an ethic of tolerance that underpins ways of working (institutions, elections, a constitution) with others who may have different ideas about what happiness looks like than we do. Like other identities, this one would help each of us define and make sense of certain relationships—with each other and with the government. And it would provide reason for action, because in seeing ourselves as Americans we would see ourselves as not only pursuing our own happiness but also taking seriously and as a matter of at least some concern the question of whether our co-citizens can pursue theirs. Not all identities demand this kind of solidarity, but this one would.

Admitting my conception of the basis for a shared identity does not mean signing up for some sort of nationalist brainwashing that requires believing that American democracy is superior to all others or that the incumbents of certain offices must be accorded some sort of indulgence. I'm not offering a plea for people just to be content with the government we've got. Ideally democratic institutions—both formal ones and the informal norms of behavior that support them—do inspire confidence and become part of the culture associated with an American political identity. But what we require to maintain and improve a political endeavor together is something less than that. We don't need a robust shared commitment to a detailed plan for the institutions and policies of a liberal democratic government in the twenty-first century. We just need to recognize that that *is* the project we're in together, and that because we're in it together, we will need to adhere to some basic ways of working in order for us to have a project at all.

The thinness of the political identity that I'm proposing is a feature, not a bug. The idea is not that my identity as an American would become newly salient or dominant as an aspect of my identity. After all, the purpose of the common enterprise we share is precisely *not* to define our individual conceptions of the good life, it is to protect our ability to seek and adopt those definitions ourselves. Most Americans would continue to see other identities as more important to their self-concept, and would appeal to these sources of identity more often in their daily lives. Their membership in other communities might be more important to how they see themselves. The inhabitants of Austin or South Dakota or Webster Groves, Missouri, might recognize themselves as part of local communities, of social structures that help them to understand their role and place in the world. There is nothing about the Americanness that I am proposing that requires pushing one's identity as a marine or teacher to the background, or pushing one's Catholic-ness or Black-ness or gay-ness or Irish-step-dancer-ness or cowboy-ness aside. The American identity should be ubiquitous, but it need not predominate.

By becoming the basis for our political identity, in some sense this American identity can simplify and unburden other aspects of our identities. By separating those identities from the task of defining political community, we are able to more freely and flexibly draw upon them and explore them in our lives, in our pursuit of happiness. Our ethic of tolerance isn't just an acceptance that others will make their own way, it is also a way of not prejudging our own. If our religion or race isn't the basis for binding us to our fellow citizens and to a state that exercises power, there is more opportunity, more space, to explore how those identities shape us, and to weave them uniquely into our personal identities and sense of self.

6.

What Americans experience today is the inverse of the vision I've laid out—an inversion from two sides, as it were. The first is the phenomenon that we colloquially call identity politics—roughly speaking that our ostensibly nonpolitical identities shape our political behaviors, the demands we make of elected leaders, and the rhetoric of those leaders in response. Identity politics is often associated, in the American context, with the political left, but as with the tango, and because identities are positively and negatively defined (you can't say who's in without also saying—or implying—who's out), it takes two.

In a way all politics is and *should be* identity politics. Ideally, we are not asked to set aside our views of the good life, which are intertwined with our identities, when we discuss political candidates or issues with neighbors at a barbecue or go to the voting booth; we must only acknowledge that others might not share our views, and, out of respect for ourselves and for others, use the democratic process to reconcile differences.

But the kind of identity politics that people complain about—where that I am a woman or gay or Black is presumed to explain my political views and choices more broadly—is a symptom of a systems failure. One reason why other identities become overtly political is that people have been treated differently *because* of those identities and have been denied some measure of their pursuit of the good life. Persistent unfairness—such as racial discrimination or sex discrimination—that gives Americans differential access to the opportunity to pursue their own happiness predictably politicizes those identities. People organize politically along the boundaries of that identity because the identity explains the unfairness.

The overall stagnation of white working class Americans' earning power in recent decades has coincided with visible demands by members of historically excluded communities—particularly people of color and women—for economic, political, and social inclusion. The election of the nation's first Black president was seen as evidence of the power of this collection of movements.[11] Many white Americans understand a perceived decline in their own economic prospects as connected to the "identity politics" of the left. There is little to suggest that what has actually happened in American society is a wealth transfer from middle- and working-class white people to brown and Black people. But that perception is one that politicians, especially in their rhetoric around immigration, have cultivated. The reason you're feeling the squeeze, they imply, is not that we've catered to corporations or failed to adjust governance to the globalized and digital economy, it's because the government spends so much on Black people and immigrants. (In reality, many of the policies around which people of color have mobilized in the last decade—like raising the minimum wage—are policies that directly help economically disempowered white workers and families.)

The perception isn't just that there is an economic transfer happening, it's also a perceived loss of moral respectability and status. The culture war battle that began in 2021 about "critical race theory" had little to do with the strand of postmodern cultural and legal criticism that had been contained to narrow corridors of academia. It was a fight about history and its lessons. It was a fight over identity, with huge numbers of white Americans seeing the call for a fresh look at history as an effort at unwinding the basis for their identity, and their sense of confidence in the goodness of that identity. For people who see themselves as figurative inheritors of Jefferson and Washington, a moral accounting of the Founders is received not as enlightenment but as accusation. When two of the white men running for the Republican nomination for U.S. Senate in Ohio in 2022 made ads declaring that they were "not racist," they weren't speaking for themselves; they were speaking for (white) Americans who see requests for civic equality or historical reexamination as a moral indictment against them.

The identity politics of white men's indignation and grievance and the claims of other Americans for redress of past and present injustice have cascaded across the political landscape in colliding waves. The two sides of this hyper-charged identity politics are symbiotic; the demands for remediation and the fears of loss are materially and morally linked. The way to neutralize the clash is to pursue a fair society that treats all Americans as equally entitled to pursue happiness by virtue of their Americanness.

The other side of the inversion is that as nonpolitical identities have become politicized, overtly political identities have become essentialized. Americans' party affiliations have long been correlated with class, racial, gender, and other lines. But increasingly partisan identities have become less a predictor of other social identities and more an essential aspect of how Americans understand themselves. Being a Republican or Democrat, or, for an increasing number of voters, refusing either identity, has become not just a political identity that establishes one's membership in a group with overlapping views on major policy questions about how our democratic society should be managed, but a quasi-religious identity that conjures deep normative convictions about the good life—about what happiness looks like. That seven in ten Democrats and half of Republicans say that they couldn't date someone who voted for Trump or Clinton, respectively, in the 2016 election is one indication.[12] In 2021 the real estate brokerage Redfin reported that more people were choosing where to live based on the prevailing politics of a given neighborhood, town, or state, and predicted that this tendency would persist—continuing a decades-long trend of Americans' self-sorting along partisan political lines.[13] Party affiliation is a deep, prominent, wide-reaching social identity in contemporary America.

A thin, shared liberal political identity works both because and only if it leaves space for people to pursue happiness in their own ways *and* it tempers the degree to which they see the triumph of their own version of happiness as a constant measure of the success of their political community. As more and more people have relinquished or given up on their unrequited hopes for a shared American identity they have reverted to a zero-sum view of politics. In this context the political parties have become more tribalistic and less deliberative. The fusing of partisan political identities with the kinds of moral meaning that people might otherwise find in nonpolitical identities—being a dentist, an outdoorswoman, a Jew—has raised the stakes of politics at the same time as it undermines its function.

7.

Imagine if you read aloud my description of the ideal—of a shared, forward-looking American identity, undergirded by ethical individualism, that recognizes that we are each entitled to pursue our own happiness—to concerned Americans, and said that *that* identity, that America, was what we were after. They would, surveying the discouraging landscape of our current politics, respond with something between a skeptically raised eyebrow and a "give me some of what you're smoking." I'll admit, this can all sound like quite a stretch, and it is ambitious in total. A genuinely liberal and pluralistic, multiracial, multi-confessional, multiethnic democracy of the kind I'm describing has never existed before. Why would we think that there is a route from the valley of our current discontent to the mountaintop? The path is steep, and maybe indiscernible at times. I want to make the case that there is reason for hope.

But first, more bad news. Not only do we lack a workable version of a national identity today, there are additional obstacles to building one together. Among these are the size of the United States (scale is a blessing and a curse), human psychology, and the nature of our current divisions.

Eighteenth-century political philosopher Jean-Jacques Rousseau famously thought the city of Geneva, where he was born and grew up, was just the right size for a democracy. In his own explorations of democratic theory, he saw that scale was a significant challenge to preserving engaged citizen participation and the common civic identity on which such participation would be based. He probably would have been surprised at the size of modern democracies. But likely wouldn't have been surprised by the challenges they face when it comes to reconciling scale and identity.

The United States' hundreds of millions of people are spread across a vast geography. It is the largest advanced democracy and longest-established. It is diverse not just with respect to race and religion but also in terms of economies and ways of life. Most of those living in a city populated by tech workers in California have no experience of what it is like to live in a tobacco-farming community in North Carolina. They probably have more familiarity with—that is to say, they would recognize echoes of their own experience in—the lives of people in Berlin or Tokyo. Among elites, globalization has strengthened trade and professional networks across the globe. The bonds of national community are less unique than they once were. It is reasonable to ask whether, in our contemporary context, even the low bar of a thin measure of common identity is too high.

It may not be that there are too many of us, really, as much as it is that we are, well, us. Could it be that democracy is destined to fail by a fundamental design flaw—that it depends on humans, with all our own enduring flaws—to become the mediocre-ocracy (or worse)? Political psychologist Shawn Rosenberg thinks we're probably doomed. His argument goes roughly this way: Proper democratic citizenship asks too much of people, and we just aren't wired for it. It calls for us to be analytically reflective; instead we're emotionally reactive. It calls for us to be objective and impartial; even the decisions we think we're making upon reflection are shaped by numerous biases. Democracy demands that we have some basic curiosity about figuring out what's good and true; most of us just want to be told what the truth is. Democracy demands that we accept losing with grace and remain committed to standards of procedural justice. Our natural response is indignation. Some of us can hold on for a while, but in the end, someone will offer up the elements of an authoritarian system and those are far less taxing on our self-control. We bite.

Thus the appeal of right-wing populist leaders and ideologies: they don't ask us to suppress so much of our lizard brain. "Right wing populism provides the lost, lonely, alienated and frightened souls of democracy with an alternative vision and practice that is readily comprehensible, morally sensible, and personally satisfying," Rosenberg says.[14] The only reason that modern democracies—imperfect though they may be—have lasted as long as they have is that they have been undemocratic in an important way: the elites have always been there to protect democracy from the masses. They mediated the effects of populist fervor on the institutions and decisions of democratic governments. And where they failed, disaster resulted. Today, because of the way that the internet has loosened elite control over the public sphere, elites are no longer distributing the "truth" and how to think about it; everyone is.

On Rosenberg's reading, which accords with the sinking sensation some of us get watching cable news or reading replies on Twitter, the problem is not that we're trying to build with what German philosopher Immanuel Kant called the "crooked timber of humanity" but rather that the timber is rotten. The challenge, Rosenberg explains, is that people are "inherently fast (as opposed to slow and considered) and sub-rational thinkers who are heuristic, schema, and emotionally driven processors of information. How they think and react is thus not circumstantial and readily remedied, but is instead indicative of *what people really are.*"[15] We started out this way. It's not that we have gone rotten over time.

To see a way forward, one has to imagine a way out of where we are today. Well-documented rising partisan antipathy makes that more difficult. When asked to rate the other party on a scale of 0 (very cold) to 100 (very warm), only 10 percent of Democrats and 7 percent of Republicans gave the other party a zero in the year 2000. Two decades later those numbers were 39 percent of Democrats and 48 percent of Republicans.[16] In a Penn State nationwide poll after the 2018 elections, just 27 percent of Republicans said that most people who voted for Democrats sincerely believe that doing so is good for the country. Democrats were only slightly more charitable about their counterparts: 42 percent of them saying that most Republicans did so for the same reasons.[17] It is difficult to build a functional politics on widespread assumptions of evil and bad faith.

But the problems go deeper than antipathy. The deliberative communications and interactions that democratic citizenship entails require some firm foundation for assessing truth and for doing it together. Participants don't need to agree; they don't even need to like each other all that much, but they do need to be able to communicate with each other about important public questions. Disagreement—the kind that characterizes vigorous debates over abortion or taxes or going to war—requires a shared set of references and bases for judgment about the truth. One participates in such debates knowing that those on the other side can make sense of what one says, even if they will always disagree, or even if they aren't listening.

In the academic world, divided as it is into spheres of knowledge, it has become common to talk about "epistemic communities," to refer to a network of experts—particle physicists, theologians, political economists, West African literature scholars—who share an intent to expand the frontiers of knowledge in their field and who have a shared way of communicating and assessing each other's contributions. Citizens of a democracy don't need to be part of a community of experts, but they do need to be able to agree on what they're arguing about. Political debates in the United States have come to reflect schisms—not just fringe movements but genuine schisms that involve more than one third of Americans on either side—that aren't just differences in opinion, or values, or interpretation of facts. They are definitional schisms. They are rejections of fundamental normative commitments such as the idea that corruption or lying is wrong. They are not normal disputes about history, but the construction of fantasy narratives. They are divides over what constitutes a scientific fact, tested by hypothesis-driven experimentation, and over what constitutes reasonable confidence for proceeding as if facts are true. Conspiracies are, after all, rooted in and fueled by community.

Nancy Rosenblum and Russell Muirhead, two longtime scholars of American government, argue that the conspiracy theories now prevalent in American politics were different from previous conspiracy theories not only in the breadth of their reach but also in their nature.[18] Unlike, say, the conspiracy theories around JFK's assassination or the 9/11 attacks, Rosenblum and Muirhead assert, the new brand of conspiracy theories are "conspiracy without the theory." And, they note, "The effect of conspiratorial thinking, once it ceases to function as any sort of explanation, is delegitimation. The new conspiracist accusations seek not only to unmask and disempower those they accuse but to deny their standing to argue, explain, persuade, and decide."[19]

The divide between Americans around the response to the coronavirus pandemic was, substantially, not a division between groups offering different preferences on policies in response to an emergency, or even between groups with different views on the origins, significance, and severity of the emergency itself, but between two groups inhabiting different worlds with different, deeply held beliefs about *what was true*, not just about what to do about it. You can have a long argument with your spouse about whether the table looks better in the dining room or the kitchen, but when your spouse says "that's not a table, that's a duck," the debate about where to place it loses its urgency and relevance.

To return to the challenge of identity, it is difficult to imagine a shared American identity to underpin democratic politics when, according to a poll in the spring of 2022, three in ten Americans, and one half of Republicans, believed the QAnon conspiracy theory that Democratic elites are involved in a child-sex-trafficking ring.[20] The American political world isn't just divided, it's unhinged. How do we come back from that? Meeting the identity test would require people to see themselves and their compatriots differently, and it would require the restoration or creation of some epistemic basis for political discourse among factions.

If the United States fails to meet the identity test, that failure will seem overdetermined. Historians will struggle to disentangle the effects of structural challenges to pluralistic democracy, the hubris of the post–Cold War era, and the failures of specific leaders; the way in which the invention of social media arrived in the wake of a disastrous war, a financial crisis, and major recession; the dismantling of core institutional features of American democracy by the Supreme Court; and decades of widening economic inequality—all of these worked as toxic forces alongside cable news to amplify the resultant passions of division, distribute the satisfying poison of illiberal populism, and accelerate the falsehoods that fractured perceptions of truth.

Failure is easy. There are plenty of reasons available to expect it today and explain it tomorrow in retrospect. But there are also reasons not to dismiss what is difficult as being impossible.

8.

And so, having piled on the bad news, it's worth recalibrating. It is easy to forget the way that a shared national identity would be experienced by human beings. The minimum requirements are sometimes set, or rather imagined, too high, especially by those determined to show why human beings will never be able to meet them. The United States does not need 330 million people to wake up each day thinking about being united in a common enterprise. The U.S. doesn't need to be transformed into a country of people in togas pondering the common weal and their obligations to one another. This is not the vision for some totalitarian state where people have to sublimate their individuality and their daily lives to some sort of deep ideological commitment. What the United States needs in terms of a national identity offers more freedom and demands less from individuals than even democratic theorists are wont to admit.

People will still support and vote for politicians who hold dumb or even evil positions that run roughshod over the interests of their co-citizens. People's positions on particular issues can be illiberal. It is possible to see oneself as part of a group and to have bad opinions about what the group should do. Democracy expects that participants will have bad ideas and good ones—it's all part of the plan. Liberalism, by embracing tolerance of diverse versions of the good life *except* with respect to the principles and constraints of political liberalism, allows democracy to substitute process where no substantive judgment about the good life can be convincingly defended to all participants. Identifying as an American in the sense that I am proposing does not require one to adopt enlightened positions about meeting the tests of fairness, investment, or scale or to have a particular position on gun rights or a fifteen-dollar minimum wage.

• • •

The thin shared identity we're imagining is intended to be a foundation for a functioning liberal democratic state. It is not meant to be—as some political identities are—a dominant source of meaning in people's personal identities. To the extent that it does enable a liberal democratic state, that identity doesn't *add* to the participatory burden placed on individuals, it allows them to effectively outsource the nuisance of governance, the burden of defending their capacity to pursue their own happiness. The common identity can make politics as such a less salient feature of people's everyday lives. This is not to dismiss the value of political participation and civic engagement by concerned citizens, but rather to acknowledge that many (most?) people may not find their most important sources of meaning in those endeavors and that's completely okay.

While some bemoan that Americans don't pay much attention to politics between elections, in some sense that's the way it should be. Not that they should be checked out and unaware of what elected leaders are doing, but they shouldn't have to fret about it, or regularly see the failure of those leaders in their daily lives. The ideal is not a bunch of citizen micromanagers. And not only because they don't have the expertise to handle the technical tasks of governing. It's also a suck of mental energy away from what individual people want to focus their lives on—their pursuits of happiness. Instead, in our current predicament, and spurred by cable news and other media consumption, we're debating questions of public policy on which we have little expertise—and not just around elections, but all the time.

We can accept that human beings are flawed, that we have certain illiberal tendencies, and that we are unlikely to collectively achieve some ideal of thorough and daily execution of reflective and deliberative citizenship without, at the same time, giving up on the idea that a bunch of ordinary people can see themselves as, for better or worse, in the same boat. And that furthermore they can understand that there are better or worse ways of organizing themselves and that the better ones may require some modest cabining of natural predilections.

The hurdle posed by the United States' scale may also be prone to overstatement. Sure, it's hard to get millions and millions of people on the same page, but what they need to be on the same page about isn't all that much. There has been plenty of discussion about how the digital era has hyper-charged division and allowed fringe movements like QAnon to metastasize into mainstream political forces. But at the same time the digital era also makes it much easier to have a shared American cultural, social, and political experience with other people in different parts of the country. For better or worse—and mostly for worse, I think—news has become nationalized. While the loss of local news has had deleterious effects on both governance and a sense of community at state and local levels, national media and digital media do allow for instantaneous shared experience. For an American in Boston in 1906, an American in San Antonio was basically a fictional character, not even a character, really, just a notion—an imaginary compatriot, whose life would never be witnessed, whose voice would never be heard.

The United States is not starting from scratch—to be an American already does mean something. This is not nation-building. Most Americans would recognize "being American" as a part of their political identity, and most would also probably see it as an important—if complicated—part of their personal identity. And there is reason to believe that a sense of being bound with compatriots in a project remains a component of most Americans' identities, and that they would prefer more emphasis on this wider circle than on partisan factions. In a 2021 survey by Harvard's Making Caring Common project, when asked their response to the statement "in the end, I care about all Americans, regardless of their political views," two thirds of Americans agreed or "completely agreed." And when asked what broad priorities President Biden should focus on in the same survey, "uniting the country" came out on top, and was rated equally by Democrats and Republicans.[21] Americans may disagree on what it means to be an American, but the epistemic breakdown in our politics doesn't include the inability to conceive of a national identity or to express preferences about it. To the extent that a more robust version of a shared American identity once existed, it has receded but not disappeared. And given the unequal access that Americans have had to that shared identity in the past, perhaps the recession of a previous incarnation of American identity is an opportunity to build, in its place, a firmer foundation for the next chapter in our national story.

In addition to the existing contours of a national identity, the United States' democratic institutions are an enormous asset—the foundation, the walls, the scaffolding for a renewal. The structure and practices of a state inevitably affect the lived experience of individuals within it and influence their understanding of themselves and their relationship to others. Notwithstanding our present discontent, American democratic institutions remain at least a reasonable approximation of the ones that one might imagine accompanying a shared commitment to a pluralistic liberal democratic endeavor. We spend so much time discussing the ways in which they fall short, or have been degraded, or have become outdated. But we should also be mindful of the ways in which they continue to work, quite remarkably. As U.S. senator Michael Bennet has remarked, reflecting on the short period between the insurrection attack on the U.S. Capitol and the 2021 presidential inauguration, "most countries that experience a January 6th don't have a January 20th two weeks later." This is not to understate the threat that has been unleashed on the United States' democratic institutions in recent years, only to say that we should also not underrate the impressiveness of their resilience, even in the face of a divided populace and feckless or destructive elected leaders.

The formal institutions of American government could use new buttresses for their independence, and they may need adjustments to restore their efficiency, or to make them more fair and representative. But these are not fatal flaws, they are fixable ones. As we wring our hands about whether the United States can meet the identity test, we should not forget: there's not only an existing social construct—a container for an American identity, there's also a collective inheritance of institutions, practices, and ideas that is still robust. As we do the work of recognizing the inadequacies of American democracy we should not lose sight of its assets, and we should remember all the reasons there are to recommend its preservation and improvement.

9.

Perhaps the greatest reason for optimism about the prospects of the United States meeting the identity test is that doing so provides such an obviously better future for Americans, and for the world, in the long term. It's not even close how much better life would be than in the alternative view. A functioning liberal democracy unlocks a collaborative, mutually beneficial relationship between citizens, where their collective engagement produces the conditions for individual lives with more genuine liberty to pursue happiness. One of our afflictions today, one of the reasons that people have begun to question their belief in American democracy, is that its dividends and its advantage have become less obvious. But that's not because democracy is wrong. It's because we're doing it wrong. And there remains immense profit—in terms of security, prosperity, and the freedom to pursue happiness—available to us if we do it right.

In addition to defending democracy to those who assail its promise and potential, we should ask ourselves, and those who posit that a better version of American democracy is not possible, about the alternatives. There are none. None that is attractive on either a moral or practical level. None that we could imagine a majority of Americans reasonably getting on board with. Right-wing populism—which defines the people that belong to the state, or what historians of political thought hauntingly refer to as the "volk," using the contours of other ethnic, racial, or religious social identities—involves institutionalized unfairness. It depends on the subordination of facts and expertise to ideology. It is by definition corrupt in that it redefines the "public" interest to exclude portions of the public. It is demonstrably susceptible to other forms of corruption because when ideology substitutes for facts, accountability becomes a fiction. It doesn't work. It is inferior. It's a source of weaknesses not strengths.

Descent into right-wing populist authoritarianism is possible, of course, and we might see elements of it in the democratic backsliding that we've witnessed in our own country and others. But with its diverse population, wealth, and long-standing democratic institutions, we should be skeptical that this slide is inexorable in the United States. The threat is real, but so are the tools at our disposal to push back against it. To believe it is inevitable, we'd have to be persuaded that tens of millions of Americans will simply permanently adapt to a new reality that persistently rolls back the democratic progress of the country. I'm not suggesting oh-it-can't-happen-here-American-exceptionalism. Quite the opposite, because of U.S. military and economic power and the U.S.'s role in world political and economic affairs, the stakes are so high that a sustained Hungary-style slide toward corrupt authoritarianism would be much worse here and would, in my view, reach a breaking point of general social and political collapse sooner than in other places. But in part because the stakes are higher, the reasons to avoid this eventuality are even more obvious.

The kind of future that an American slide into semipermanent right-wing populism portends would be violent, chaotic, poorer, and intolerable. That something would be a colossal error does not mean that people won't do it. But it does give a basis for making the case to them not to. And that has to count for something: for those interested in seeing the emergence of a shared political identity that can underpin a functioning, diverse, liberal, democratic United States, it has to be relevant that it is actually better for most Americans in the short and medium term and for all Americans in the longer term than the alternatives.

10.

The identity test presents a "chicken and egg" puzzle: For people to adopt a sense of themselves as co-participants in a collective enterprise along the lines of a genuinely liberal democratic state, they need to see the value and importance of that enterprise. And yet it's hard to imagine addressing the dysfunction and imbalances that imperil American democracy without having at least some progress on addressing the divisions, and in particular the insufficiency of whatever identity is shared among Americans today. People won't buy in unless it works, and it won't work unless people buy in. The operative question then, is what comes first—the identity chicken or the democracy egg?

Absent an enormous shock event, building the content of a shared identity, like the experience of building trust, is likely to be an incremental process rather than a social sea change. As with a crowbar, the lever will have to push a bit toward a better-functioning democracy and then a bit toward a more fully shared sense of identity, then a bit more toward improving American success as a collective enterprise, then back toward identity, and so on. No waving a magic wand here, just patient wedging to pry our future loose from our present predicament.

11.

One of the civic virtues that American leaders should spend more time cultivating and advocating is a sense of what might be called patriotic empathy. The individualism prized in American culture and the litigiousness, figurative and literal, of American society has led to deficiencies of both practicality and humility. Responsibility is an important ethical principle, but sometimes the urgency of the problems we face demands that we set aside the question of whose fault it is that we ended up in the ditch and leave it for historians. As citizens we need to ask what we, the Americans who are here now, can do to get out of the ditch and get, together, back to the task of living. Sometimes we wrongly leap from the righteousness of our entitlement to pursue our own happiness to a confidence that we have figured it all out. To put ourselves in the position of fellow Americans who have different lived experiences is both a useful invitation to find meaning in the identity of being American, and a reminder that our fellow Americans are people with whom we share a meaningful project.

We can have empathy for those who struggle to make sense of the world in new ways, even as we demand that they do. As a matter of successful political progress, empathy is more likely to deliver results than condemnation. Most people want to see themselves as good people. It is likely easier for them to get on board with something that is good or necessary than it is for them to acknowledge that what they previously held true was bad. We should still be interested in correcting historical narratives that have whitewashed the role of racism in the U.S. History should not be constrained by the discomfort of reckoning with truth. Politics, however, is constrained by psychology and behavior. As my colleague Rachel Kleinfeld has written, "the prodemocracy community must remain inclusive and liberal." To dismiss compatriots as "racist or unsaveable simply thrusts them closer together," she observes, and "brings out the worst in many individuals who also have better selves."[22]

Patriotic empathy might moderate our tendencies to indulge in outrage and enhance our ability to focus on positive democratic change. Americans on both sides of the political divide have become accustomed to a number of prominent media personalities and political actors and their legions of supporters publicly shaming those who are culturally or politically associated with the other side. But there is a cost to indignation, even righteous indignation, about the comments or behaviors of public figures on the other side of societal polarization. Because this high-volume oppressive national psychodrama is a sideshow and distraction. It suggests that the real problem is cultural or personal, rather than structural. It persuades us that people—compatriots—are irredeemable rather than that parts of the system are broken. It serves the interests of those who benefit from the unfairness of the current system. And it exonerates those who are in a position to change it by depicting the power to do so as out of their hands.

12.

Recall the fairness dividend: the additional benefit, over and above whatever transactional value participants in an interaction take away from it, that they perceive from having participated in a fair interaction. The extra benefit we experience is a reflection of our feeling "seen" and our feeling recognized as having equal dignity and worth when we are treated fairly. The links between the fairness test and the identity test are profound. Making America more fair would reinforce a national identity because it would make Americans more likely to harvest the fairness dividend, and to see their status as Americans as an indication of their participation in a group whose participants commit to, and whose ways of working reflect, a modicum of mutual respect.

It can be tempting to see the partisan acrimony and dysfunction of Washington as a result of polarization and division among voters. But the idea that Washington is broken because Americans are polarized inverts cause and effect. Americans are increasingly polarized in large part because of the failure of the United States to update our social contract for the twenty-first century, and to address regulatory and democratic shortcomings that would make our society more fair and our citizens more resilient in the face of shocks like a global financial crisis or a pandemic. It is a set of policy failures, enabled and encouraged by the influence of money in U.S. politics, that has created a reality where inequality has been rising persistently for over four decades, the bottom 90 percent of Americans have seen zero to modest growth in their earnings, and have been set back by the faster-than-inflation rise in the costs of essential elements of a secure life: education, health care, and housing. It's not just that reaching a recognizably middle-class life has become harder, it's also that people have a sense that the systems in which they participate and that produce that outcome are out of whack.

Inequality, even significant inequality, is not in and of itself the problem. One can imagine a fair society that protected a baseline of welfare, that took on consolidated economic power before it calcified, and that still produced some people who were tremendously richer than most. But *persistent expansion* of inequality over more than a generation is an indicator that the net economic benefits of being American are not being shared fairly. Closer examination reveals the mechanics of how this is so—including corporate capture of public decisions, disinvestment from essential public goods, and racism and other persistent barriers. The significant divergence in the economic well-being of the richest Americans and that of the vast majority of Americans making up the working and middle class in the last forty years has created an America with two economic pies. One of these—the rich one—has grown, the other has stagnated and shrunk. The fairness test, in many respects, is about merging the two pies—one country, one pie, so to speak—and the investment test is about ensuring its continued growth.

Of course, the two pies aren't just a coincidence. It's not that there are two economies, one where things are going well and one where things aren't. The separate pies are the product of real fairness deficits. The rapid expansion of the pie for the top 10 percent of Americans, and really for the top 1 percent, has been made possible in part by the shifting of economic power and its benefits from the bottom of the pyramid to the top, and the denial of benefits by the top to the bottom. Many Americans reasonably feel themselves to be working for a piece of a shrinking pie, and that puts them in a beggar-thy-neighbor relationship with their compatriots. Instead of working to merge the two pies, political leaders beholden to elites have been willing to encourage voters to focus their attention on blaming their neighbors for denying them a growing piece of the shrinking pie.[23] It's hard to build a shared identity premised on mutual concern in that context.

13.

Investments—in a business, in a relationship, in a shared endeavor—are a statement of intent about the future. The investments that the United States needs to make to ensure that it is not wasting human capital, and that it is sufficiently developing that capital to compete in the coming decades, would also reinforce shared identity. This is so, first and foremost, because the act of preparing together for the future is such a strong indicator of preparing for a future *together*—it is an expression of purpose that invites people to see some durability in the idea of being American; it makes that identity secure.

And because the investments that the United States needs to make are investments in the ideas, industries, and human capacities that can be a foundation for collective success, those investments can also be contributions to the foundation for a shared national identity. An investment in universal health care, or in making early childhood education universal, is an investment that defines a community. An investment in research and development of emerging technologies and in industrial policy to incubate new industries is a statement about the intention for the country to actively pursue high-quality jobs and a technical edge in the global economy. When the state takes an interest in providing prerequisites for the effective pursuit of happiness in the modern world—such as health care or education or affordable housing and sustainable public transport—it telegraphs that the national community will endure, and will face the future together.

One idea that would entail significant investment and would buttress the development of a more widely shared American identity, cultivate patriotic empathy, and reinforce the rationale for a liberal political identity is a program of national service. Because many of the investments that the United States must make to meet the investment test are investments in human capital, and because such investments are themselves labor-intensive, a new, near-universal program of national service could be a mechanism for investing in human capital—particularly in the care economy. And the period of service itself could become part of an investment in ensuring that all Americans have a minimum level of skills.

In addition to marshaling resources to support human capital development, such a program could—as the military did for male Americans before the end of conscription—provide contexts in which a Black American from rural Alabama and a Latino Catholic from Denver and an Asian from suburban New Jersey and a Jew from California and a farm kid from Ohio all work together. This is not an alchemic prescription for comity. But as geographic mobility has declined alongside social mobility in America, the chance for Americans to meet and know compatriots who don't share their background by working together for a few months is one that can assist in their working together in a democracy too, and in helping them to see themselves as part of a shared venture.

While making a program compulsory would be objectionable—no one should be sent to jail for refusing to participate—there are ways to create incentives that would make it attractive, and thereby nearly universal. Consider a supplementary highly progressive tax that might attach to those who choose not to participate and would ensure that Americans who have wealth, or who believe themselves likely to accumulate it, have incentives to participate in a national service program. If I'm going to pay 7 percent higher income tax when I become a partner at a law firm if I haven't participated, the financial benefits of participating become much more compelling. If I plan to live as a playboy off my inheritance, and nonparticipation attracts a significant supplemental wealth, capital gains, or inheritance tax, I might see

THE FOUR TESTS

value in joining my compatriots. Public funding for education might be used to reward service, as with Reserve Officers' Training Corps (ROTC) participants today.

14.

Conflict is a final potential catalyst for the development of a shared identity among Americans and is, human history would suggest, at once the most efficient and the least attractive.

Our domestic political convulsions are not happening in a vacuum. They are connected to shifts in the international political economy and are unfolding in ominous and dissonant concert with what foreign policy pundits call "the return of great power competition." The decline of American hegemony presents a new world for others to adjust to—friends, potential friends, potential adversaries—in addition to generating specific challenges for the United States itself.

As countries jockey for position in international politics, the most obvious path to a resurgence in shared American identity would be through a geopolitical crisis, or a war, that posed a real threat to Americans and our way of life. As Gareth Evans, the former Australian foreign minister and former head of the International Crisis Group, has put it:

> The sense of national identity is never stronger than when countries are at war with each other, at imminent risk of war, or remembering war. Cultural achievements can stir national pride, and sporting contests can excite national emotion in memorable ways, but it is war, the prospect of war, and the memory of war that has traditionally shaped and defined that collective national

sentiment and sense-of-self we think of as being at the core of national identity.[24]

Perceived threats catalyze identity formation more readily than perceived achievements. That's why, as Evans colorfully assesses, in contemporary Britain the dominant source of national identity is not a glorified narrative about the British Empire but instead "the magnificently phlegmatic way in which the country collectively responded to the threat of Nazi invasion."[25]

Part of my motivation for writing this book is my conviction that the threats associated with geopolitics in the twenty-first century are real. Though its influence remains substantial, the relative decline of U.S. power raises real challenges for the security and prosperity of the United States and its citizens. The concomitant relative rise of an authoritarian state is a legitimate concern. In today's world, China and Russia, in different ways, present the most obvious counterparties in a real or potential confrontation with the United States and its allies. Russia has the power to damage and even destroy essential elements of the old order, China's rise raises concerns that it may attempt to assert a new one. Democratic governments—and people everywhere—have an interest in ensuring that neither happens. It would be a moral catastrophe. It would be inherently unstable and impermanent, and for that reason would entail massive amounts of human suffering.

We should take these threats seriously—after all Russia is, as I write, prosecuting the second year of the largest war in Europe since World War II, a brutal act of unabashed aggression in violation of international law that destabilizes a continent. And China has backed Russia with a "no limits" partnership. But we should be wary of the temptation to welcome confrontation, and especially military confrontation, as a potential solution to our own divisions. In great power competition it is not enough to not *want* to go to war. Leaders have to want *not* to go to war.

One reason that geopolitical confrontation as a source of identity formation is unattractive is that identities forged in fear are rarely liberal. Their us-versus-them nature requires othering, and is unavoidably dehumanizing. Moreover, consolidation of national identity spurred by external threat alone generates an identity that functions as a defensive shell more than a strong core. That identity can be useful for near-term mobilization to confront the crisis—in an emergency even those who loathe each other can work together—but it is unlikely to be the basis for sustained cooperation of the kind that a democratic society requires. There is no content to the identity other than the common experience of an external threat, no moral material in which to root institutions or ongoing mutual respect among citizens.

While we remember the moments of unity in the face of Nazi and Axis power aggression, and remain inspired by Churchill's radio addresses or Roosevelt's speech to Congress after Pearl Harbor, we should also remember that national identities that emerge based on threats can also encourage strategic miscalculations. At 90 percent, George W. Bush had the highest recorded approval rating of any modern president in the wake of September 11, higher even than Harry Truman in June 1945 at the end of World War II.[26] While disapproval of the president doesn't necessarily indicate a lack of a common political identity, unified approval for the president is a reasonable indicator of a shared sense of political community, however fleeting. It would be hard to explain the miscalculations that led to the strategic blunder of the invasion of Iraq, and the political environment that encouraged and enabled it, without reference to the post-9/11 political identity shared by many Americans as citizens of a country engaged in a "war on terror."

It is not uncommon in Washington, D.C., these days to hear a hint of nostalgia in reminiscences about the Cold War. Looking at the decades that have passed since its end, people pine for a sense of national purpose like the one they remember or ascribe to the Cold War era. That's part of why even those who purport to bemoan the prospect of a "new Cold War" with China can seem to be a bit relieved or even secretly gleeful at the prospect of a return of a bipolar contest. It's attractive for the crude clarity it provides, the way it focuses the mind, and the way that it might reconsolidate a sense of national identity by accepting a kind of perpetual emergency for the foreseeable future.

There is obvious appeal in this perspective, but also enormous risk. For one, it would entail embracing the prospect of actual conflict—the Cold War was only called that because it was an alternative to actual "hot" war, which was always on the table. There's no such thing as a Cold War without the very real prospect of it jumping the fence. In retrospect, it is at least as much a credit to magnificent good fortune as it is to prudent leadership that there was not a direct conflict or a nuclear exchange between the two superpowers in the Cold War. And even if we avoided nuclear war, there were enormous human and economic costs to the U.S.- Soviet contest. The idea that the U.S. should welcome an increase in tensions with China rather than seek to manage competition in a way that defuses them, is dangerous.

At a deeper level, an identity that arises out of a "new Cold War" with China, or some other similar frame, is unavoidably intertwined with the logic of great power competition, that is to say, the idea of a world of endless contest between big countries armed with thousands of nuclear weapons. We don't want our identity to sign us up for a world that we don't want. And we don't want our identity to commit us to that particular version of world politics at a time when the U.S.'s relative power is declining rather than growing as it was at the outset of the actual Cold War. We should want America to succeed in the geopolitics of the time that we are living through, but not to have its destiny determined by that geopolitics.

Addressing the multidimensional puzzle of how to deal with China's increasing economic and military power is inescapably part of the challenge facing U.S. leaders today and for the foreseeable future. But we should beware the feedback loop between the reality of that challenge and the popular sentiment, fanned by some leaders, that urges confrontation and depends on an "us versus them" mentality. That feedback loop threatens to short-circuit judicious, creative thinking about how the U.S. can best navigate the central geostrategic question of our time. A bipolar confrontation may be unavoidable, and we should be prepared to win it, but we shouldn't welcome it. And the world, and especially the Chinese government, should know that we do not.

International competition inspires a sense of urgency. And if a competitive world in which America's relative weight is declining can force introspection and reassessment, so much the better. But jingoism is not a substitute for strategy. And the focus on the external threat can distract from or provide an excuse to avoid the internal work necessary for long-term success. External threats, real or perceived, provide excuses for quelling dissent, papering over differences, accepting existing unfairness in the name of expediency. If the contest with China pulls us together based on little more than geopolitics, the unity that it provides will be temporary. We cannot find what we need from without, it must be found within. We need more than unity in the face of external challenges. We need renewal. An America that meets the four tests will have internal strength on which to build new ways of leading in the world, and new ways of shaping world politics.

15.

The last lines of both "My Country 'Tis of Thee" (the anthem Samuel Francis Smith wrote in 1831 that Americans sing to the tune of "God Save the King") and of "The Star-Spangled Banner" make reference to the concept of "home." To feel at home in a place is, in part, to feel that one belongs, that one has a role and an identity there, an identity that is satisfying and safe. One of the messages from the 2016 election was that tens of millions of Americans no longer feel at home in a place they once did. One can ascribe this alienation from home to sympathetic or unsympathetic reasons; it doesn't change the fact of their feelings of dislocation and its unsettling effects on our politics. At the same time, millions of other Americans are still waiting to feel at home. Trump voters and the founders of the Black Lives Matter movement have this idea in common—both want to feel at home in America. And America can only be as successful as it needs to be if both do.

Calls for a more civil form of political discourse in the United States often invite criticism, particularly by those on the political left, for tone policing, that is, for demanding a lowering of the volume in the face of outrage, for requesting moderation in the face of radical injustice. To be sure, there are some who use demands for civility to cover their own discomfort at confronting urgent challenges. But there's another way to understand this desire for civility—to see it not as recommending complacency but instead as an expression of longing for a world in which vitriol will be drained because a shared identity is restored, because partisan tribes just don't matter as much to people. That's not yet the world in which we live. But it is possible to feel a kind of anticipatory nostalgia (from the Greek, *nostos*—for home or homecoming, and *algia*—for pain or longing) understood not as a pining for some lost paradise, but rather a hope for the future home we might build together.

6

WHAT CHOICE DO WE HAVE?

1.

Reading a novel of the French Revolution, seeing a headline about the Wright brothers, watching an old newsreel about D-Day, we wonder what it was like to live through a historical moment of great consequence. It's rare that we stop to realize that we have lived through such moments, rarer still that we realize at the time that we are living through one.

Because we know what happened in documented history, or at least we think we know, the world of history feels more determined than the world we experience. After all, what happened happened; the counterfactuals did not. We learn about history in narrative threads. Especially for those who didn't live through it, who know only what they have learned, the year 1963 in American history is a rope in time made up of threads about the Cold War, the civil rights movement, rock 'n' roll, space exploration, Kennedy's assassination. We know what came before 1963 in those threads and what came after; they have a structure. We can see with hindsight how strands of culture and politics and art in 1963 intertwine. But that's not how we see the present. We don't experience the present as a twisting together of narrative threads. We experience it as swimming in a soup—opaque, inchoate, confusing, everything happening all at once, and with no certainty about what comes next.

Looking back, we can identify those people who had special effect on how history unfolded. We marvel at their courage, and we do so with the benefit of knowing its consequence. It's easy to forget that they experienced their time the way that we experience ours: one confusing day at a time and with no certainty about whether their efforts were properly directed or would be enough to change outcomes. Even the ones who seem most confident on the pages of a biography were muddling through, just as we are.

Idealists are worriers at heart. To believe in the possibility of progress toward a set of ideals is to be concerned about achieving it. To embrace agency is to carry it as a burden. But the way we think about history can cause us to be more depressed than we ought to be about the present. Progress is the product of that muddling through, of taking opportunities as they arise and not knowing when or how they will. And although we tend to see major shifts as single episodes, they are really accumulations of events and interactions—the Protestant Reformation, women's suffrage, Reaganomics, the end of apartheid—we may mark specific dates that attach to these but none of them actually happened in a day. We can be living through a transformation, experiencing the nonlinear unfolding of change, without being aware that it will all add up to something historic.

2.

As I write, the world is responding with a mixture of amusement, derision, wonder, and fear to the latest developments in artificial intelligence. It occurs to me that this book might be one of the last to be written without the assistance of AI. Who knows? Authors in 1983 couldn't imagine writing on something other than a typewriter. The advent of the word processor and personal computer had more consequential societal impacts than the way that it changed book publishing. AI will too.

There is an idea that finds expression in the Bible, in Marx's writings on revolution, in a quotation apocryphally attributed to Lenin, and elsewhere about the way that history periodically breaks from the regularity of time. One version of this was offered by Mexican poet and novelist Homero Aridjis in 1991: "There are centuries in which nothing happens, and years in which centuries pass."[1] We are living through a moment when history seems to move faster than time. We're in the midst of a period—a few years, a decade, maybe longer—in which there is a reordering, a transformation in economy and society, with political implications and consequences for human dignity.

Political economy—the way that political structures and economic arrangements interplay with each other—both anticipates and lags behind politics. New inventions create new forms of power and productivity that are, for a time, ungoverned or ungovernable by old systems. Their economic effects reconfigure the relationships between people within societies and between societies themselves. These shifts change people's lives in unequal ways and spring-load tensions in politics. Those moments when history seems to happen faster than time are often those when the spring releases, and political economy catches up to politics.

If we meet the four tests, a principal upshot would be a change in the political economy of the United States. Political economy would catch up to politics. Our politics is already there—people are dissatisfied with the status quo, they are alarmed by the effects that world trends are having on their everyday lives. Whether it's climate change, globalization, technological advance, they are worried about the future of their country and its ability to provide a future for their families—people on both sides of the political spectrum are united in their desire to see something different. And beyond our borders, the shifts in power that are also products of economic changes in the last seventy-five years demand a new, more coherent, more competitive American political economy too.

3.

Of course, the shift in our political economy will require our politics to break through its present apparent stalemate. It's understandable to wonder how likely that kind of political progress is. After all, the challenges we face feel impossibly large and innumerable.

The four tests are composites. There is no single policy, no awakening, no cultural shift that can address any one of them. They are a way of organizing some of the biggest challenges we face, so that the list is not innumerable. They are a way of grouping together steps that may appear incremental on their own but that can add up to something transformative. They are a way of suggesting the possibility of positive momentum when progress on one test unlocks second-order effects that help us meet the other tests, because they are mutually reinforcing. The four tests are not a color-coded division of a laundry list of problems, they are sets of opportunities for the United States to meet the moment. We don't have to address the tests completely or all at once to succeed.

If we allow ourselves to contemplate silver linings of the coronavirus pandemic, one is that it ushered in what one might call the "era of big numbers." In part because of lessons learned from the inadequate response to the 2008 financial crisis, Congress repeatedly unleashed hundreds of billions of dollars at a time to blunt the pandemic's impact. It is hard to imagine a world in which legislation like the Bipartisan Infrastructure Bill or Inflation Reduction Act would have passed without the recent precedent of the pandemic response having reset expectations of scale for a major piece of legislation. And we will need additional investments of that size in the years to come.

Part of the reason I'm optimistic that we will make progress is that while many of the changes that we need can be supported by moral arguments rooted in proper respect for each other as human beings, getting people to support these changes does not require persuading them of social justice claims. As the United States faces more competition in the world, we are more likely to secure the futures of individual Americans and their families if we have all Americans working together to compete. The four tests are a foundation for doing that. We can be Machiavellian rather than missionary about meeting these tests.

Here's the rub, the purpose of this book, really. My arguments may ultimately be unpersuasive. My case that catastrophizing about the irreparable lack of a common American identity and the decline of American democracy is premature, and my suggestion that, despite flaws rooted in our past and fractures that characterize our present, the United States has more going for it than we sometimes realize, may not be enough to counterbalance the reasons for pessimism. It may still seem far-fetched and Pollyannish to suggest that we can develop a social contract and an ethic of citizenship that unites us in a common story in order to enable flourishing in our individual stories. Indeed, what we've experienced as a country in recent years and what we know about human psychology may tilt the odds against it. And, on this, history can be no guide because any example of liberal ideals put into reality has not only been incomplete but has only been possible *because of* its incompleteness—because of the oppression and exclusion of Black people, of women, of workers, of queers, of immigrants. Liberalism has been parasitic on illiberal substructures. A delusion.

And yet, though there may be no precedent for what the United States must now achieve, that is not in itself proof that it is *not* achievable. We *must* aspire to it. There is no acceptable other course. The alternative is not some sort of passive permanent acceptance of an imperfect, off-kilter democracy. It must get better or it must get worse, the status quo is not sustainable. At this world-historical inflection point, the tectonic shifts around us will continue, and we will not be able to stand still. If we can't salvage our politics, or if human beings really are biologically and psychologically incapable of adapting to the changes we face without jettisoning the values we need, then the existing systems of republican democratic governance will indeed collapse on the rotten ground of the flawed nature of those who have increasingly seized power. Tribalism will tear apart what has not been torn apart already. On this view, it's not a house in disrepair that we must cope with, but rather a house doomed to collapse.

But wait: Why would we entertain this possibility? We already know that this is intolerable. This is not an experiment that needs running! There is no reason to think that human beings are permanently content to sublimate their selves to the state. And I'm not just talking about intellectuals and artists. So-called ordinary people are extraordinary in their diverse expressions of self, in their variegated pursuits of happiness. Ordinary people *don't* want that directive authoritarianism, especially in a heterogeneous society like the United States where so many versions of the good life already proliferate. The doomsday predictions about our inexorable descent toward lobotomized complacency with the evaporation of human freedom and fulfillment are themselves predicated on a hellish fantasy. Reversing the deterioration of recent years, achieving a sustainable liberal democracy prepared for our time, is surely no *more* unrealistic than the idea that Americans would settle in to authoritarianism.

We don't know whether the ideal is possible. But we do know that the alternative is morally abhorrent and practically likely to lead to chaos and violence. Where does that leave us? Surely we cannot defend the idea that we should just give up and passively accept a long slide toward the intolerable. Whether one thinks the odds of America's future success are long or short is immaterial. There's only one answer for what a concerned citizen today should do: set aside the debate over our odds, and focus on trying to make progress. We can allow ourselves to be inspired by the possibility of a genuine liberal, pluralistic democracy, and the contribution that creating one would make to humanity. We can take a leap of faith. In the end, really, what choice do we have?

Acknowledgments

I'm grateful to my family: to Mom and Steve, Ron and Carolyn, Bill and Sue, Peter and Natalia, Merritt and Landon, Eileen, Katie, and Lyle. My grandmother, Nancy Van Buren, died in March 2023 as I was in the final throes of editing. After her husband walked out when she was twenty-five, she raised two children as a single mother in the 1950s and 1960s. She was smart, funny, and open to changing her mind, even in her mid-nineties. I'm glad for her example.

I'm thankful to have had so many friends in my life to learn from and laugh with. Classmates and roommates at college and in grad school and, later, colleagues at BCG, at Harvard and Georgetown, at the U.S. Department of State and the U.S. Mission to the OSCE, at the Colorado Department of Higher Education and on the campaign trail, and, now, gratefully, at Carnegie, where my coworkers challenge and inspire me.

Sarah Labowitz has cheered me through this project and so many others with loyalty and love. Abby Rezneck's friendship is a talisman in my life. Kate Dresser coached me through the book process with expertise and caring. Maggie Goodlander really wanted there to be three tests not four—her honesty about things like this, and her patriotism, endear her to me. Ellie Yuan's earnest idealism encourages me. Laurie Richardson inspires brain envy and makes me laugh as hard as she makes me think. Craig Wilson and Jack Cahill set an example with their partnership and love for each other. Michael Bennet was a friend when I needed one, and after that, too. Alex Soros, Sarah Margon, and their Open Society Foundations colleagues have been generous in supporting my work, and with encouragement. Eileen Koob is a friend and retiree from Wheat Ridge, Colorado, who asked a question in late 2021 that gave me the idea for this book.

I first met my agent, Brettne Bloom, when I was in college and a mentor of mine, the late Reverend Peter Gomes, asked his agent, Ike Williams, to take me on for a book project. Ike assigned a young associate to me—a thankless project—and Brettne worked dutifully to sell my unsellable book way back then. For a quarter century since she has continued to support me, listen to my ideas, and take me out to lunch when I come to town. This would be a lovely story about playing the long game if this book becomes a runaway international bestseller. More likely it will remain a lovely story about friendship.

It is a joy to know Ben Loehnen—he has the kind of Wildean wit that seems an anachronism in any age. It is also a lesson in grace. Even when I didn't know how to make good on his editing suggestions I never felt anything other than fortunate to be the beneficiary of his expert attention. I marvel at what he and Jofie, together with their wonderful colleagues, have built at Avid Reader Press.

Most of this book was written during two stints at Lovel Dene, an eighteenth-century house on the edge of Windsor Forest that once belonged to the Queen of England's dressmaker—Queen Elizabeth II's coronation gown was made there—and the house has been a second home to me for more than twenty years, since the Dunn family welcomed me when I was a graduate student in England and my father was dying at home in Colorado. A book is a measly thing to have to show for the generosity that Jigga, Trish, Andrew, Liz, Will, Bibby, and Baxter have bestowed on me. I'm grateful for the meals, the cheeky pints, and the quiet library in which to write.

In D.C., our friends old and new, but mostly new, have made returning to that city an unexpected delight in so many ways. I hope they consider this my small effort to make the case that there is still idealism and purpose to find and create there.

As I type, Brian hasn't read a word of this book, but he has given me reason to write every one. His commitment to the future enlarges my own. Life with him is exciting.

Washington, D.C.

June 2023

Notes

Chapter 1: A Wager on the Future

1. Govind Bhutada, "The U.S. Share of the Global Economy Over Time," Visual Capitalist, January 14, 2021, https://www.visualcapitalist.com/u-s -share-of-global-economy-over-time/.

Chapter 2: From Hegemon to Cooperator-in-Chief: The Scale Test

1. Melissa Kearney and Phillip Levine, "Will Births in the US Rebound? Probably Not.," Thinktank, *Brookings* (blog), May 24, 2021, https://www .brookings.edu/blog/up-front/2021/05/24/will-births-in-the-us-rebound -probably-not/.

2. Anna Brown, "Growing Share of Childless Adults in U.S. Don't Expect to Ever Have Children," *Pew Fact Tank* (blog), November 19, 2021, https:// www.pewresearch.org/fact-tank/2021/11/19/growing-share-of-childless -adults-in-u-s-dont-expect-to-ever-have-children/.

3. "OECD Population by Age Group 2021" (OECD), accessed February 20, 2023, https://stats.oecd.org/Index.aspx?DataSetCode=EDU_DEM.

4. Ellis, Stefanie, "St Louis: The US City Transformed by Heartbreak," *BBC* (blog), January 17, 2022, https://www.bbc.com/travel/article/20220117 -st-louis-the-us-city-transformed-by-heartbreak.

5. Robert Kagan, *The Jungle Grows Back* (New York: Alfred A. Knopf, 2018).

6. SIPRI, "World Military Expenditure Passes $2 Trillion for First Time," *Stockholm International Peace Research Institute* (blog), April 25, 2022, https://www.sipri.org/media/press-release/2022/world-military-expendi ture-passes-2-trillion-first-time.

7. SIPRI, "SIPRI Military Expenditure Database" (Stockholm: Stockholm International Peace Research Institute), accessed February 21, 2023, https://milex.sipri.org/sipri.

8. Congressional Budget Office, "Projected Costs of U.S. Nuclear Forces, 2021 to 2030," May 24, 2021, https://www.cbo.gov/publication/57240.

9. Melanie Hansen, "U.S. Public Education Spending Statistics [2023]: Per Pupil + Total," *Education Data Initiative* (blog), accessed March 5, 2023, https://educationdata.org/public-education-spending-statistics.

10. "World Trade to GDP Ratio 1970-2023," accessed February 22, 2023, https://www.macrotrends.net/countries/WLD/world/trade-gdp-ratio.

11. See: Levinson, Marc, *The Box* (Princeton: Princeton UP, 2016).

12. Evan A. Feigenbaum and Adam Szubin, "What China Has Learned from the Ukraine War," *Foreign Affairs*, February 14, 2023, https://www.foreign affairs.com/china/what-china-has-learned-ukraine-war.

13. Jon Bateman, "U.S.-China Technological 'Decoupling': A Strategy and Policy Framework," Carnegie Endowment for International Peace, accessed February 23, 2023, https://carnegieendowment.org/2022/04/25/u.s.-chi na-technological-decoupling-strategy-and-policy-framework-pub-86897.

14. Arzan Tarapore, "AUKUS Is Deeper than Just Submarines," *East Asia Forum* (blog), September 29, 2021, https://www.eastasiaforum .org/2021/09/29/aukus-is-deeper-than-just-submarines/.

15. Martijn Rasser, "Rethinking Export Controls: Unintended Consequences and the New Technological Landscape," accessed February 22, 2023, https://www.cnas.org/publications/reports/rethinking-export-con trols-unintended-consequences-and-the-new-technological-landscape.

16. See: Andrew Imbrie et al., "Privacy Is Power," *Foreign Affairs*, January 19, 2022, https://www.foreignaffairs.com/articles/world/2022-01-19/privacy -power; Imbrie, Andrew et al., "Democracies Must Empower a Biotech Future for All," Lawfare, November 20, 2022, https://www.lawfareblog .com/democracies-must-empower-biotech-future-all.

17. Anu Bradford, *The Brussels Effect: How the European Union Rules the World* (Oxford: Oxford University Press, 2020).

Chapter 3: From Monopoly to Start-up: The Investment Test

1. Christopher Witko, "How Wall Street Became a Big Chunk of the U.S. Economy—and When the Democrats Signed On," *Washington Post*, March 29, 2016, https://www.washingtonpost.com/news/monkey-cage

/wp/2016/03/29/how-wall-street-became-a-big-chunk-of-the-u-s-econo my-and-when-the-democrats-signed-on/.

2. St. Louis Fed, "Federal Reserve Economic Data (FRED)," FRED, accessed March 20, 2023, https://fred.stlouisfed.org/.

3. U.S. Census Bureau, "Children as a Percentage of the Population: Persons in Selected Age Groups as a Percentage of the Total U.S. Population and Children Ages 0–17 as a Percentage of the Dependent Population, 1950–2021 and Projected 2022–2050," Child Stats, accessed March 20, 2023, https://www.childstats.gov/americaschildren/tables/pop2.asp.

4. Garcia, Jorge Luis et al., "Quantifying the Life-Cycle Benefits of a Proto-typical Early Childhood Program," Working Paper (Cambridge, MA: National Bureau of Economic Research, 2017, Rev 2019).

5. Nathaniel Hendren and Ben Sprung-Keyser, "A Unified Welfare Analy-sis of Government Policies," *Quarterly Journal of Economics* 135, no. 3 (2020): 1209–1318.

6. Chloe East et al., "Multi-Generational Impacts of Childhood Access to the Safety Net: Early Life Exposure to Medicaid and the Next Generation's Health" (Cambridge, MA: National Bureau of Economic Research, September 2017), https://doi.org/10.3386/w23810. P. 5 (emphasis added).

7. Children's Defense Fund, "The State of America's Children 2021—Early Childhood" (Children's Defense Fund), accessed March 10, 2023, https://www.childrensdefense.org/state-of-americas-children/soac-2021-early-childhood/.; Kids Count Data Center, "Head Start Enrollment by Age Group," accessed March 10, 2023, https://datacenter.kidscount.org/data/tables/9786-head-start-enrollment-by-age-group.

8. U.S. Census Bureau, "CPS Historical Time Series Tables," Census.gov, accessed March 10, 2023, https://www.census.gov/data/tables/time-series/demo/educational-attainment/cps-historical-time-series.html.

9. Max Roser and Esteban Ortiz-Ospina, "Literacy," *Our World in Data*, August 13, 2016, https://ourworldindata.org/literacy.

10. OECD, "Country Note: China," Education at a Glance, 2019, https://www.oecd.org/education/education-at-a-glance/EAG2019_CN_CHN.pdf.

11. I say most because it's not all: thousands—disproportionately women of color—get scammed by certain for-profit schools; millions—also dispro-portionally women—end up with mountains of debt in low-paying but es-sential jobs like teaching.

12. Jeff Cox, "It's Never Been This Hard for Companies to Find Qualified Workers," CNBC, February 19, 2020, https://www.cnbc.com/2020/02/19/its-never-been-this-hard-for-companies-to-find-qualified-workers.html.

13. Quoctrung Bui, "Map: The Most Common* Job in Every State : Planet Money : NPR," accessed February 24, 2023, https://www.npr.org/sections/money/2015/02/05/382664837/map-the-most-common-job-in-every-state.

14. Annie Lowrey, "How ChatGPT Will Destabilize White-Collar Work," *The Atlantic*, January 20, 2023, https://www.theatlantic.com/ideas/archive/2023/01/chatgpt-ai-economy-automation-jobs/672767/.

15. Sophia Laderman, "State Higher Education Finance Case Study: Ten Years Out, State Recovery from the Great Recession" (State Higher Education Executive Officers Association, 2019), https://sheeo.org/shef-2018-case-study-ten-years-out-state-recovery-from-the-great-recession/.

16. Center for Analysis of Postsecondary Education and Employment, "By the Numbers: For-Profit Colleges," *For Profit Colleges by the Numbers* (blog), accessed February 24, 2023, https://capseecenter.org/research/by-the-numbers/for-profit-college-infographic/. There are some effective for-profit institutions, and they can be part of the mix, but public funding should come with expectation of performance and fair dealing.

17. Kriston McIntosh et al., "Examining the Black-White Wealth Gap," February 27, 2020, https://www.brookings.edu/blog/up-front/2020/02/27/examining-the-black-white-wealth-gap/.

18. Stephanie Cellini, Designing an Intuitive Measure of Value for Higher Education Programs: A conversation with Professor Stephanie Cellini, 2023, https://www.arnoldventures.org/stories/designing-an-intuitive-measure-of-value-for-higher-education-programs.

19. National Science Board, "The State of U.S. Science and Engineering 2022" (National Science Foundation, January 2022), https://ncses.nsf.gov/pubs/nsb20221/u-s-and-global-research-and-development#:~:text=Based%20on%20R%26D%20expenditures%2C%20a,global%20R%26D%20(Figure%2012).

20. *Financial Times* journalist Rana Foroohar lays out a broader vision for re-localization of economic activity in the wake of the failures of globalization and neoliberal economic orthodoxy to deliver. Rana Foroohar, *Homecoming: The Path to Prosperity in a Post-Global World* (New York: Penguin, 2022).

21. National Center for Science and Engineering Statistics, "Businesses Performed 60% of Their U.S. R&D in 10 Metropolitan Areas in 2018," Info-Brief, accessed March 11, 2023, https://ncses.nsf.gov/pubs/nsf21331.

22. Nicholas Bloom et al., "The Diffusion of Disruptive Technologies," SSRN Scholarly Paper (Rochester, NY, June 28, 2021), https://doi.org/10.2139/ssrn.3875827.

23. Anne Applebaum, "What America's Vaccination Campaign Proves to the World," *The Atlantic*, April 10, 2021, https://www.theatlantic.com/ideas/archive/2021/04/mass-vaccination-show-american-might/618559/.

24. McKinsey Global Institute, "The Net-Zero Transition: Its Cost and Benefits," accessed March 11, 2023, https://www.mckinsey.com/capabilities/sustainability/our-insights/the-net-zero-transition-what-it-would-cost-what-it-could-bring.

25. Emily Kos et al., "Solving the $290 Billion Care Crisis," BCG Global, November 10, 2022, https://www.bcg.com/publications/2022/solving-the-care-crisis.

26. Theda Skocpol, *Protecting Soldiers and Mothers* (Cambridge: Harvard University Press, 1995).

27. Isaac Jabola-Carolus, Stephanie Luce, and Ruth Milkman, "The Case for Public Investment in Higher Pay for New York State Home Care Workers: Estimated Costs and Savings" (New York: CUNY Graduate Center, 2021), https://slu.cuny.edu/wp-content/uploads/2021/03/The-Case-for-Public-Investment-in-Higher-Pay-for-New-York-State-H.pdf.

Chapter 4: Right Makes Might: The Fairness Test

1. Daniel Baer, "The Death Penalty Isolates America," *Foreign Affairs*, September 16, 2020, https://www.foreignaffairs.com/articles/united-states/2020-09-16/death-penalty-isolates-america.

2. Carroll Doherty, "Millennials Want an Economy That Works Better and More Fairly—No Matter What You Call It," *The Catalyst: A Journal of Ideas from the George W. Bush Institute* (blog), 2019, https://www.bushcenter.org/catalyst/capitalism/doherty-pew-millennials-want-economy-that-works-better-and-more-fairly/.

3. Social Security itself had a fairness problem from inception: the exclusion of domestic workers disproportionately affected Black Americans, particularly Black women workers.

4. See: William A. Galston and Hendrickson, Clara, "A Policy at Peace

with Itself: Antitrust Remedies for Our Concentrated, Uncompetitive Economy," January 5, 2018, https://www.brookings.edu/research/a-pol icy-at-peace-with-itself-antitrust-remedies-for-our-concentrated-uncom petitive-economy/.; "GDP (Current US$) - United States | Data," ac cessed February 26, 2023, https://data.worldbank.org/indicator/NY .GDP.MKTP.CD?locations=US.; *Fortune*, "*Fortune* Announces 2022 Fortune 500 List," accessed February 26, 2023, https://www.prnews wire.com/news-releases/fortune-announces-2022-fortune-500-list-3015 52608.html.

5. Galston and Hendrickson, Clara, "A Policy at Peace with Itself." The au thors reference the work of David Autor.

6. "Vast Corporate Profits Are Delaying an American Recession," *The Economist*, accessed February 26, 2023, https://www.economist.com /finance-and-economics/2022/08/30/vast-corporate-profits-are-delaying -an-american-recession.

7. Galston and Hendrickson, Clara, "A Policy at Peace with Itself."

8. Fiona M. Scott Morton, "Reforming U.S. Antitrust Enforcement and Competition Policy," *Equitable Growth* (blog), February 18, 2020, http:// www.equitablegrowth.org/reforming-u-s-antitrust-enforcement-and-com petition-policy/.

9. Isaac Chotiner, "What a Ban on Non-Compete Agreements Could Mean for American Workers," *The New Yorker*, January 10, 2023, https://www .newyorker.com/news/q-and-a/what-a-ban-on-non-compete-agreements -could-mean-for-american-workers.

10. "FTC Proposes Rule to Ban Noncompete Clauses, Which Hurt Workers and Harm Competition," Federal Trade Commission, January 4, 2023, https://www.ftc.gov/news-events/news/press-releases/2023/01/ftc-pro poses-rule-ban-noncompete-clauses-which-hurt-workers-harm-competi tion.

11. Elise Gould and Jori Kandra, "Inequality in Annual Earnings Worsens in 2021: Top 1% of Earners Get a Larger Share of the Earnings Pie While the Bottom 90% Lose Ground," accessed February 26, 2023, https://www.epi .org/publication/inequality-2021-ssa-data/.

12. Rana Foroohar, *Makers and Takers* (New York: Crown Business, 2016).

13. OECD, Tax to GDP Ratios, 2021, https://www.oecd.org/coronavirus/en /data-insights/tax-to-gdp-ratios.

14. Christopher Pulliam and Richard V. Reeves, "The SALT Tax Deduction

Is a Handout to the Rich. It Should Be Eliminated Not Expanded," *Brookings Up Front* (blog), September 4, 2020, https://www.brookings.edu/blog/up-front/2020/09/04/the-salt-tax-deduction-is-a-handout-to-the-rich-it-should-be-eliminated-not-expanded/.

15. Lily Batchelder, "Leveling the Playing Field between Inherited Income and Income from Work Through an Inheritance Tax," The Hamilton Project (Washington DC: Brookings, January 28, 2020), https://www.brookings.edu/research/leveling-the-playing-field-between-inherited-income-and-income-from-work-through-an-inheritance-tax/.

16. John Guyton et al., "Tax Evasion at the Top of the Income Distribution: Theory and Evidence," NBER Working Papers (National Bureau of Economic Research, 2021), https://www.nber.org/system/files/working_papers/w28542/w28542.pdf. p. 4.

17. TRAC Center, "IRS Audits Poorest Families at Five Times the Rate for Everyone Else," March 8, 2022, https://trac.syr.edu/tracirs/latest/679/.

18. John Guyton et al., "Tax Evasion at the Top of the Income Distribution: Theory and Evidence." p. 3.

19. U.S. Department of the Treasury, "The American Families Plan Tax Compliance Agenda" (Washington DC, 2021), https://home.treasury.gov/system/files/136/The-American-Families-Plan-Tax-Compliance-Agenda.pdf.

20. Eric Katz, "House Sends Package That Includes an IRS Hiring Boost and USPS EV Funding to Biden," *Government Executive*, August 12, 2022, https://www.govexec.com/workforce/2022/08/house-sends-package-including-irs-hiring-boost-usps-ev-funding-bidens-desk/375802/.

21. Karl Evers-Hillstrom, "Most Expensive Ever: 2020 Election Cost $14.4 Billion," OpenSecrets News, February 11, 2021, https://www.opensecrets.org/news/2021/02/2020-cycle-cost-14p4-billion-doubling-16/.

22. Open Secrets, "Who Are the Biggest Donors?," Database, OpenSecrets, accessed February 25, 2023, https://www.opensecrets.org/elections-overview/biggest-donors.

23. David Edward Burke, "A Realistic Strategy for Overturning Citizens United," *Washington Monthly* (blog), July 25, 2020, http://washingtonmonthly.com/2020/07/25/a-realistic-strategy-for-overturning-citizens-united-within-10-years/.

24. Steven Kull, "Americans Evaluate Campaign Finance Reform" (University of Maryland, 2018), https://www.documentcloud.org/documents/4455238-campaignfinancereport.

25. Matt Vasilogambros, "Polling Places Remain a Target Ahead of November Elections," September 4, 2018, https://pew.org/2MCsiBT.
26. U.S. Commission on Civil Rights, "Assessment of Minority Voting Rights Access," Statutory (Washington DC: US Commission on Civil Rights, 2018), https://www.usccr.gov/files/pubs/2018/Minority_Voting_Access_2018.pdf. p. 13.
27. U.S. Commission on Civil Rights.
28. Daniel Baer, "How to Make American Democracy More Democratic," *UnHerd*, January 7, 2021, https://unherd.com/thepost/how-to-make-american-democracy-more-democratic/.
29. Josiah Ober, *Democracy and Knowledge: Innovation and Learning in Classical Athens* (Princeton: Princeton UP, 2008).
30. Julian Gewirtz, *Never Turn Back: China and the Forbidden History of the 1980s* (Cambridge, MA: Belknap Press, 2022).
31. Sebastian Heilmann, "Policy Experimentation in China's Economic Rise," *Studies in Comparative International Development* 43 (2008): 1–26. pp. 2–3.
32. Sarah Labowitz, "What More Climate Disasters Mean for U.S. National Security," Carnegie Endowment for International Peace, accessed April 23, 2023, https://carnegieendowment.org/2023/04/10/what-more-climate-disasters-mean-for-u.s.-national-security-pub-89484.
33. Michela Wrong, *It's Our Turn to Eat: The Story of a Kenyan Whistle-Blower* (London: Harper Collins, 2009).
34. A recent, accessible, provoking example is Isabel Wilkerson, *Caste: The Origins of Our Discontents* (New York: Random House, 2020).
35. U.S. Census Bureau, "Educational Attainment in the United States: 2020," Census.gov, accessed February 25, 2023, https://www.census.gov/data/tables/2020/demo/educational-attainment/cps-detailed-tables.html.
36. Anthony P Carnevale et al., "The Cost of Economic and Racial Injustice in Postsecondary Education" (Washington DC: Georgetown Center on Education and the Workforce, 2021).
37. McGhee, Heather, *The Sum of Us: What Racism Costs Everyone and How We Can Prosper Together* (New York: One World, 2021).
38. McGhee, Heather., p. 30.
39. Golnaz Tabibnia, Ajay Satpute, and Matthew Lieberman, "Are Humans Hardwired for Fairness?," Association for Psychological Science—APS,

accessed February 25, 2023, https://www.psychologicalscience.org/news/releases/are-humans-hardwired-for-fairness.html.

40. G. Tabibnia and M. D. Lieberman, "Fairness and Cooperation Are Rewarding: Evidence from Social Cognitive Neuroscience," *Annals of the New York Academy of Sciences* 1118, no. 1 (September 5, 2007): 90–101, https://doi.org/10.1196/annals.1412.001.

41. Shelby R. Buckman et al., "The Economic Gains from Equity," *Federal Reserve Bank of San Francisco, Working Paper Series*, April 7, 2021, 1.000-30.000, https://doi.org/10.24148/wp2021-11.

42. Ani Turner, "The Business Case for Racial Equity" (Battle Creek, MI: W. K. Kellogg Foundation, 2018), https://onlinelibrary.wiley.com/doi/10.1002/ncr.21263.

43. See, for example, Dani Rodrik, "Growth Strategies," Working Paper, NBER Working Papers (Cambridge, MA: National Bureau of Economic Research, 2003), https://www.nber.org/system/files/working_papers/w10050/w10050.pdf.

44. International Monetary Fund, "World Economic Outlook (October 2022) - GDP per Capita, Current Prices," 2022, https://www.imf.org/external/datamapper/PPPPC@WEO.

45. David Marchese, "Thomas Piketty Thinks America Is Primed for Wealth Redistribution," *The New York Times Magazine*, April 3, 2022, https://www.nytimes.com/interactive/2022/04/03/magazine/thomas-piketty-interview.html.

Chapter 5: Take a Chance on We: The Identity Test

1. As Francis Fukuyama puts it "These political ideas come directly out of the Enlightenment and are the only possible basis for unifying a modern liberal democracy that has become de facto multicultural." Francis Fukuyama, *Identity*, paperback (New York: Farrar, Strauss, and Girooux, 2019). p. 158.

2. Francis Fukuyama, "A Country of Their Own," *Foreign Affairs*, April 1, 2022, https://www.foreignaffairs.com/articles/ukraine/2022-04-01/francis-fukuyama-liberalism-country.

3. The dismantling of identity for particular groups of people often emerges in tandem with other mechanisms to force their social and political disempowerment. Sociologist Orlando Patterson describes how the experience

of chattel slavery in the United States also purposefully undermined the ability of enslaved people to constitute the kinds of social relationships in which a sense of identity is grounded. Orlando Patterson, *Slavery and Social Death: A Comparative Study* (Cambridge, MA: Harvard University Press, 2018).

4. Claudia Wallis, "Another Tragic Epidemic: Suicide," *Scientific American*, accessed April 11, 2022, https://doi.org/10.1038/scientificamerican08 20-23.

5. Emily Stewart, "Why Do We Buy What We Buy?," *The Goods by Vox* (blog), July 7, 2021, https://www.vox.com/the-goods/22547185/consum erism-competition-history-interview.

6. Elena Renken, "Most Americans Are Lonely, and Our Workplace Culture May Not Be Helping," *NPR*, January 23, 2020, sec. Shots—Health News, https://www.npr.org/sections/health-shots/2020/01/23/798676465/most -americans-are-lonely-and-our-workplace-culture-may-not-be-helping.

7. Carli N Conklin, "The Origins of the Pursuit of Happiness," *Washington University Jurisprudence Review* 7, no. 2 (2015): 69.

8. Conklin.

9. Ronald Reagan, "Inaugural Address 1981" (Presidential Inauguration, Washington DC, 1981), https://www.reaganlibrary.gov/archives/speech /inaugural-address-1981.

10. Kwame Anthony Appiah, *The Ethics of Identity* (Princeton, NJ: Princeton UP, 2007). p. 47.

11. Never mind that that particular president did not effect a pronounced left turn in national policy; in fact, he has been criticized by members of his own party for being particularly attentive to avoid accusations of serving the interests of Black Americans, to the point of erring on the side of indulging the status quo.

12. Anna Brown, "Most Democrats Who Are Looking for a Relationship Would Not Consider Dating a Trump Voter," *Pew Research Center* (blog), accessed February 27, 2023, https://www.pewresearch.org/fact -tank/2020/04/24/most-democrats-who-are-looking-for-a-relationship -would-not-consider-dating-a-trump-voter/.

13. Daryl Fairweather, "Redfin Predicts a More Balanced Housing Market in 2022," Redfin Real Estate News, November 18, 2021, https://www.redfin .com/news/housing-market-predictions-2022/.

14. Shawn Rosenberg, "Democracy Devouring Itself: The Rise of the Incom-

petent Citizen and the Appeal of Right Wing Populism," June 28, 2021, p. 23, https://escholarship.org/uc/item/8806z01m.

15. Rosenberg. p. 20 (emphasis added).

16. Harry Enten, "Statistically, Democrats and Republicans Hate Each Other More than Ever | CNN Politics," *CNN*, November 20, 2021, https://www.cnn.com/2021/11/20/politics/democrat-republican-hate-tribalism/index.html.

17. Eric Plutzer and Michael Berkman, "Americans Not Only Divided, but Baffled by What Motivates Their Opponents" (Penn State McCourtney Institute, 2018), https://democracy.psu.edu/wp-content/uploads/sites/14/2020/08/Poll-Report-November-2018.pdf.

18. Muirhead, Russell and Rosenblum, Nancy L., *A Lot of People Are Saying* (Princeton, NJ: Princeton UP, 2019), https://press.princeton.edu/books/hardcover/9780691188836/a-lot-of-people-are-saying.

19. Russell Muirhead and Nancy Rosenblum, "The New Conspiracists," *Dissent* 65, no. 1 (2018): 51–60, https://doi.org/10.1353/dss.2018.0012, p. 54.

20. Economist / YouGov, "Which Groups of Americans Are Most Likely to Believe Conspiracy Theories? | YouGov," accessed February 28, 2023, https://today.yougov.com/topics/politics/articles-reports/2022/03/30/which-groups-americans-believe-conspiracies. See also: Public Religion Research Institute Staff, "The Persistence of QAnon in the Post-Trump Era: An Analysis of Who Believes the Conspiracies," *PRRI* (blog), accessed February 28, 2023, https://www.prri.org/research/the-persistence-of-qanon-in-the-post-trump-era-an-analysis-of-who-believes-the-conspiracies/.

21. Richard Weissbourd et al., "Do Americans Really Care For Each Other?," Making Caring Common Project (Cambridge, MA: Harvard University, 2021). p. 17.

22. Rachel Kleinfeld, "Five Strategies to Support U.S. Democracy," Carnegie Endowment for International Peace, p. 21, accessed April 24, 2023, https://carnegieendowment.org/2022/09/15/five-strategies-to-support-u.s.-democracy-pub-87918.

23. Jacob S. Hacker and Paul Pierson, *Let Them Eat Tweets* (New York: Liveright (Norton), 2020), https://wwnorton.com/books/9781631496844.

24. Gareth Evans, "War, Peace and National Identity," http://www.gevans.org/speeches/speech440.html.

25. Gareth Evans.

26. Gallup Inc, "Presidential Approval Ratings—Gallup Historical Statistics and Trends," Gallup.com, March 12, 2008, https://news.gallup.com/poll/116677/Presidential-Approval-Ratings-Gallup-Historical-Statistics-Trends.aspx.

Chapter 6: What Choice Do We Have?
1. David Clark Scott, "Mexican Novelist Sees 1492 as 'A Year of Centuries,'" *The Christian Science Monitor*, October 11, 1991, https://www.csmonitor.com/1991/1011/11101.html.

Index

Adelson, Miriam, 141
Adelson, Sheldon, 141
Affordable Care Act, 154
AI (artificial intelligence), 103–4, 221
Albright, Madeleine, 63
"America First" foreign policy, 43
American Rescue Plan Act (2021),
    30
anomie, 179–81
antitrust issues and fairness, 122–23. *see
    also* legal and regulatory issues
Appiah, K. Anthony, 184
Aridjis, Homero, 221
Aristotle, 183
artificial intelligence (AI), 103–4, 221
AUKUS (U.S., Australia, United
    Kingdom joint agreement, 2021),
    57
Australia
    purchasing power of U.S. vs., 167
    Quadrilateral Security Dialogue
        (Quad), 61
    U.S. alliance with, 41, 57
authoritarianism
    "cross-pollination" of knowledge and
        expertise in, 151

democracy vs., as oversimplification,
    172
doomsday predictions of, 224–25
economic integration/growth and
    effect on, 53–54
identity, democracy, and right-wing
    populist authoritarianism, 193–98,
    203–5
international relations and test of
    scale, 40
investment in science and technology
    and ethical considerations, 103–4

Baer, Daniel, career of, 43, 135, 139,
    143
Batchelder, Lily, 133–34
Bennet, Michael, 202
Biden, Joe
    on defense spending, 44
    on "foreign policy for middle class,"
        5–6
    on immigration, 36
    on IRS staffing, 136
    on nuclear war restraint, 50–51
    partisanship and, 202
    presidential election (2020), 147

Biden, Joe (*cont.*)
  State of the Union (2023) address, 1
  on technological innovation, 57
Bipartisan Infrastructure Bill (2021), 13
birthrate decline (2007–2020), 27, 29–
    32. *see also* children, childbearing,
    and parenthood
Black Lives Matter, 217
Blackstone, William, 183
Bosnia, immigration to St. Louis from,
    35
Boston Consulting Group, 104
Britain. *see* United Kingdom
Bureau of Democracy, Human Rights,
    and Labor (U.S. State Department
    "human rights bureau"), 143
Bureau of International Organization
    Affairs, U.S. State Department
    ("foreign service"), 63–64
Bush, George H. W., 78
Bush, George W., 39, 214–15

campaign finance, 137–44, 207–9
Canada, purchasing power of, 167
capital gains taxes, 131–32
Capital in the Twenty-First Century
    (Piketty), 168
carbon tax, 136–37
care economy
  investment needed in, 79–80, 104–7
  national service proposal for, 211
Census Bureau, U.S., 84–85
children, childbearing, and parenthood.
    see also education
  birthrate decline (2007–2020), 27,
    29–32
  child care and investment in care
    economy, 104–7
  child care cost, 83–84
  child poverty rate, 30
  investment needed in, 79–84
  population replacement and
    economic scale, 26–33
  poverty among children, 125
  prenatal care, 82–83
Children's Defense Fund, 83
China
  COVID vaccine development, 99
  Deng's economic reforms, 151
  economic growth of, 23, 54
  international relations and leadership
    of U.S. vs., 60, 61, 66
  literacy rate in, 84–85
  "new Cold War" predictions about,
    9–11, 47, 171–72, 215–17
  purchasing power of U.S. vs., 167
  research and development spending,
    96
  Russia-Ukraine war and, 213–14
  U.S. economic competition from, 74
Chinese Exclusion Act (1882), 146
CHIPS Act (2022), 13, 97–98
Churchill, Winston, 115
citizens, U.S. *see also* democracy;
    immigration; political ideology
  coronavirus response by, 197–98
  cynicism vs. confidence of, 149–56,
    164–69
  identity and democratic citizenship,
    196
  identity and "pursuit of happiness,"
    185, 210
  power of, 1–2
*Citizens United v. Federal Election
    Commission* (2010), 141–44
"city on a hill" speech (Reagan), 113
City University of New York, 107
civility, identity and, 217–18

climate change
   birthrate decline due to, 29, 31–32
   carbon taxes, 136–37
   international alliances for, 62
   investment needed for, 100–102
   Paris Agreement, 155
Clinton, Hillary, 147, 192
Cold War
   American hegemony at end of, 21–23
   China and "new Cold War"
      predictions, 9–11, 47, 171–72,
      215–17
   post–Cold War expansion of trade,
      53
   scale of U.S. vs. USSR, 19–22
   Soviet communism vs. American
      democracy as world hegemon,
      7–10
Colorado
   higher education in, 89–90, 135
   U.S. Senate races in, 139, 141
Commission on Civil Rights, U.S., 145
communism and socialism. *see also*
      China; Cold War; Russia
   American democracy as world
      hegemon vs., 7–10
   U.S. public opinion on, 118–21
Comprehensive and Progressive
      Agreement for Trans Pacific–
      Partnership (CPTPP), 66
confidence in government. *see* political
      ideology
conflict, national identity bolstered
      by, 212–17. *see also* international
      relations
Congress, U.S.
   Colorado and U.S. Senate races, 139,
      141
   Congressional Budget Office, 136

House of Representatives and
      proportional representation,
      147–48, 179
   Senate and nonrepresentative nature,
      147, 179
conspiracy theories, 197–98
Constitution, U.S., 146, 183
coronavirus pandemic
   Americans' response to, 197–98
   Congress' response to, 223
   investment and vaccine development,
      99–100
corporations and corporate profits. *See
      also* taxes
   corporate political action committees
      (corporate PACs), 139, 141–44
   market consolidation and fairness,
      121–24
"critical race theory," 191
"crooked timber of humanity," 195
cynicism about government. *see* political
      ideology

Déclaration des Droits de l'Homme et
      du Citoyen (France), 182
Declaration of Independence, U.S.,
      181–89
Defense Advanced Research Projects
      Agency (DARPA), 57
democracy. *see also* United States
      political system
   democratic institutions for shared
      national identity, 193, 199–203
   identity, right-wing populist
      authoritarianism, and, 193–98,
      203–5
   prioritizing identity vs. ("identity
      chicken" vs. "democracy egg"),
      205–6

democracy *(cont.)*
    right-wing populism ideology and,
        193–98, 203–5
    shared national identity and obstacles
        of, 193–98 *(see also* identity)
Deng Xiaoping, 151
Department of Higher Education
    (Colorado), 135
The Division of Labor in Society
    (Durkheim), 180
Doherty, Carroll, 119
Durkheim, Émile, 179–81

early childhood education, 79–84, 95
Early Head Start, 83
economics. *see also* employment; GDP;
        health care; income gap and class
        issues; investment
    alliances and leadership, 60–64
    alliances and strategic partnering,
        55–60
    alliances and trade agreements,
        65–67
    Biden on "foreign policy for middle
        class," 5–6
    collective social investment, UCLA
        experiment, 162–64
    corporations and corporate profits,
        121–24, 139, 141–44
    dollar as currency standard, 12
    fairness and income gap, 124–29
    fairness and market consolidation,
        121–24
    Great Depression, 12, 78, 105, 158,
        168
    identity as societal crisis, 177–81
    political economy and, 221–23
    population and net immigration
        needed for, 34–38
    population and productivity for scale
        in, 19–22, 26
    population replacement and growth
        needed for, 26–33
    post–Cold War expansion of trade, 53
    post–World War II collective
        social investment from federal
        government, 89, 91, 108, 128–29
        (see also investment)
    tax revenue for social investment,
        129–37
    2008 financial crisis, 34, 54, 161–64,
        223
    U.S. output as of 1960, 10, 22
education
    birthrate decline and investment in,
        31
    defense spending vs., 50, 51
    early childhood, 79–84, 95
    fairness and federal spending on, 134
    fairness and income gap, 125–26,
        233n11
    higher education, 86–94, 157
    investment in early childhood
        education, 79–84, 95
    investment in K-12 education, 84–85,
        88
    race/ethnicity and educational
        attainment, 157
    technological innovation and scale,
        57
    white recipients of public education,
        159
Eisenhower, Dwight, 49, 105
elder care, 104–7. *see also* care economy
Electoral College, 147–48
empathy, 206–7, 211
empires
    British Empire's end, 40

"civilizing" by, 20
U.S. as expansionist vs. imperial,
    21–22
employment
    in care economy, 79–80, 83–84,
        104–7, 211
    decoupling health care from, 105
    higher education credentials and,
        86–94
    income gap and wages statistics,
        125–26
    industrialization and anomie, 179–81
    manufacturing jobs and trends, 73
    market consolidation and fairness,
        122
    minimum wage, 191
    national service proposal, 210–12
    noncompete agreements, 123–24
    race/ethnicity and educational
        attainment, 157
    return on investment for R&D
        employees, 97
    skilled workforce investment for,
        69–70, 79–80, 84–94, 211
    state and local tax (SALT) deduction,
        131–32, 155
    taxes on capital gains vs. earned
        income, 131–32
"epistemic communities," 196–97
ethics and morality
    identity and judgment of, 175
    identity and patriotic empathy,
        206–7, 211
    immigration as social justice issue,
        37
    "pursuit of happiness" as ethical
        individualism, 181–89, 210
    racism and national competitiveness,
        156–61

shared national identity and
    upholding democratic institutions,
        193, 199–203
social contract, 127–29, 208, 224
of technological governance, 59, 103
eudaimonia, 183
European Union (EU)
    Germany's purchasing power,
        167
    technological governance, 59 (*see also*
        France)
Evans, Gareth, 212–13

fairness, 113–69. *See also* ethics and
    morality
    of campaign finance, 137–44, 207–9
    citizens' cynicism vs. confidence in
        fairness, 149–56, 164–69
    defined, 115–17
    economic consolidation and, 121–24
    economic welfare and poverty,
        124–29
    fairness experiment (UCLA), 162–64
    freedom narrative of U.S., 113–15
    gender issues of, 165
    geopolitical success and changing
        global competition, 13–14
    identity and Otherness, 159
    identity and perception of, 207–9
    investment and discrimination,
        108–11
    investment in higher education and,
        94
    political polarization and, 161–64
    as practical vs. moral, 117–18
    racial issues of, 156–61, 165
    scale and, 65–67
    social contract and, 127–29, 208,
        224

fairness (*cont.*)
  tax revenue for social investment, 129–37
  of voting rights, 137–38, 144–49, 152
federal government spending (U.S.). *see also* investment; taxes
  CHIPS Act (2022), 13, 97–98
  collective social investment from federal government needed, 108–11, 162–64
  food stamps and white recipients, 159
  ideology about government size and, 77–78, 105, 109–11
  Inflation Reduction Act (2022), 13, 97–98, 100, 101
  marginal value of public funds (MVPF), 82
  natural disaster aid, 152–53
  private vs. public investment in research and development, 94–102
  tax gap and, 134–36, 234n16 (*see also* taxes)
Federal Trade Commission, 124
Fifth Amendment (U.S. Constitution), 183
Financial Action Task Force (FATF), 61
"foreign service" (Bureau of International Organization Affairs, U.S. State Department), 63–64
Fortune 500, revenue, 121
Fourteenth Amendment (U.S. Constitution), 183
four tests. *see also* fairness; identity; investment; scale; United States and future success
  as composites, 222

fairness test, defined, 13–14
identity test, defined, 14–15
importance of, 223–25
investment test, defined, 12–13
political economy changed by, 221–23
recognizing historic change as it happens, 219–20
scale test, defined, 12
France
  Déclaration des Droits de l'Homme et du Citoyen, 182
  international relations of, 41
freedom narrative, 113–15
Fukuyama, Francis, 177, 239n1

GDP
  care economy and, 104
  corporate revenue and, 121–22
  defense spending and, 44–45
  energy infrastructure, 100
  globalization and, 53
  income tax and, 128–30
  market consolidation and fairness, 121–22
  population and productivity, 26, 77–78, 167
  purchasing power of U.S. vs. other countries, 167
  race/gender discrimination and effect on, 165
  research and development spending, 96
  women in labor force and, 28–29
gender and sexism. *See also* income gap and class issues
  fairness and voting rights, 146
  fairness issues of, 165
  identity politics and, 190–91

investment and fairness, 108–11
sexism as structural, 107, 179
wages in care economy jobs, 107
women in labor force, 28–29
generational issues. *See also* children,
    childbearing, and parenthood
elder care, 104–7
of identity, 180–81
Millennials and Gen Z on capitalism,
    119
Georgetown University Center on
    Education and the Workforce, 157
George W. Bush Institute, 119
Germany, purchasing power of U.S.
    vs., 167
G.I. Bill, 89, 91
globalization
    "global governance," 64–67
    higher education credentials and,
        86–87
    identity of voters and Trump's
        election, 179
    as megatrend, 70–74
    regional economic crises and, 165
Gorbachev, Mikhail, 50
grassroots fundraising, 140
Great Britain. *see* United Kingdom
Great Depression, 12, 78, 105, 158, 168
groups, identity of, 176. *see also* identity

Hart, Gary, 140–41
Harvard University, 81, 201–2
Head Start, 83
health care
    Affordable Care Act, 154
    defense spending vs., 51
    investment in care economy, 104–7
        (*see also* care economy)
    Medicaid, 82–83, 159

Medicare, 78
    universal, 106
Heckman, James, 81
Hickenlooper, John, 139, 141
Hidden Figures (film), 87
higher education
    for-profit colleges, 90
    high-skill apprenticeships, 93
    investment needed in, 86–94
    race/ethnicity and educational
        attainment, 157
    student loan debt, 90–94
    transparency in potential earnings
        needed, 92
Hillbilly Elegy (Vance), 177
historic change, recognizing, 219–20
Hodges, Ben, 42
home concept, identity and, 217–18
House of Representatives, U.S.,
    proportional representation of,
    147–48, 179

identity, 171–218
    civility and home concept, 217–18
    democracy vs. right-wing populist
        authoritarianism and, 193–98,
        203–5
    fairness and Otherness, 159
    geopolitical success and changing
        global competition, 14–15
    of groups, 176
    identity politics and, 189–93
    importance and difficulty of,
        171–73
    national identity and upholding
        democratic institutions, 193–94,
        199–203
    national identity bolstered by
        conflict, 212–17

identity (*cont.*)
    national identity needed for success,
      173–74
    national identity obstacles, 193–98
    national service proposal for,
      210–12
    patriotic empathy needed for, 206–7,
      211
    perception of fairness and, 207–9
    prioritizing democracy vs. ("identity
      chicken" vs. "democracy egg"),
      205–6
    "pursuit of happiness" and, 181–89,
      210
    in relation to others, 174–76
    as societal crisis, 177–81
immigration
    Chinese Exclusion Act (1882), 146
    freedom narrative about U.S. and,
      113–15
    identity politics and, 190–92
    population replacement via, 26,
      34–38
    technological innovation and scale,
      56–57
    to U.S., between Civil War and
      World War II, 3
income gap and class issues. *see also*
    taxes
    Biden on "foreign policy for middle
      class," 5–6
    campaign finance and, 137–44,
      207–9
    child poverty rate, 30
    fairness and poverty, 124–29
    fairness deficits as inefficient and
      damaging, 164–69
    identity and liberal values, 177–81,
      193, 199–203

identity and "pursuit of happiness,"
    184–85, 210
    identity as societal crisis, 177–81
    investment and race, 91–92
    natural disaster aid and, 152–53
    political polarization and, 161–64
India
    literacy rate in, 85
    Quadrilateral Security Dialogue
      (Quad), 61
    U.S. economic competition from, 74
    U.S. technology initiative with, 57
individualism
    identity in relation to others, 174–76
    libertarianism and, 108, 114, 186
    "pursuit of happiness" as ethical
      individualism, 181–89, 210
Inflation Reduction Act (2022), 13,
    97–98, 100, 101, 135–36
Internal Revenue Service (IRS), 135–36
International Monetary Fund, 167
international relations
    alliances, economic, 55–64
    alliances, military, 44–45
    alliances as substitute for scale,
      43–44
    conflict and national identity, 212–17
    international system and U.S.
      leadership, 38–40, 60–67
    political engagement in, 60–64
    research collaboration and, 97–98
    trade agreements, 65–67
interstate highway system (U.S.),
    105
investment, 69–111
    in care economy, 79–80, 104–7, 211
    in children, 79–84
    collective social investment, UCLA
      experiment, 162–64

collective social investment from federal government, 108–11 (*see also* federal government spending)

defense spending and scale, 44–52

future intent and, 210–12

geopolitical success and changing global competition, 12–13

identity and maximizing human assets, 172–73

megatrends of scale, globalization, and technological innovation, 70–74

quality measures and, 67

scale test and, 65–67

in science and technology, 75–80, 94–104

in skilled workforce, 69–70, 79–80, 84–94, 211

U.S. economic competitiveness as challenge, 74–80

Iraq, U.S. war with (2003–2011), 23, 214–15

It's Our Turn to Eat (Wrong), 153

January 6, 2021 insurrection, 202–3

Japan

    Quadrilateral Security Dialogue (Quad), 61

    tax revenue in, 129–30

Jefferson, Thomas, 181–89, 191

The Jungle (Sinclair), 128

Kagan, Robert, 40

Kant, Immanuel, 195

Kenya, political system of, 153

Kleinfeld, Rachel, 207

leadership

    "global governance," 64–67

hegemony vs., 23–24

international system and U.S. leadership, 38–40, 60–67

legal and regulatory issues. *See also* Congress, U.S.

    Affordable Care Act, 154

    American Rescue Plan Act (2021), 30

    antitrust issues and fairness, 122–23

    Bipartisan Infrastructure Bill (2021), 13

    Chinese Exclusion Act (1882), 146

    CHIPS Act (2022), 13, 97–98

    Citizens United v. Federal Election Commission (2010), 141–44

    fairness and income gap, 128

    illegal (or irregular) immigration, 36–37

    immigration as law-and-order issue, 37

    Inflation Reduction Act (2022), 13, 97–98, 100, 101, 135–36

    "justice" vs. fairness definitions, 116

    laws targeted by political opposition, 153–56

    R&D infrastructure and, 96, 102

    Shelby County v. Holder (2013), 144–46

    U.S. competitiveness and deregulation policies, 74–75

    voting rights, 137–38, 144–49, 152–53

Leonard, Franklin, 179

liberal values, identity and, 177–81, 193, 199–203

libertarianism, 108, 114, 186

Lieberman, Matthew, 162

literacy, world rate in, 84–85

Locke, John, 182

Making Caring Common (Harvard University), 201–2
marginal value of public funds (MVPF), 82
McCain, John, 154
McConnell, Mitch, 142
McGhee, Heather, 158
media, identity and, 177–81, 199–203
Medicaid, 82–83, 159
Medicare, 78
megatrends, challenge of, 70–74. *see also* investment
middle class. *see* income gap and class issues
military. *see also* U.S.-Iraq War (2003–2011); World War II
    defense spending, 44–52
    military alliances, 41–45
    military and societal strength, 52–55
    military power, 10–11, 22
    nuclear forces, 50–51
    service members' recognition, 49–50
    spending efficiency, 48–51
    strategic investment, 47–48
    strength measurement, 46–47
Modi, Narendra, 57
morality. *see* ethics and morality
Morton, Fiona M. Scott, 123
mRNA vaccines, 99–100
Muirhead, Russell, 197–98
"My Country 'Tis of Thee" (Smith), 217

NASA, 87
National Bureau of Economic Research (NBER), 135
national identity. *see* identity
national service proposal, 210–12

Native Americans, voting rights and, 146
natural disaster aid, 152–53
neoliberalism experiment, 121
New Jersey, voting rights in, 146
New START, 50
New Zealand, U.S. alliance, 41
Nineteenth Amendment (U.S. Constitution), 146
noncompete agreements, 123–24
North Atlantic Treaty Organization (NATO), 41, 45
North Carolina, voting rights in, 145
nostalgia, identity and, 217–18

Obama, Barack
    on defense spending, 45
    election of, 190, 240n11
    GDP and government spending by, 78
    on trade, 65–66
Ober, Josiah, 150
oil industry
    Russia's economic growth and, 23, 54
    U.S. early and sustained role in, 26
Organization for Economic Co-operation and Development (OECD), 27, 85, 129
Otherness, 159

parenthood. *see* children, childbearing, and parenthood
Paris Agreement, 155
patriotic empathy, 206–7, 211
Patterson, Orlando, 239–240n3
Pennsylvania, voting rights in, 146
Pennsylvania State University (Penn State), 196

Perkins, Frances, 120
Pew Research Center, 28
Philippines, U.S. alliance, 41
Piketty, Thomas, 168
Pledge of Allegiance, U.S., 116
political economy, 221–22
political ideology. *see also* democracy
  about government size, 77–78, 105,
    109–11
  communism and socialism, 7–10,
    118–21 (*see also* China; Russia)
  identity and liberal values, 177–81,
    193, 199–203
  isolationism, 38–39
  January 6, 2021, insurrection, 202–3
  libertarianism, 108, 114, 186
  neoliberalism experiment, 121
  partisan identity, 192–93, 202
  political divisions and dysfunction,
    modern-day, 3–4
  right-wing populism, 193–98, 203–5
  Tea Party movement, 34
political system of United States. *see*
  United States political system
polycrisis/polyprogress concepts, 2
population size and statistics
  benefits of population size, 25–26
  birthrate decline (2007–2020), 27,
    29–32
  China population statistics, modern-
    day, 16
  net immigration, 34–38
  population replacement and growth,
    26–33
  scale as territory, population, and
    productivity, 19–22 (*see also* scale)
  United States population statistics,
    modern-day, 12, 26
  world literacy rates, 84–85

poverty. *see* income gap and class issues
public swimming pools, segregation
  of, 158
"pursuit of happiness" (Declaration of
  Independence), 181–89, 210
Putin, Vladimir, 8, 43, 46, 50–51, 54.
  see also Russia

QAnon conspiracy theory, 197–98
Quadrilateral Security Dialogue
  (Quad), 61

race and racism. *see also* income gap and
  class issues
  achievement gap and, 94
  Black Lives Matter, 217
  "critical race theory," 191
  fairness and income gap, 125–26,
    233n11
  housing and, 91–92
  identity and perceived threat by
    whites, 177–79, 239–240n3
  identity politics and, 190–91
  investment and fairness, 108–11
  investment in care economy wages,
    107 (*see also* care economy)
  racial issues of fairness, 156–61,
    165
  racism and national competitiveness,
    156–61
  racism as structural, 107, 179
  racist segregation, 117, 158
  slavery and, 182, 239–240n3
  social programs and perception
    about, 159
  Social Security and, 235n3
  voting rights and, 144–49
RAND Corporation, 81
Rasser, Martijn, 58

Reagan, Ronald
  "city on a hill" speech, 113
  deregulation by, 74–75
  first inaugural address by, 183
  on nuclear war restraint, 50
  on social programs, 159
Redfin, 192
regulatory issues. *see* legal and
  regulatory issues
religion
  childbearing and, 32–33
  partisan identity and, 192–93
  St. Louis and Muslim immigration,
    35
  Trump's migration ban, 36
Republic of Korea, U.S. alliance, 41
Romney, Mitt, 139
Rosenberg, Shawn, 194–95
Rosenblum, Nancy, 197–98
Rousseau, Jean-Jacques, 193–94
Russia
  COVID vaccine development,
    99
  defense spending by, 46–47
  on nuclear war restraint, 50–51
  oil industry and economic growth of,
    23, 54
Russia-Ukraine war
  drones used in, 44
  identity and conflict, 213–14
  Russian invasion, 8–9, 42
  sanctions imposed for Crimea and
    Ukraine invasions, 54
  U.S. support for Ukraine, 155

San Francisco Federal Reserve, 165
Satpute, Ajay, 162
scale, 19–67
  decline in U.S. economic scale

  as megatrend, 70–74 (*see also*
    investment)
  expansionism vs. imperialism, 21–22
  geopolitical success and changing
    global competition, 12
  importance of, 25
  international alliances as substitute
    for, 43
  international relations and political
    engagement, 60–64
  international relations and strategic
    partnering, 55–60
  international system and U.S.
    leadership, 38–40, 60–67
  market consolidation and fairness,
    121–24
  military alliances and, 41–45
  military and defense spending, 44–52
  military and societal strength, 52–55
  population and net immigration,
    34–38
  population replacement and growth
    for, 26–33
  population size, geographic size, and
    productivity, 19–22
  population size and benefits of,
    25–26
  shared national identity and, 193–94,
    201–3
  structural challenges to U.S., 22–24
  test of, defined, 24, 37, 40, 65–67
Schor, Juliet, 180–81
Schumer, Chuck, 142
science and technology. *see also* climate
    change
  artificial intelligence (AI), 103–4,
    221
  governance, 59, 103
  international alliances for, 60–64

investment for societal advantage, 102–4

investment needed in, 75–80, 94–104

megatrend of technological innovation, 70–74

military and scale, 46–47, 55–60

patents and geographic "super clusters," 98

skilled workforce needed for, 69–70, 79–80, 84–94, 211

STEM (science, technology, engineering, mathematics) education, 76–77

Second Treatise (Locke), 182

Senate, U.S.

Colorado and U.S. Senate races, 139, 141

nonrepresentative nature of, 147, 179

September 11 terrorist attacks, 214–15

shared national identity. *see* identity

Shelby County v. Holder (2013), 144–46

Sinclair, Upton, 128

Skocpol, Theda, 104–5

slavery

identity and social relationships undermined by, 239–240n3

Jefferson and, 182

Smith, Samuel Francis, 217

social contract, 127–29, 208, 224

socialism. *see* communism and socialism

Social Security

defense spending vs., 51

fairness and federal spending on, 134

GDP and government spending by, 78

inception of, 120, 235n3

Southeast Asia Treaty Organization (SEATO), 41

Soviet Union. *see also* Cold War; Russia

Soviet communism vs. American democracy as world hegemon, 7–10

on U.S. racist segregation, 117

St. Louis, Bosnian immigrants in, 35

Starr, Evan, 124

state and local tax (SALT) deduction, 131–32, 155

State Department, U.S.

Bureau of Democracy, Human Rights, and Labor ("human rights bureau"), 143

Bureau of International Organization Affairs ("foreign service"), 63–64

fairness and federal spending on, 134

State of the Union (2023) address, 1

structural challenges to United States

cultural challenges vs., 159, 207

defined, 22–24

policy choices and, 126–29

racism and sexism as, 107, 179

suicide, 180–81

The Sum of Us (McGhee), 158

Syracuse University, 135

Tabibnia, Golnaz, 162

taxes

on capital gains vs. employment, 131–32

carbon tax, 136–37

estate tax, 132–34

income tax inception, 128

national service incentive proposal, 211–12

property tax, 134

as revenue for social investment, 129–37

tax gap, 134–36, 234n16

Tea Party movement, 34. *see also* political ideology

technology. *see* science and technology
tests of future success. *see* fairness; four
  tests; identity; investment; scale;
  United States and future success
Thailand, U.S. alliance, 41
"The Star-Spangled Banner," 217
TRAC Center, Syracuse University, 135
Trans-Pacific Partnership (TPP), 66
Trump, Donald
  on climate change, 155
  on defense spending, 44, 45
  on foreign policy, 43
  GDP and government spending by,
    78
  identity of voters and election of,
    177–79, 217
  on immigration, 36
  partisan identity and, 192
  presidential race (2020), 140
  on taxes, 131–32, 154–55
  on voting rights, 145
Turner, Ani, 165
2008 financial crisis
  China's economic growth and, 54
  COVID response as lesson learned
    from, 223
  political polarization resulting from,
    161–64
  Tea Party movement, 34

UCLA, fairness experiment by, 162–64
Ukraine, Russia and. *see* Russia-Ukraine
  war
Ukraine Defense Contact Group, 42
United Kingdom
  British national identity, 213, 214
  end of British Empire, 40
  former geopolitical dominance of,
    6, 7

purchasing power of U.S. vs., 167
U.S. alliance with, 41, 57
United States. *see also* citizens, U.S.;
  Cold War; federal government
  spending (U.S.); GDP;
  immigration; international
  relations; legal and regulatory
  issues; military; *individual names
  of agencies; individual names of
  presidents*
Constitution, 146, 183
Declaration of Independence,
  181–89, 210
defense budget as percentage of
  global military spending, 44
foreign policy (*see* international
  relations)
freedom narrative of, 113–15
interstate highway system of, 105
"My Country 'Tis of Thee" (Smith),
  217
national security and changing nature
  of threats, 9–10
Pledge of Allegiance, 116
population size, geographic size, and
  productivity, overview, 19–22 (*see
  also* scale)
structural challenges to, 22–24, 107,
  126–29, 159, 179, 207
"The Star-Spangled Banner," 217
U.S.-Iraq War (2003–2011), 23,
  214–15
United States and future success, 1–18
  communism vs. U.S. as world
    hegemon, 7–10
  expectations for, 1–2, 16–18
  four tests and importance to, 12–16,
    223–25 (*see also* fairness; identity;
    investment; scale)

functioning of democratic system
and, 4–6 (*see also* United States
political system)

geopolitical success and changing
global competition, 11–16

geopolitical success and U.S. military
power as insufficient, 10–11

national identity needed for success,
173–74

political economy and, 221–23

polycrisis and polyprogress concepts,
2

post–World War II influence vs.
future influence, 6–7

recognizing historic change as it
happens, 219–20

societal evolution without political
revolution in U.S., 3–4

United States domestic policy. *See also*
federal government spending;
taxes

American democracy as objective
for, 5

discrimination as geopolitical
problem vs. domestic issue, 160
(*see also* gender and sexism; race
and racism)

literacy rate in, 84–85 (*see also*
education)

United States political system. *See also*
political ideology

campaign finance, 137–44, 207–9

citizens' confidence vs. cynicism,
149–56, 164–69

constitutional democracy, 115

"cross-pollination" of knowledge and
expertise in, 151

economic elites and influence on, 130

Electoral College, 147–48

"one person, one vote," 146

polarization in, 161–64

power of citizens in, 1–2

public opinion on, 118–21

societal evolution without political
revolution in, 3–4

U.S. investment in global public good
and, 102–4

voting rights, 137–38, 144–49, 152

U.S.-Iraq War (2003–2011), 23,
214–15

Vance, J. D., 177

voting rights, 137–38, 144–49, 152–53

Voting Rights Act (1965), 138, 144,
146

Winthrop, John, 113

Works Progress Administration (WPA),
158

World War II

American post-war influence vs.
future influence of, 6–7

British national identity and, 213, 214

Wrong, Michela, 153

About the Author

DANIEL BAER is senior vice president for policy research and director of the Europe Program at the Carnegie Endowment for International Peace. Under President Obama, he was US ambassador to the Organization for Security and Co-operation in Europe (OSCE) from 2013 to 2017. He has appeared on CNN, Fox, MSNBC, BBC, PBS *Frontline*, Al Jazeera, Sky, and *The Colbert Report*. His writing has appeared in *The Washington Post*, *The Wall Street Journal*, *POLITICO*, *Foreign Affairs*, *Foreign Policy*, and numerous other publications. He holds a doctorate in international relations from Oxford, where he was a Marshall Scholar, and a degree in social studies and African American studies from Harvard. He is married to Brian Walsh, an economist at the World Bank.